CATCH THE DEVIL

CATCH THE DEVIL

A True Story of Murder,
Deception, and Injustice
on the Gulf Coast

PAMELA COLLOFF

Alfred A. Knopf
New York 2026

A BORZOI BOOK
FIRST HARDCOVER EDITION
PUBLISHED BY ALFRED A. KNOPF 2026

Published by Alfred A. Knopf, a division of Penguin Random House LLC, 1745 Broadway, New York, NY 10019.

Page 307 constitutes an extension of this copyright page.

Library of Congress Cataloging-in-Publication Data
Names: Colloff, Pamela, author.
Title: Catch the devil : a true story of murder, deception, and injustice on the Gulf Coast / by Pamela Colloff.
Description: First hardcover edition. | New York : Alfred A. Knopf, [2026] | Includes bibliographical references.
Identifiers: LCCN 2025054369 | ISBN 9780593230862 hardcover | ISBN 9780593230879 ebook
Subjects: LCSH: Skalnik, Paul | Informers—Florida | Prisoners—Florida | Judicial error—Florida | Evidence, Criminal—Florida | Murder—Florida | LCGFT: Case studies.
Classification: LCC HV9468.S585 C66 2026
LC record available at https://lccn.loc.gov/2025054369

penguinrandomhouse.com | aaknopf.com

Printed in the United States of America

2nd Printing

For Chad, Jake, and Lucy

How easy it is to make people believe a lie,
and how hard it is to undo.

—MARK TWAIN

CONTENTS

Prologue 3

PART I

1. Skalnik 9
2. Fool Me Once 16
3. Sunshine State 29
4. Confidence Man 39
5. False Witness 48
6. The Closer 56

PART II

7. Jim 67
8. Shelly 78
9. Jack 85
10. Dark Waters 98
11. Snitch 107
12. A Simple Lie 119
13. Conviction 128

PART III

14. Starke 139
15. The Art of the Deal 149
16. An Unreal Dream 161
17. Six by Nine Feet 173
18. Small Fictions 181
19. Fail-Safe 190
20. E. Paul Smith, Esq. 194
21. The Call 200

PART IV

22. Eleventh Hour 219
23. Zombie Case 230
24. Catch the Devil 244
25. Lockdown 254
Epilogue 261

Acknowledgments 269
Notes on Sources 275

CATCH THE DEVIL

PROLOGUE

I first met Paul Skalnik in the fall of 2018, when he was serving time in federal prison. All I knew then were the broad strokes of his story, pieced together from court filings in Florida: He was a small-time con artist, married nine times, whose testimony prosecutors had relied on, decades earlier, to win a staggering number of felony convictions. Skalnik had a gift: Whenever his luck ran out and he ended up in jail, men confessed their crimes to him. More than thirty years after he had testified against them, some remained in prison. One sat on death row, awaiting an execution date.

Yet from the beginning, these men told a different story: They said Skalnik had made it all up. I wanted to know: Were they lying—or was he? How did he get these confessions? And how did a con man become the state's most valuable witness?

I had tracked Skalnik down to a federal penitentiary in Texas, southeast of Dallas: a squat, redbrick building, ringed by a double perimeter fence and razor wire, where I was granted entry one October morning. To my surprise, he had agreed to meet with me—though the prison limited us to just an hour. A correctional officer led me through a series of locked metal gates to the sparsely furnished visitation room where Skalnik was waiting.

Time had eroded his once-roguish appeal; at sixty-nine, he was

Falstaffian in scale, his bulk straining against the wheelchair he sat in. His thinning gray hair was greasy, and his complexion had the waxy pallor that comes from years spent in confinement. But his eyes remained sharp and alert, bright with anticipation, and he thanked me effusively for coming to see him. Then, without warning, he began to cry. His voice swelled with emotion as he confided that he had been diagnosed with late-stage colon cancer. From his waistband, he pulled out a soiled rag, stained with dried, rust-colored blood. He thrust it toward me, as if offering it as evidence, and his voice dropped to a whisper. "I'm dying," he said.

Like much of what he told me during our brief time together, it was impossible to know if this was true. He blamed his imprisonment on a vendetta, which he said had been orchestrated by an ex-lover's daughter and a U.S. marshal. He boasted of money he'd stashed in offshore accounts in the Cayman Islands and Abu Dhabi, and of his time as a star witness in Pinellas County, Florida. His reputation there, he said, had been so fearsome that the mere possibility of his testimony could sway the outcome of a case. "If I was on the witness list, people would take deals," Skalnik said. "I never lost a case—never ever." He thumped the table in front of him for emphasis.

When I pressed Skalnik to explain how he had extracted so many confessions from so many men in a single jail, he sidestepped my questions. Soon the correctional officer rapped on the visitation room's window: five minutes left. Our time was nearly up.

Skalnik acknowledged my obvious frustration with a smile, assuring me that this would be the first of many conversations. He told me to send him my questions so we could correspond, and he encouraged me to visit him as often as the warden allowed. The more sensitive details about his work with prosecutors in Pinellas County, he said, could only be shared in person. "This is a story that needs to be told," he said when I stood to leave, "and I want to help you tell it."

Elated that he had agreed to cooperate, I drove home to Austin, where I pored over jail logs, case files, and trial transcripts, and wrote him letters that brimmed with questions. I contacted the prison to set up another interview and messaged him through an email system that connects federal inmates to the outside world. He wrote often, describing the daily indignities of prison life and his fear of dying alone—but never a word about Pinellas County. There was always a holdup: He had not received my most recent letter because the mailroom was short-staffed, or he felt too unwell to write. Still, he assured me that as soon as he regained his strength, he would be ready to talk.

I refused to admit to myself, until it was much too late, that Skalnik had been stringing me along. Months after our visit, when I was still holding out hope that he might talk, he wrote to say that my questions were making him uneasy. Then he went dark on me.

PART I

1

SKALNIK

In Friendswood, Texas, the only disturbance to the order of things came during hurricane season, when storm surges in Galveston Bay left the creeks with nowhere to drain and floodwaters could rise in an instant. Some seven thousand people lived there in the mid-1970s, when it still retained the austere calm of its early days as a Quaker settlement. Halfway between Galveston and Houston, it remained, as the county's sole dry town, a world unto itself—a stubborn holdout against modern excess. Lisa Rogers had never lived anywhere else, and apart from school she spent most of her waking hours at her grandparents' horse farm. At fourteen, she preferred the company of horses. She liked the quiet sameness of her days, the predictable hum of life. Her mother, Penny, longed for something different.

Penny often told her stories about an earlier, more exhilarating time, when she had been a regular on *The Larry Kane Show,* Houston's own version of *American Bandstand.* Of all the bright-eyed teenagers who were chosen to appear on the show each Sunday in the late 1950s and early 1960s, it was Penny who stood out. Her heart-shaped face, framed by dark, dramatic eyebrows and high cheekbones, often drew comparisons to Elizabeth Taylor. But no modeling contracts followed; no acting career bloomed. After high school, she married and divorced three men, in quick succession, and suffered a shattering loss when her twin sister died of leukemia. By early 1977, at thirty-three, she was raising two children on her own, working as a receptionist at the funeral home her parents owned, and still living in Friendswood.

It was that spring, at the funeral home, that Penny first encountered a man named Paul Skalnik. He cut a striking figure in a three-piece suit, his blue-gray eyes tracking her from across a roomful of mourners. At twenty-seven, he was six years Penny's junior, but he spoke with the polished assurance of a trial lawyer or politician, leaning in just close enough to make the conversation feel private without being intrusive. He told Penny that he had grown up in nearby League City and that, after college, he had quickly ascended the corporate ladder to become a top executive at Southwest Airlines. Then a scrappy Texas upstart, Southwest was known for outfitting its flight attendants in hot pants and go-go boots. Skalnik, with his outsized ambition, seemed to reflect the company's brash confidence.

When Penny brought him home to meet Lisa and her younger brother, Lynn, Lisa was put off by his heavy-handed efforts to win over her mother. Penny, however, was enthralled by his attention. Skalnik held out the promise of a life that was bigger, brighter, grander, and he made it feel thrillingly within reach, carrying a business-sized checkbook with him whenever he took her out. Restraint, Lisa noticed, was not his strong suit. He cultivated a maximalist style, accenting his wide-lapelled suits with gold chains, a Rolex watch, and

PENNY ROGERS IN FRIENDSWOOD, TEXAS, IN THE EARLY 1970S

plush sideburns, and he encouraged Penny to live large, too. After a brief courtship, he spirited her away to Las Vegas for a weekend, and they returned to Friendswood as Mr. and Mrs. Paul Skalnik.

Skalnik moved into Penny's condo, where he soon settled into a routine. On weekday mornings, he bounded out the door with his briefcase in hand, telling her that he was headed to the airport, to fly to Southwest's headquarters in Dallas, and that he would be back home in time for dinner. On weekends, he took Penny, Lisa, and Lynn to the best hotels in Dallas and Austin, where he ran up the tab on room service, summoning platters of chocolate-covered strawberries and bottles of champagne. He bought Penny a fur coat and jewelry, and outfitted their home with the latest technology, including a microwave and another modern marvel, a VCR. He gave Penny both a baby-blue Lincoln Continental and a customized Dodge van, complete with red velvet curtains, a TV, and CB radios.

Only Lisa seemed to see Skalnik's idiosyncrasies: how he filched the robes and towels from their luxury hotel suites and squirreled away the purple velvet bags that held his Crown Royal. It didn't escape her attention, either, that he always kept his handgun within reach, even stashing it under the driver's seat when he was behind the wheel. What these details added up to, she could not be sure, but she took note of each peculiarity. Once, on a drive through League City, he pointed out the house where he said his parents lived, and Lisa stared at the sun-blistered paint and shabby yard. The tiny frame house, she thought, seemed oddly untouched by his largesse.

When Skalnik was in an expansive mood, he would regale the family with stories of his extraordinary achievements. He was skilled at weaving a narrative, and he knew how to hold a listener's attention with a perfectly timed pause or an anticipatory smile. He frequently boasted of having helped the University of Texas clinch a national football title when he was a college student, before a knee injury sidelined his athletic career—always making a point, as he told this story, to flash his jumbo-sized championship ring. He was the hero of every story. No one else was ever as bold, or as quick thinking, or as clever. Lisa thought he seemed happiest when he was holding court, his hands shaping the air as he spoke.

Once, Skalnik promised Penny and the kids a trip to New York City—a trip he announced they would take on a Learjet that he had commandeered for the occasion. Lisa was elated until their departure day came, and she, her mother, and her brother found themselves in an empty airport hangar, watching Skalnik pace back and forth. As the day wore on, and the Learjet did not materialize, Skalnik became more distressed, shouting into the receiver as he made a series of frenzied calls from a nearby phone. Lisa watched as he waved his arms in what appeared to her, in a moment of sudden clarity, to be a pantomime of fury. Despite his show of outrage, he seemed to enjoy being the center of attention, she thought. As he barked orders, Lisa wondered if anyone was on the other end of the line. At the end of the day, Skalnik shook his head and told Penny the trip would have to be postponed. Engine trouble, he said.

Lisa kept her questions to herself, but she studied Skalnik as he moved about the house, which he did, increasingly, in nothing but his white Jockey briefs. She had failed to notice his crudeness at first, but as he grew more familiar, it was all she could see: the gold chain beneath his collar, grazing his dark pelt of chest hair; his gaudy self-regard; his obsessive need to accumulate newer and ever more expensive things; his taste for ersatz splendor. She grew exhausted with his grandiose stories and his thirst for praise and adulation. His wolfish appetite for all things—alcohol, spending money, her mother's attention—seemed to have no limits. One evening when she was in the shower, she thought she felt his gaze, but when she turned to look, she saw nothing. She heard only the click of the bathroom door.

Her uneasiness was not lost on Skalnik. That Christmas, to win her over, he presented her with a lavish gift: a glittering Seiko watch that he told her was made of 24-karat gold and inlaid with diamonds. It glittered in the light.

Lisa looked up at him, unsmiling, and asked if it was real.

Skalnik broke into a grin. "Looks real to me," he said.

That January, a series of typewritten letters addressed to Skalnik began arriving at the condo in Friendswood. The first, from Amco Jewelry Company, informed him that three different checks of his had failed to clear. The tenor of the letter was professional but urgent. If the total of $1,879 was not received by February 1, it warned, the matter "will be out of our hands." Days later, an attorney representing Oshman's Sporting Goods wrote to insist on the immediate remittance of $1,307. Taken together, these were sizable amounts: today, adjusted for inflation, nearly $16,000.

More letters came in the months that followed—from banks, a local grocery store, a pharmacy, a men's clothier. Skalnik carried on as he always had, striding down the front walkway with his briefcase each morning, only to reappear at dinnertime, loosening his tie and heading for the liquor cabinet. He did not share the letters with Penny, but the strain he was under showed. He drank heavily, and any perceived slight could set him off, his face suddenly going taut with anger. Lisa saw her mother emerge from the bedroom more than once, after a night of Skalnik's rages, with a poorly camouflaged black eye.

As Skalnik's behavior became more and more unpredictable, he began heading out of town on business, always returning a few days later. But one such absence in the spring of 1978 stretched on and on—first for weeks, then for more than a month. Lisa did not know where her stepfather was or what had become of him, and Penny, if she knew more, offered no explanation. Freed from Skalnik's grip, their household resumed its quiet rhythm. Just as suddenly as Skalnik had barreled into their lives, he was gone.

Kenny Rodgers, an investigator in the Harris County District Attorney's Office in Houston, was sitting at his desk one day that May when the phone rang. Rodgers worked in the Special Crimes Bureau, a division of the DA's office that specialized in investigating and prosecuting organized crime, money laundering, and major fraud and narcotics cases. Located above a thriving import-export business, it was not listed on the building directory, and its detectives, many of whom wore street clothes, accessed the office through an unmarked sliding glass door on an adjacent side street. If anyone called the unpublished number that was dedicated to undercover operations, whoever picked up the phone was supposed to answer, "Austin Street and Bridge Company. How may I help you?"

Rodgers hunted down the witnesses whom prosecutors needed to bring their cases to trial. The Houston native was a natural people person, skilled not only at locating uncooperative citizens but at winning them over. The phones at the Special Crimes Bureau were always buzzing with tips from contacts he had all over the city. When Rodgers picked up, he expected it to be one of his sources.

"Hey, Kenny," he heard a familiar voice say. "It's Paul Skalnik."

Rodgers had not heard from Skalnik in years. They had met a decade earlier, in 1968, when they were first-year cadets waiting in line for buzz cuts at the New Mexico Military Institute, a predominantly male junior college in Roswell, southeast of Albuquerque. Both were Texans far from home, and they immediately hit it off, despite their different approaches to the regimented nature of a military college. Rodgers established himself as the school's resident bootlegger, sneaking six-packs of beer onto campus in guitar cases, selling them at a steep markup, and running a counterfeit driver's license operation on the side. Skalnik was a model cadet, a stickler for the rules who won the favor of the school's top brass and an appointment to the honor board. "I'll be running this school in no time," he told Rodgers the day they met.

Skalnik signed a contract with the Marine Corps, all but guaranteeing that he would begin active duty upon graduation. He already looked the part, with his stiff-backed stride and the set of his jaw, and he acted it too, going out of his way to cultivate the steely persona of a drill sergeant. Rodgers suspected it was all for show; he doubted his friend had the self-discipline for the Marines' punishing regimen of physical and mental conditioning. Skalnik remained resolutely out of shape when they played together on the junior college's baseball team, and he was a lazy, disinterested student. When Skalnik returned from summer training in Quantico, Virginia, sporting a conspicuous white neck brace, Rodgers was certain Skalnik had feigned an injury to get out of his Marine contract. "You're nothing but a big old pussy," he ribbed his friend.

They saw little of each other after graduation, but when Rodgers ran into him a few years later, Skalnik proudly announced that he was a cop, too. He had never become a Marine; he had spent a few semesters at the University of Texas, then dropped out and enrolled in the Austin Police Academy.

Now Rodgers was holding the receiver to his ear, pleased to hear from his old friend. "Where in the hell are you?" he said.

"The Harris County Jail," Skalnik said, without further explanation. "I need you to come and get me. I've got something to tell you—something that will interest you." He had information in one of the highest-profile criminal cases in Houston, a case he knew the DA's office had to win.

2

FOOL ME ONCE

The case that had gripped Houston for more than a year began on a muggy spring night in 1977, a few blocks from the bayou in the city's East End. José Campos Torres, a slim, black-haired Army veteran, had been out at a hole-in-the-wall bar called Club 21, where the mood was celebratory; the date was May 5, Cinco de Mayo, and Torres had been drinking for the better part of the day. Some time before midnight, he began sparring with customers, and the manager asked him to leave. Torres refused, and when a scuffle ensued, the manager asked that someone call the police. It took three officers to subdue the twenty-three-year-old, and his obstinacy, which continued after they wrestled him to the ground and dragged him, cursing, into a patrol car, enraged the officers. Rather than take him to jail, they drove him to a secluded spot on the bayou they called the Hole.

His body was found three days later, by a tour boat operator who was steering past the canebrakes that fringe the bayou. Torres was clad in a T-shirt, fatigue pants, jump boots, and a belt with a southwestern-style buckle: the same clothes he was seen wearing to Club 21. Bruises bloomed along the length of his body, from his face to his shins.

At the time, the Houston Police Department held the distinction of being one of the most violent big-city police forces in the country. It boasted a long history of shooting, beating, and terrorizing citizens, particularly people of color, and its officers operated with impunity. No internal affairs division existed to investigate wrongdoing, and those who tried to probe police misconduct were stymied by the force's pervasive code of silence. Bucking a culture that prized loyalty above all else was one officer who saw what happened at the Hole that night: a rookie, not yet indoctrinated by the brotherhood, who had been on the force for just two months. He reported seeing his fellow officers beat Torres over the span of hours. One of them, he recounted, had pushed Torres off a steep embankment into the bayou, crying out, "Let's see if this wetback can swim."

Public outrage over the killing quickly spilled into the streets, provoking city leaders to reckon with Houston's twin legacies of racism and police violence. But the hope that the city might finally hold lawless cops accountable proved to be short-lived. That fall, an all-white jury found two of the officers guilty only of a misdemeanor charge of negligent homicide, for which they received probation. When they and a third officer were tried and convicted of federal civil rights violations the following spring, they were afforded leniency yet again; a sympathetic judge sentenced each of them to just a year in prison.

Weeks later, on May 7, 1978, thousands of people gathered at a Cinco de Mayo celebration at Moody Park, in a predominantly Mexican American neighborhood north of downtown. It had been almost exactly a year since Torres's body had been pulled from the bayou, and the usually joyous event was marked by a sense of grievance. Early that evening, police officers who responded to a disturbance call were met with rocks and bottles, and when more law enforcement moved in, the collective anger of the crowd broke loose. Park goers flooded the streets, looting shops, overturning squad cars, and setting vehicles ablaze. A patrolman was hit by a car, and two reporters were attacked: One was struck with a brick, the other stabbed. As officers advanced in riot gear through the park, people chanted Torres's name. By the time the sun rose, fifteen people had been hospitalized and dozens more were under arrest.

Skalnik watched the Moody Park riot unfold on the local news, on a small black-and-white TV he could glimpse through the bars of his cell. He had been arrested two weeks earlier, when his habit of writing bad checks finally caught up with him, and he was charged with misdemeanor theft. Because he was a former police officer, jailers placed him in a single cell on the jail's sixth floor, where high-profile defendants and men awaiting trial who needed special protection were housed apart from the general population.

That May, Skalnik spotted a fresh arrival, twenty-four-year-old Thomas Hirschi, whose name was all over the news. The Oklahoma City native was one of the "Moody Park Three," a trio of anti-police-brutality activists whom the DA's office had charged with inciting the riot. The unrest at the Cinco de Mayo celebration had been a spontaneous expression of pent-up rage, but rather than concede that years of maltreatment had sparked the uprising, city leaders quickly reframed events, blaming the melee on "outside agitators." Prosecutors echoed this narrative, charging Hirschi and two other young activists, Travis Morales and Mara Youngdahl, with stirring the crowd of thousands to violence. If convicted, they faced up

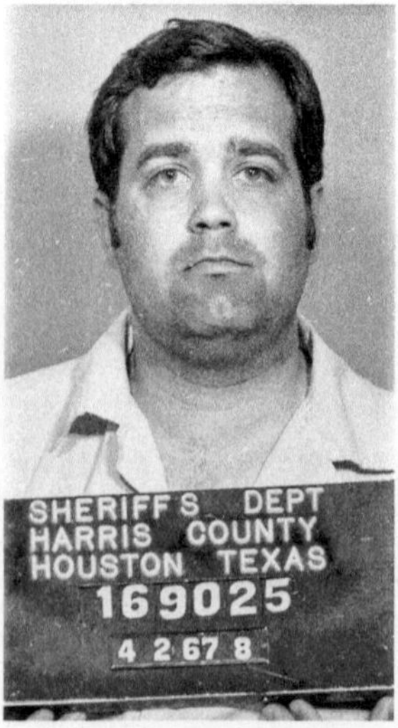

PAUL SKALNIK AT THE HARRIS COUNTY JAIL IN HOUSTON, TEXAS, ON APRIL 26, 1978

to twenty years each behind bars—nineteen more years than the police officers who were charged with Torres's killing would ever serve.

Standing six feet five, with a mop of unruly reddish-brown hair, Hirschi was hard to miss. The son of an oral surgeon, he had left behind a life of privilege to devote himself to the cause of revolutionary communism. He and his two co-defendants were members of a local group called People United to Fight Police Brutality, which had spent the previous year organizing rallies across Houston to demand police reforms and accountability, including prison terms for the officers involved in Torres's killing. When the police arrested Hirschi at gunpoint the week after the riot and informed him that he would be held on a bond of half a million dollars, he felt a surge of pride. He was no longer just an armchair intellectual, he thought; his work was meaningful enough to have pissed off the city's most powerful people.

Hirschi was adamant that he and his friends had played no role in the violence at Moody Park. For them, that Cinco de Mayo had played out much like any other day: They handed out leaflets about police abuses, standing in the park under a banner that read, "Justice for Joe Torres, Jail the Murderers for Life, Justicia para José Torres, Cadena Perpetua a los Asesinos." (Torres went by both José and Joe.) Later, they went to a barbecue, and when word of the unrest reached them, they returned to the park. Exactly what they then shouted over a bullhorn—whether they urged people to stop looting, as they insisted, or egged on the destruction—was the crux of the case.

Kenny Rodgers hurried over to the jail as soon as he hung up the phone with Skalnik. The investigator soon learned that Skalnik was already on probation in Orlando, where he had pleaded no contest to charges of grand larceny and hot-check writing the previous year. His arrest in Houston violated the terms of his release in Florida, as did his failure, for six months running, to report to his probation officer. He was being held at the Harris County Jail without bail.

Rodgers signed him out and drove him the two blocks to Special Crimes, ushering him inside through the side entrance. As soon as they sat down, Skalnik cut to the chase: He had gotten one of the Moody Park Three talking, he said, and he thought he could do the same with the capital murder defendant in the cell next to him, too.

And so began a ritual that stretched into the summer: Most mornings, on his way into the office, Rodgers would stop by the jail to have Skalnik pulled out of protective custody, then bring him in an unmarked car to Special Crimes. Once inside, Skalnik would meet with prosecutors, reading from a small spiral notebook in which he scribbled notes about conversations he claimed to have had with men at the jail. While he wagered that the DA's office would ultimately, in return, go easy on his theft charge, he reaped more immediate rewards: the simple joys of the free world. In the midst of a sweltering Houston summer, the Special Crimes office had ice-cold air-conditioning. Fresh coffee. Freedom of movement. Phone privileges. The privacy afforded by a bathroom stall.

The DA's office offered Skalnik an attractive plea deal: He would receive ninety days in jail—time he had already served—if he pleaded no contest. And rather than extradite him to Florida right away, prosecutors would let him stay in Houston until they needed his testimony at trial. The rules for the former police officer were so loose that Rodgers signed him out of the jail more than a month before the deal was finalized and simply never brought him back.

When the pressures of work threatened to overwhelm him, Rodgers would retreat to the beach town of Matagorda, to a modest, tan-colored cottage on stilts, perched high above the sand dunes. The deck afforded a panorama of Matagorda Bay and, beyond it, the Gulf of Mexico: an expanse of blue that extended, luminous and calm, to the horizon. Rodgers had bought the place on the cheap, since Matagorda, which lies one hundred miles southwest of Houston, is not on the way to anywhere. Flanked by tidal flats and marshy wetlands, it is a sparsely populated place, accessible only by a single, two-lane road.

During the months leading up to the Moody Park Three trial, Rodgers headed to Matagorda whenever he could steal a day away from work. Sitting on the deck, cold beer in hand, his mind often drifted back to Skalnik. The investigator needed him to stay in the Houston area, and out of trouble, until prosecutors called him to testify. Initially, Rodgers felt sure his friend would come through. "Call me every day and let me know where you are," Rodgers told him—instructions that seemed simple enough. Skalnik had been diligent at first, regularly calling to check in. But gradually, his calls grew less frequent, and then they stopped altogether.

It was while Skalnik was incommunicado that Rodgers happened to meet a jeweler named Aron Frank. Upon learning that Rodgers worked at the DA's office, the jeweler began to describe his difficulty recouping his money from a customer who had written a string of checks that turned out to be worthless. Frank explained that the stranger, who had made off with a valuable diamond ring, was a smooth talker with an unusual last name that he struggled to remember.

Rodgers's eyes narrowed as he listened. Then he offered his guess as to the thief's name; it was the same name Frank had been trying to recall. "I'll get your ring back," Rodgers promised.

The investigator spent several days trying to track down Skalnik, calling around to anyone who might have seen him. When Skalnik finally called to check in, he struck a breezy tone. "Hey, Kenny, what's wrong?"

Rodgers ripped into him, leaving no room for misunderstanding: Skalnik could not pull another disappearing act, and he had to return the diamond ring he had stolen. Otherwise, Rodgers would be taking him back to jail.

"What ring?" Skalnik asked.

The investigator went quiet. "I'm the wrong guy to fuck with," he finally said.

Soon afterward, a package was left for Rodgers at the Special Crimes Bureau. There was a shoe box inside, and inside the shoe box were a few sheets of wadded-up newspaper, and inside the wadded-up newspaper was a diamond ring.

That Skalnik had committed some petty financial crimes did not, as far as Rodgers was concerned, compromise his role as a trial witness. Jailhouse witnesses, by definition, were never squeaky clean. The prosecutors and investigators working on the Moody Park Three case, who knew the evidence far better than Rodgers, thought Skalnik's information checked out, and that was as much consideration as Rodgers gave it.

The trial, which got under way in the spring of 1979, fell along ideological fault lines: law-and-order establishment on one side, and the shaggy-haired defendants—represented by civil rights attorneys from San Francisco, including a longtime defender of the Black Panthers—on the other. The state's case would prove to be short on evidence and long on culture-war provocations, with prosecutors spending at least as much time on the Moody Park Three's political ideology as on the facts themselves. Hirschi, Morales, and Youngdahl stood accused not of committing acts of violence but of stirring others up to commit them. To prove this, prosecutors called a series of witnesses, many of them police officers, who claimed to have heard them whipping up the crowd with exhortations like "Get the pigs!"

But as the state sought to make its case, the picture that emerged was a hazy one. One officer admitted that critical details he described to the jury could not be found in his written report about the riot. A veteran police reporter, who said he saw one of the defendants encouraging park goers to attack law enforcement, conceded that he only offered his eyewitness account ten months later, as prosecutors readied for trial. Others claimed to have seen the trio wreaking havoc in the park during the same time frame when multiple witnesses placed them at a barbecue.

To bring clarity, the assistant district attorney Andy Tobias called another witness before he rested his case. "Tell the ladies and gentlemen of the jury what your name is, please, sir," he began.

"Paul Skalnik."

"Mr. Skalnik, I ask you to direct your attention to the three defendants seated here and tell us whether or not you know either one of the three?"

"Yes, sir, I do."

"Which one, please?"

"Tom Hirschi."

Hirschi, who was wearing a blue T-shirt that read, "Justice for Joe Torres," leaned forward in his chair. He had never spoken to this man before in his life.

The prosecutor led Skalnik through a series of questions that quickly tied his witness and the defendant together. "Back on May the 12th of 1978, did you have occasion to be in jail?" Tobias asked.

"Yes, sir, I did," Skalnik said.

"Were you charged with an offense?"

"Insufficient funds check."

Under the prosecutor's questioning, he laid out what he said Hirschi had told him over the course of six different conversations: "I was allowed out of my cell block two or three times a day, and when I went out during the afternoon to take a shower, I went and talked to Mr. Hirschi in front of his cell." Their first conversation,

Skalnik said, quickly turned to what had happened at Moody Park: "He opened up and spoke about how really, he was not the leader—Travis Morales was."

"Did he tell you what Travis Morales's plans were for Moody Park?" Tobias asked.

"Mr. Morales's plans were to incite the Mexican-American youngsters," Skalnik said. "He knew that if the kids were drunk or got enough alcohol in them, they would be easily led." Weapons were to be supplied as well, Skalnik added: "Mr. Hirschi stated Mr. Morales was providing a truck with rocks and bricks."

"Did he tell you what those rocks and bricks would be used for?"

"To throw at the police," Skalnik said.

And, Tobias asked, did everything go according to plan?

"The youngsters did do exactly what Travis Morales thought they would," Skalnik said.

In just a few minutes on the stand, Skalnik had supplied exactly what prosecutors needed to win a conviction: premeditation, intent, and evidence of a conspiracy. His testimony moved beyond the abstractions of *inciting* a riot; it suggested that one of the defendants had personally delivered the rocks and bricks that rained down on police.

As Skalnik spoke, Hirschi sat at the defense table in disbelief. He was not naive; he knew people did not always tell the truth in court. He already thought that law enforcement would say or do anything to make the charges stick, and he figured an ex-cop like Skalnik was no different. But to actually see such a thing unfold—to witness a man lying when three people's lives were on the line—floored him. How effortlessly Skalnik had done it, Hirschi thought. As if it were nothing.

. . .

On May 11, the jury found the Moody Park Three guilty. Morales and Youngdahl were saddled with felony convictions, while Hirschi, who was portrayed as a more peripheral figure, escaped with a misdemeanor. Jurors declined to give the defendants prison time, but prosecutors were satisfied; they had secured a symbolic victory. Tobias took Rodgers aside afterward to say how pleased he was with Skalnik's testimony.

Skalnik still had to be extradited to Florida, where he faced possible imprisonment for violating his probation, but in the wake of the trial the DA's office allowed Skalnik to stay in Texas a little while longer. Prosecutors told Florida authorities that they were considering calling him to testify again in an upcoming capital murder trial. Until then, he was allowed to live as he wanted—his reward for having helped to secure guilty verdicts for the Moody Park Three. The arrangement was highly unusual; normally, someone with an outstanding warrant for an out-of-state felony is jailed while awaiting extradition.

Rodgers was to remain Skalnik's handler, a task he approached with cheerful pragmatism. Having spent plenty of time around opportunists and swindlers, Rodgers considered himself a clear-eyed appraiser of character. His own grandfather had been a bookmaker in Houston for decades, boasting a rap sheet several pages long. As a kid, Rodgers had tagged along as the old man made the rounds of East End bars, pocketing the spoils in a cigar box stuffed with rubber-banded rolls of bills. He saw Skalnik and his small-time cons as something that could be managed and contained, and at that moment he had only one concern: His charge was unemployed and restless. Skalnik needed to be kept busy enough that he stayed out of trouble.

Sitting on his deck in Matagorda one spring weekend, Rodgers had an idea: He could pay Skalnik to do some work around the beach house. There was tall grass to cut and corroded pipes that needed replacing. He drew up a list of odd jobs that would take Skalnik a while to knock out. Skalnik was amenable to the idea, and the following weekend Rodgers was pleased to see that he had already gotten started.

Rodgers did not make it back out to Matagorda for several weeks, but as soon as he returned to the beach house, he knew something was wrong. First, he noticed that his deck chairs were missing. Then, when he stepped inside, a few other odds and ends. Walking from room to room, he could see that the place looked lived in. Skalnik had made no effort to hide that he was living there, though this had never been part of their arrangement. There was no phone at the beach house, so before Rodgers turned around and walked out the door, he scrawled an angry note, which he stuck on the refrigerator, demanding the immediate return of his key and missing belongings.

Rodgers drove back to Houston, and not long after he sat down at his desk, a call was forwarded to Special Crimes with a complaint about Skalnik. The caller explained that he knew Skalnik—they had been fraternity brothers at the University of Texas, he said—and he had given Skalnik a place to stay in Houston during the Moody Park Three trial. Afterward, he realized that Skalnik had pocketed one of his credit cards and used it to buy a TV. This had not required much detective work, the caller explained; Skalnik had signed his own name to the charge slip. Listening, Rodgers grew livid. Skalnik had broken the law the same week that he had testified for the DA's office.

After Rodgers hung up the phone, he called a friend at the Matagorda County Sheriff's Office, in the warrant division. He felt certain that Skalnik had slunk back to the beach house by then. "You'll find a guy at my house who's wanted out of Florida," he said. "Paul S-K-A-L-N-I-K." Within an hour came the call: Sheriff's deputies had picked up Skalnik there, along with a woman who identified herself as his wife.

Rodgers got in his unmarked car and headed south, out of the city, to the Matagorda County Jail. The investigator needed to get Skalnik back to Houston, where he would face a new theft charge and remain behind bars until he was extradited to Florida. As Rodgers drove, he stewed, furious that Skalnik had thumbed his nose at the trust the DA's office had placed in him.

When Rodgers finally laid eyes on Skalnik in a holding cell at the Matagorda County Jail, he stared in disbelief. His onetime friend was wearing Rodgers's own clothes: his baseball cap, his shirt, his belt, his shorts. Even the paperback Skalnik held, a police thriller, belonged to the investigator. Skalnik returned his stare without any trace of embarrassment. All he said was, "Why the handcuffs, Kenny?"

In Friendswood, seventy miles northeast of the jail, Lisa had been searching for her mother. All the tenth grader knew was that Penny had reconnected with her stepfather, then vanished, leaving her and her brother in the care of their grandmother. So abrupt and total was her absence that Lisa came to believe Skalnik had kidnapped Penny. Frantic, she began stealing away in her grandmother's black Cadillac DeVille, slowly coasting down the streets of nearby towns, scanning the sidewalks and passing cars, hoping that she might catch a glimpse of her mother and know that she was still alive.

Lisa would later find out that her mother had been with Skalnik at the beach house in Matagorda when the deputies arrested him. They brought Penny to the sheriff's office, where Rodgers had the opportunity to speak to her. Stroking a brown terrier she held in her arms, Penny expressed no surprise or concern about her husband's arrest, seemingly unfazed by the events unfolding around her. To Rodgers, she appeared almost as if she were in a daze. Though he asked her a few questions, she said little in return, and the investigator, who was eager to get Skalnik into custody in Houston, did not probe further. Wordlessly, Penny turned her attention back to the dog.

Penny would later tell her daughter that she had not wanted to stay away, but that Skalnik had grown violent and controlling not long after they reconciled, telling her that she could never leave him. By then, he had wiped her out financially, having drained her checking account, plundered her savings, and wrecked her good credit. She had nothing left, and despite Rodgers's gentle inquiries she had no assurances that anyone would care if she reported the abuse she had endured. Domestic violence was then largely seen by law enforcement as a personal matter between a husband and a wife, and rape, so long as it occurred within the confines of marriage, was not considered a crime in Texas.

In the aftermath of Skalnik's arrest, Penny did not immediately cut ties with him. It would take time, and the help of a psychiatrist, to free her mind from his grip. She corresponded with him when he served a sixty-day sentence in Houston on the new theft charge, in the summer of 1979, and when he was extradited to Orlando that fall, she sent a letter to the judge who would oversee his probation violation case. "I ask you to show him mercy," read her tidy longhand. "He is not a threat to society in any way. He is a good person."

Skalnik was sentenced to a year in the Orange County Jail, but he spent only a few months there before he was placed in a work-release program and then freed. He departed Orlando as quickly as he came, leaving no forwarding address. Penny, who filed for divorce in the summer of 1980, had to publish legal notices in the newspaper announcing her intent to end the marriage. "To: Paul E. Skalnik," the notices read, "whose residence and whereabouts are unknown."

3

SUNSHINE STATE

The early Spanish explorers who made their way to the western coast of Florida, to what is now Pinellas County, came searching for treasure. But they found only primeval forest, which stretched to the Gulf of Mexico, and a slender chain of barrier islands edged with aquamarine water and bone-white sand. Fortune seekers continued to flock there for centuries afterward, lured by myths of a Shangri-La, but it wasn't until 1887, when a railway line connected the peninsula to the mainland, that the area finally made good on its long-imagined riches. Tourism and citrus farming gave rise to two major cities, St. Petersburg and Clearwater, and by the middle of the twentieth century an influx of retirees and veterans of World War II fueled a population boom.

Subdivisions and strip malls swallowed up the ancient pine forests and orange groves, and Pinellas County became a showy, if despoiled, new world: a patchwork of swimming pools and retention ponds, manicured retirement communities and RV parks, sleek new condos and Easter-egg-hued motels. Rapid change was taking place all across Florida, where the postwar years brought more new residents, development, and commerce than the previous four centuries combined. The pull of the Sunshine State never let up, drawing successive generations of newcomers.

People came to Pinellas County because it promised to be better than whatever they left behind. They were northerners fleeing bleak winters and the higher cost of living; southerners who had run out of money, or ideas, or goodwill back home; retirees from the upper Midwest who yearned for an easier, more carefree way of life. Scientologists were among the many people who made their way to Pinellas County, and in 1975 the Church of Scientology began buying up swaths of property in Clearwater. Its disciples would remake the city's downtown into a mecca of their own. Turning a once-grand, run-down hotel into their opulent base of operations, they created a marble-and-gold-leaf fantasia that would have left Florida's early European explorers speechless.

It was a wedding—Skalnik's fourth—that brought him to Pinellas County in the spring of 1980. He had met his new wife, a faithful, clean-living young evangelical named Suzanne Bourdeau, while she was vacationing in Orlando, and they married in her Clear-

PAUL SKALNIK AND SUZANNE BOURDEAU'S WEDDING ANNOUNCEMENT, WHICH RAN IN THE *ST. PETERSBURG TIMES* ON APRIL 20, 1980

water church on a cloudless April afternoon. "The bridegroom," read their wedding announcement, "served in the U.S. Marine Corps and is general manager of Pro Chem Inc." In the accompanying photo, Skalnik stood beside his jubilant bride, gazing soberly at the camera. He wore a businessman's suit and tie, his dark mustache barely obscuring a smile, apparently untroubled that he was still married to Penny.

Suzanne did not know that three Mrs. Paul Skalniks had preceded her. (Her husband's first two unions, to a nurse in Austin and a young woman from a small town outside Waco, lasted eleven months and eighteen months, respectively.) Cheerful and unguarded, Suzanne was the sort of person who assumed the best of others, not out of ignorance, but from a generous spirit. She felt lucky to have found a husband who not only doted on her but shared her strong faith. Skalnik, who claimed to be a new believer, accompanied her to worship services every Sunday, and her church community eagerly welcomed him into the fold.

They settled in St. Petersburg, in a duplex enclosed by a white picket fence. Half an hour's drive away was Stetson University College of Law, which had, for generations, produced many of the area's judges and prosecutors, and that spring Skalnik told Suzanne that the law school had accepted him into its incoming class.

Suzanne was thrilled that he was going to be an attorney, but being married to a law student, she soon learned, was lonely. Her husband was rarely around, and no sooner was he home than he was off again—telling her that he had to prep for moot court, or study into the early morning hours at the law library. His fierce work ethic only underscored, for her, the scope of his ambition, but she dreaded eating dinner alone, looking out from the dining room table at the law textbooks he left scattered around. This was not how she had envisioned their first year of marriage. While she supported the two of them, doing back-office work for a local defense contractor, and kept busy volunteering at their church, she reminded herself that the sacrifice was temporary. Everything he was doing was to build them a better future.

On May 22, 1981, thirteen months and a day after their wedding, Suzanne received a phone call from the city jail in St. Petersburg. Skalnik was on the other end of the line. He provided no details, saying only that he would explain everything later—but first she needed to bail him out. When she arrived at the bail-bond agency across the street from the jail, Suzanne was floored to learn that her husband had been charged with a felony: a single count of grand theft, for which he faced up to five years in prison. The bail-bond woman who assisted her looked unfazed as Suzanne began to cry and offered her some unsolicited advice. "Just leave him there," the woman said with a tired wave of her hand. "Walk away and don't look back."

This was not the first time someone had tried to warn Suzanne about her husband. A married couple who employed him for a short time in Orlando had hinted at bookkeeping inconsistencies, telling Suzanne that they had noticed "problems with the receipts" when he worked for them. Her own mother said that she felt there was something off about him. But at the bond woman's words, Suzanne offered a weak laugh, trying to brush off the advice as a joke. Suzanne was trusting, and her husband always had an answer for everything, even the most head-scratching behavior. After she secured his release, he assured her that the theft charge was a simple mistake. He promised he would get it all straightened out.

Skalnik's arrest merited a short article in the back of the *St. Petersburg Times,* running under a small but catchy headline: "False Promise, Fake Diamond, Phony Practice—Real Trouble." While Suzanne had been having solitary dinners at home, her husband had been having an affair with a local dietitian. After presenting the young woman with a fake diamond ring, he bilked her out of thousands of dollars under the premise that he was a successful out-of-town lawyer who needed investors for his new local practice. He had also persuaded her to give him power of attorney, with which he had drawn additional money from her bank account. She had become suspicious when he kept disappearing on business trips and she was unable to reach him. "If he channeled his energies into something productive, it's amazing what he could do," a detective told the paper.

Suzanne did not subscribe to the newspaper, and Skalnik, hoping to buy himself some time, decided it would be best if they got out of town. He volunteered to drive her and some of her missionary friends, who needed to catch a flight to their next assignment in Haiti, to the airport in Miami, telling her that they would make a little getaway out of it. But leaving Pinellas County was a violation of his bail agreement. Word of his unauthorized trip to South Florida quickly made its way to the bail-bond agency, and after a little more than a week of freedom he was taken back into custody. Suzanne was once again blindsided. Her husband was to remain in the Pinellas County Jail until his case went to trial in August.

That summer was unusually hot. The peninsula's subtropical splendor was outmatched by the intensity of the sun, which burned too brightly, and by the oppressive, almost suffocating, humidity. Within the stultifying confines of the jail, Skalnik was left to contemplate his uncertain future. He was now a repeat offender who, if convicted, would be looking at time in state prison. He faced five years behind bars, far longer than his jail stints in Houston and Orlando. June ground on, then July. One day he walked over to the bank of pay phones inside the jail and placed a collect call to the state attorney's office in Clearwater. He asked to speak with an investigator.

. . .

Ten days before his grand theft case went to trial that August, Skalnik was quietly escorted from the jail to the state attorney's office. He had information, he said, about three different men who were awaiting trial. All of them were charged with murder. And all of them, he said, had made full or partial confessions to him. By his telling, one man had admitted to shooting his ex-wife's lover. Another had acknowledged pulling the trigger on a friend. A third had described hiding his grandfather's body.

There were easy ways for Skalnik to gather the information he needed. Three daily newspapers—the *Clearwater Sun*, the *St. Petersburg Times*, and *The Tampa Tribune*—circulated freely around the jail, providing basic details about arrests and charges. More valuable was his position working in the jail's law library, which allowed him to present himself as a helpful adviser to the lockup's less savvy arrivals. Some of them kept their legal paperwork in their cells—arrest warrants, indictments, and investigative reports that laid out critical facts of the state's case against them—which Skalnik, playing the role of legal strategist, could ask to see.

The cursory information he provided on the first two defendants closely mirrored facts that had already run in the *Times;* the third defendant, about whom Skalnik offered the most detail, had unwittingly handed over documents in his case and asked for Skalnik's advice.

Prosecutors did not challenge the idea that Skalnik had obtained three confessions in three different murder cases in less than a summer: a more impressive track record than all but the most storied of homicide investigators. Instead, they offered him a deal. If he pleaded guilty to grand theft, rather than go to trial, they would recommend to the judge overseeing his case that he spend no more than three years in prison—two less than he was facing. They also left open the possibility that he could secure a sweeter deal if he cooperated further. So significant was the reward they dangled before him that it merited an exclamation point when it was recorded in the state attorney's files: "Probation was discussed!"

Skalnik took the plea, and his sentencing was postponed while he went back to work inside the jail as a snitch. Prosecutors would hold off on making a sentencing recommendation until they saw exactly how much he had to offer them.

Skalnik made himself busy in the months that followed. Not long after meeting with prosecutors, he came forward with information on a fourth defendant, Jerome Hall—a bit player in a highly publicized drug-trafficking conspiracy case. The trial was dragging into its third week when Skalnik got word to the state attorney's office that Hall had approached his cell and made a full confession. The timing raised obvious red flags, coming just days before jury deliberations were to begin, as did the fact that Skalnik's account contained only details already reported in news coverage of the trial. Nevertheless, the prosecutor Larry Bergman was quick to add Skalnik to the witness list. The prosecutor had him repeat, for the jury, the remarks he asserted Hall made, beginning with the oddly specific declaration "We were loading the boat with 24,000 pounds of marijuana in Colombia." Hall was found guilty of drug trafficking and received the maximum punishment of fifteen years in prison.

Skalnik next tried to make himself valuable in the case of Peter Pfluger, one of the three men charged with murder whose confessions he had claimed to have extracted in jail. He told the state attorney's office that the "zombie-like appearance" of Pfluger, accused of bludgeoning his grandfather to death, was all a put-on. The twenty-five-year-old, he said, was actually a canny tactician who had solicited his advice about whether to "try to play crazy" at trial—exactly the kind of ammunition prosecutors needed to counter an insanity defense. Evidence in the state attorney's own files, however, made clear that Pfluger was not bluffing. An investigation report found that he had "a history of psychiatric problems" and that multiple witnesses possessed "direct knowledge and evidence of Mr. Pfluger's troubled mental state." A neighbor reported that Pfluger had repeatedly tried to starve himself to death. He had been placed under observation at a psychiatric hospital after reporting that he heard voices; he later told police that he believed his grandfather transmitted pain to him telepathically.

The gulf between the young man's fragile state of mind and the picture that Skalnik painted of him in a pretrial hearing was so conspicuous that Pfluger's lawyer, Susan Schaeffer, sounded the alarm, warning in a motion to the court that "Mr. Skalnik has not overheard those conversations which he says he has regarding this defendant," and accusing him of "making up certain information." Schaeffer, who would go on to become a respected state circuit court judge, speculated that he was lying "about other inmates as well, to assist himself out of an uncomfortable situation of his own."

Yet if her appraisal of Skalnik, or Skalnik's own documented history of fraud, stirred concern in the state attorney's office, there is no indication of it. The following month, prosecutors put him on the witness list in another drug-trafficking trial, in which an auto body shop owner named Melvin Glazener was charged with trafficking marijuana and cocaine. The state's case hinged on the word of a coke dealer who, after his arrest in a sting operation, tried to win favor with police by offering information on Glazener. Prosecutors would rely on Skalnik—who said Glazener admitted his guilt—to advance their case that the body shop owner was a major drug supplier. It was the fifth time since Skalnik's arrival at the jail that he claimed to have procured a stranger's confession.

. . .

For all of this, Skalnik was amply rewarded. Larry Bergman, the prosecutor who had tried the drug-trafficking conspiracy case, rose to speak on his behalf at his sentencing hearing on June 30, 1982, telling the court that Skalnik's assistance had been invaluable. Without him, the state attorney's office could not have successfully prosecuted at least three different men, Bergman said. Presiding over the hearing was the circuit court judge Thomas E. Penick Jr., a straight-backed former city attorney who would see Skalnik in his courtroom more than once in his career. "I have never violated the trust of a judge," Skalnik had assured Penick in a letter he wrote before his sentencing, "and promise you I will not in the future."

With the backing of the state attorney's office, Penick gave Skalnik the lightest possible penalty: probation. Given that Skalnik had fled the state the last time he was on probation and racked up seven criminal charges in Florida in as many years, it was a breathtaking leap of faith.

Suzanne, who sat in the courtroom that day, having spent the past year struggling to come to terms with her husband's infidelity, was heartened to learn just how meaningful his help had been to the state attorney's office. She was further encouraged by the judge's decision to give him probation. Her confidence grew when two detectives at the sheriff's office helped secure him a job upon his release. The detectives, who had benefited from Skalnik's jailhouse tips, recommended him to a Belleair Beach police officer named Johnny Touchton who supplemented his income moonlighting as a private investigator. Touchton needed help with his side business, and he agreed to bring Skalnik on board.

Skalnik promised Suzanne that he was not the same man he had been at the time of his arrest. If the judge and the state attorney's office could give him a second chance, he reasoned, why shouldn't she? On Sundays, he accompanied her to church, expressing his faith with a fervor she had not seen before; during the week, he pursued leads around town for Touchton. The men hit it off right away, and one day after work Touchton brought his gregarious new partner by his brother's house in Seminole.

That evening, they sat outside swapping stories, nursing beers in the fading light. Skalnik was in a celebratory mood, and as he entertained the brothers with one wild tale after another, he kept them doubled over with laughter. The peninsula spread out before him, under a sky shot through with streaks of pink and tangerine and violet. Whatever he wanted, it seemed, was his for the taking.

4

CONFIDENCE MAN

Karen Parker was twelve years old during the long, restive summer of 1982, when she pedaled her bike down Seminole's familiar streets, longing for the day when she could finally get her driver's license. Always, for as long as anyone could remember, she had been in a hurry to grow up; her mother liked to joke that she was born with a drink in one hand and a cigarette in the other. Her closest confidante was a high schooler named Evelyn, who lived next door on their cul-de-sac. Evelyn was four years older, though the age gap was one that Karen, by virtue of her self-assuredness and occasional acts of daring, easily overcame. But Karen's freckled face, fringed with feathered blond hair that faithfully mimicked Farrah Fawcett's, still held the soft roundness of childhood.

Like the other kids in her neighborhood, Karen had tremendous freedom, and the rhythm of the summer was loose and improvisational. Her parents worked long hours—her father as a nurse and her mother as a cosmetologist—and she was often left to her own devices. Sometimes she would jump the fence that separated her subdivision from the Bardmoor Golf and Tennis Club and dash across the manicured lawn, past the fairway, to dip in the swimming pool. Other times she found ways to be alone with one of the neighborhood boys—in her family's garage, where they came to gawk at her father's collection of *Playboy* magazines, or in a nearby park, where their hands, damp and eager, fumbled with her bra clasp. Karen longed for affirmation; there was none at home, where her father was cold and critical, often launching into cruel tirades.

His mood always brightened, though, when Paul Skalnik dropped by. Every so often Skalnik and Evelyn's uncle, Johnny Touchton, would swing by the cul-de-sac as their workday wound down, stopping at the house next door where Touchton's brother lived. The adults in Karen's orbit were captivated by him, none more so than her father, and the few times Skalnik came on his own, gliding up the Touchtons' driveway in his silver Cadillac, it felt like a special occasion. He spent hours entertaining them with outsized stories about his days working undercover. What he was doing for Johnny had little of the same cachet; he was working as a process server, hand delivering divorce papers, notices of lawsuits, and court summonses around Pinellas County. But he carried himself with the bravado of a seasoned private eye.

He struck Karen as impossibly cool, a sharp dresser with a certain louche charm. His presence put into relief everything she felt her life lacked: adventure, excitement, sophistication. She had never given much thought to how much money her parents made, but she noticed that Skalnik seemed well-off by comparison. She marveled at his generosity—once he invited her family and the Touchtons out to dinner at a sit-down restaurant and then footed the bill—and at his flash. His silver Cadillac stood out to her in a neighborhood whose driveways were lined with sensible station wagons and economy cars.

KAREN PARKER IN 1982

On those warm summer evenings when Skalnik came around, he always made a point of talking to Karen. He treated her as if she were interesting in her own right, asking her opinion and drawing her into the larger conversation. If the other adults were lost in discussion, he would glance over at her and smile or wink. Whenever his gaze settled on her, she felt a flush of pride. His attention was exhilarating.

One Saturday afternoon in late July, the Touchtons headed to the lake in nearby Largo, and Karen, glad for any pretext to escape her house and the monotony of the day, accepted Evelyn's invitation to join them. Evelyn's boyfriend and Skalnik came along as well. The adults spent the afternoon fishing, casting their lines from banks grown thick with vegetation, while the girls sunned themselves on the shore.

When it was time for dinner, Skalnik ferried part of the group back to the Touchtons' house to order some pizza and restock the cooler. The plan was to return to the lake for the evening after picking up supplies. As people filed into the house, Skalnik stayed in the car. Casually, he summoned Karen back to the Cadillac. By then, everyone had gone inside except for Evelyn, whom he waved into the house, telling her to go help her mother. He smiled at Karen and told her to get in. Gamely, she opened the passenger door of the Cadillac and slid onto the seat beside him.

All afternoon, Karen had felt Skalnik's eyes on her. His interest hadn't scared her; it made her feel powerful. Now he was sitting very, very close, so close that she could smell the sun on his skin and the sweat on his neck. Seeming unconcerned that someone might spot them sitting in the Touchtons' driveway, Skalnik leaned over to kiss her.

She was enthralled at first. She was startled, too—by his tongue in her mouth, by the roughness of his face. As they kissed, he slipped his hands under her T-shirt.

Karen could hear the far-off voices of her neighbors, an occasional screen door slapping shut in the distance. She wondered where everyone had gone, where Evelyn was, whether her parents were home. Time slowed as he pressed in. She felt his hands in her cut-off jeans, then his fingers inside her.

Her happiness quickly gave way to something more complicated: a jumble of shock and a heart-thudding curiosity and a small but potent sense of fear. She pulled away when he began tugging open his shorts, but he grabbed her hand and pulled it into his waistband. He guided her hand until he ejaculated.

Later, she could not remember the drive back to the lake. She could not recall what was spoken between them or what remained unsaid. She could not remember when she returned home that evening or whether her parents were still awake.

All she could retrieve about the rest of that evening was the change that came over Skalnik when he spotted her speaking privately to Evelyn. The sight of the two girls, heads bent together, enraged him. Gone was the look of longing he had given her hours earlier. His face hardened, and he grabbed her by the arm. "One of these days you're going to open your mouth too many times," he snapped.

His meaning was unambiguous: She was to keep quiet about what had happened.

If she wasn't careful, he added, she could end up in "JDC"—juvenile detention. "The only one who is going to be in trouble," he warned, "is you."

Suzanne wanted to believe in her husband's redemption and the future of their marriage. But within weeks of his release from jail, he had gone back to keeping the same odd hours he had before, sometimes vanishing for days with little explanation, telling her only that he was doing work for Johnny. Money materialized and disappeared as unpredictably as he did. When Suzanne expressed her misgivings to her pastor and several church friends, they urged her to see the promise they saw in him. Everyone deserved grace and mercy and a second chance. She just needed to be more patient.

Skalnik, by then, had already embarked on a new business venture. His silver Cadillac was his conversation starter, an easy way for him to draw out people who had a taste for nice cars. If someone showed interest, he would let them in on a secret: He had purchased the Cadillac at a steep discount through his law enforcement contacts, and he could buy other vehicles the state confiscated in narcotics cases, too. He told an older couple, Harry and Edith Garner, that he could purchase a 1981 Thunderbird for them if they gave him the marked-down price he quoted—$3,216—up front. The Garners did not hesitate. They had first met Skalnik while he was still in jail, when they visited their son, also a former police officer, and they took such a liking to him that they visited him in jail after their son's release and vouched for him at his sentencing hearing. Skalnik never delivered the Thunderbird or returned their money.

He also made off with roughly $40,000 from at least three other unsuspecting people. There was Robert Seidenberg, a wealthy man from Fort Myers whom Skalnik befriended on a cruise to the Bahamas he took Suzanne on, a grand gesture meant to reassure her of his fidelity. Skalnik extracted a total of $22,175 from Seidenberg for three vehicles—a Mercedes, a custom Ford van, and a Winnebago—that never materialized. There was Jerry Custer, a member of Suzanne's church, who forked over $12,500 on similar promises. And there was Jackie Millner, a Clearwater travel agent Skalnik persuaded to partner with him in buying the near-bankrupt agency where she worked. While setting up their partnership, he pocketed nearly $5,000 of her money.

Skalnik counted on a cruel fact of grifting: Victims of fraud rarely turn to law enforcement for help. Many are too embarrassed or ashamed, blaming themselves for being too trusting, or too inattentive to warning signs that only later seem obvious. Many more fail to understand that their exploitation amounts to a criminal act. Skalnik would later admit to embezzling money from the private investigation firm that he and Johnny Touchton operated, J & P Investigations, though Touchton never pressed charges. Skalnik also likely scammed some, or all, of the women he spent time with outside his marriage that summer and fall. These included a nurse who worked in the surgical intensive care unit at a local hospital, a wealthy Jehovah's Witness, the single mother of a child with a developmental disability, and a divorcée in Sarasota.

That November, however, Robert Seidenberg stepped forward and went to the police. Jackie Millner followed. It would take the Garners many more months to come to terms with the fact that Skalnik, whom they thought of as a second son, had swindled them. They trusted him "implicitly," Harry would later tell a detective, so much so that they had "put aside normal inquisitive behavior." Searching for the right words to explain why he and his wife had not been more guarded even though they had met Skalnik while he was serving time for theft, Harry told the detective, "We had a great deal of *confidence* in Paul." The detective wrote in block letters at the top of his notes, "CONFIDENCE MAN."

Seidenberg, Millner, and the Garners all pressed charges. Custer, the friend from church, told the sheriff's office that after searching his Bible for answers, he did not wish to prosecute. The criminal charges leveled at Skalnik—initially two counts of grand theft, and later a third—almost certainly represented a fraction of the damage he had wrought. But they were enough to cut short his winning streak. On November 19, 1982, he was arrested and booked back into the Pinellas County Jail. He had been out for less than five months.

• • •

Karen struggled to categorize what Skalnik had done to her. As a twelve-year-old, "sexual assault" was not a phrase in her vocabulary, but the encounter sat uneasily in her memory. Mindful of his warning to her, and fearful that she was somehow to blame, she did not talk to anyone except Evelyn about what had happened. The assault would only come to light after Skalnik was jailed, when his arrest spurred the adults on the cul-de-sac to reappraise the man they had come to trust, and to ask Karen and Evelyn, who had spent time with Skalnik away from adults, some hard questions. Two days before Thanksgiving, Karen's parents took her to the sheriff's office to make a report.

Few law enforcement agencies at the time had protocols in place for interviewing victims of sex crimes or gave much thought to the way in which questioning a survivor of rape or assault should differ from interrogating a suspect. When a male detective escorted Karen, alone, to an empty conference room, his questions only reinforced for her the possibility that she was the one at fault. The detective asked her to explain why she did not get out of the Cadillac. Did she ever tell Skalnik to stop? Had Skalnik used any physical force or coercion? Karen shook her head both times.

Skalnik, when interviewed by the same detective, insisted that there had been a simple misunderstanding. Yes, he conceded, he and Karen were briefly alone that night in his car, but the Touchtons had been in and out of the house the whole time, loading the trunk with provisions. Their stop at the house was so quick, he added, that he had kept the motor running. He scoffed at the idea that he and Karen had been alone for long enough for an assault to take place. During that short interlude in the car, he said, it was Karen who behaved inappropriately; she had leaned over and given him a quick kiss on the lips. "The suspect states that the victim is sexually promiscuous," the detective wrote in his report. "He alleges the victim is flirtatious towards all men."

Skalnik went on to theorize that Karen had falsely accused him of assaulting her in order to exact revenge. His only offense, he told the officer, was sharing his suspicion with the Touchtons that Karen was engaging in "sexual activity with adult boys"—news that, he presumed, the Touchtons had passed on to her parents.

There were, in fact, two eyewitnesses to back up the story Karen told about Skalnik, a rarity in such cases. Even before Karen had confided in Evelyn that night, Evelyn, coming and going from the house, had glimpsed some of the activity in the car. So had her boyfriend. Evelyn reported to the police that she had seen Skalnik kiss and embrace her friend—who, she added, liked Skalnik "a lot." Evelyn's boyfriend went further. He said he approached the Cadillac that night and saw, according to the formal language of the police report that documented his statement, "movement in the suspect's lap (suspect's hand or victim's) of a masturbatory nature."

Yet it was Karen, a slight and freckled seventh grader, who was asked to submit to a polygraph exam. This was common practice in sexual assault investigations in the early 1980s, when the credibility of the victim was often scrutinized as much as, if not more than, the evidence itself. A detective secured pneumographs, thin rubber tubes that would measure respiration, around Karen's chest and abdomen. He attached electrodes to her fingers, and a blood pressure cuff to her arm. Then he led her through a number of questions, each of which had an unmistakably accusatory ring:

> Were you untruthful when you said Paul Skalnik fondled your breast?
> Were you untruthful when you said Paul Skalnik placed his finger in your vagina?
> Did you lie about Paul Skalnik placing your hand on his penis?
> Are you now concealing any facts concerning your sexual contact with Paul Skalnik?

Anyone else might have been scared off by such an ordeal—maybe, Karen later wondered, that was the real purpose of the exercise?—but she was defiantly not. She answered the polygraph examiner's questions one by one: No, she had not been untruthful. No, she did not lie. *No, no, no.*

Polygraphs have since been shown to be unreliable measures of a person's honesty. No evidence exists that the physiological responses they quantify, like increases in heart rate and perspiration, reveal deception; at best, polygraphs assess whether someone is nervous when they undergo the exam. But in 1982, so-called lie detector tests were central to the work of many law enforcement agencies, shaping the direction of investigations and helping to determine which suspects to pursue. Despite the great faith detectives and prosecutors put in polygraphs, Skalnik was not asked to sit for a test too; instead, he was allowed out of jail on bond on the grand theft charges.

The detective found Karen to be credible, noting in his report that her answers demonstrated "definite indications of truthfulness." So powerful, at that time, was the act of passing a polygraph that almost immediately doubts as to the soundness of her story fell away. She was finally believed.

With two eyewitnesses, and a victim who could articulate what had happened to her and was willing to testify, Karen's case was a strong one, and ready for prosecutors. On December 16, the sheriff's office issued a warrant for Skalnik's arrest. The case was referred to the state attorney's office on charges of "lewd and lascivious conduct on a child under fourteen," a felony punishable by up to fifteen years in prison.

5

FALSE WITNESS

The state attorney James T. Russell stood just five feet five, but he enjoyed a fearsome reputation as a bare-knuckle courtroom adversary. He had little patience for prosecutors who did not approach the job with the same zeal, and anyone in his office whose performance fell short of his expectations became the target of his volcanic temper. As a teenager during World War II, Russell had served with the Navy in the Pacific, operating landing craft in the Battles of Iwo Jima and Okinawa, and as a prosecutor he still saw the world as a brute struggle between good and evil. His success, he believed, could be measured by the sheer number of men and women he locked up who got religion in the Pinellas County Jail. "I probably made more people find God than any preacher in the city," he once boasted.

Like many chief prosecutors of his day, Russell came to power amid a national surge in violent crime, and it was this immutable fact that shaped his office's sense of mission. Crime rates soared across the country in the late 1960s and kept climbing through the 1970s; from 1965 to 1980, the number of homicides nearly tripled. Criminologists do not agree on what caused this rise, only that many factors were at play, perhaps most unmistakably the postwar baby boom, which created a demographic spike in young men, who commit more violent crime. In Florida, this uptick was especially pronounced. Roughly 70 percent of all marijuana and cocaine coming into the country passed through Miami, and by the early 1980s the resulting turf wars left the city with the highest murder rate in America. The medical examiner's office was forced to keep a refrigerated truck on hand to ease overcrowding in the morgue.

Before lawlessness subsumed the city, Russell had staked his claim in Clearwater, three hundred miles northwest of Miami. He grew the state attorney's office from half a dozen lawyers in 1969 to more than eighty by the dawn of the Reagan era, and he pursued a law-and-order agenda whose mandate was to put away as many people as possible for as long as possible. "Put more criminals in prison," he told a local civic group in 1981, "and there will be less crime on the streets." His hard-nosed approach left little room for modulation. When a white New Yorker named Bernhard Goetz made national news in 1984 for shooting four unarmed Black teenagers on the subway after one of them demanded $5, Russell spoke out in support of the gunman. "If a man doesn't have a right to defend himself, he doesn't have a right to do anything," Russell said of Goetz, whose bullets left one teenager paralyzed and brain damaged.

The revelation that Skalnik had been charged with molesting a twelve-year-old girl brought Suzanne to her knees. She could not make any sense of it or integrate it with the man she thought she knew, but her husband, she came to realize, had been a stranger to her all along. Her pastor and members of her church urged her to stand by him, reminding her that no sinner was ever beyond redemption and that such adversity served as an opportunity to remember the sufferings of Christ.

Suzanne could not stomach staying with him, but it was not until she began trying to unwind their life together—contacting creditors and closing bank accounts and eventually fielding calls from collection agencies—that she came to understand the full scope of his predation. He had forged her signature on credit card applications, paying off one card with another. He had taken out loans under her name. He had siphoned away her savings. When she looked inside her jewelry box, she saw that nearly everything of value was gone, including a black-onyx-and-diamond ring, a prized family keepsake that her mother had given to her. No longer sure what to believe, she called Stetson University to inquire about her husband's status at the law school. The university informed her that it had no record of anyone by Skalnik's name.

Suzanne decided to end their marriage by delivering the most humiliating blow she could think of: She had Johnny Touchton go down to the jail and personally serve Skalnik with divorce papers. Afterward, she told everyone who continued to stand by him—including a detective in the sheriff's office who, at Skalnik's urging, called her to say that she should take him back—that they were being duped. "Listen to me," she pleaded. "He is not who you think he is. You've been taken in by him." But Skalnik had an instinct for what people wanted to hear. He understood that skepticism rarely won out to the power of belief—that fundamental, irresistible human need to invest ourselves in narratives that we want to be true.

With two eyewitnesses who could corroborate Karen's story, the lewd-and-lascivious case against Skalnik posed few of the usual challenges. Karen was willing to testify in open court, and she wanted Skalnik to be held to account. "I don't think it's fair," she told prosecutors, "that he's calling me a liar when I am not."

Taking the case to trial was not without its risks. The defense could try to smear Karen's character by portraying her as promiscuous, or cast doubt on her credibility, or question why she had not spoken up sooner. Yet her case was not ambiguous. The law recognizes that a twelve-year-old cannot give meaningful consent, and the Florida statute defining lewd-and-lascivious conduct left no doubt that Skalnik's actions constituted a crime. Few violations better demonstrated the moral decay and corrosion of public safety that James Russell so often railed against. All told, the state had a case they could present to a jury. Child sexual-assault cases are routinely tried on far less.

But Skalnik would never be prosecuted. In an astonishing about-face, the state attorney's office abandoned the case three months after Karen passed the polygraph exam. Its notice to the court dismissing the lewd-and-lascivious conduct charge, which bore Russell's name, consisted of just eight words: "There is insufficient evidence available at this time."

The decision not to prosecute Skalnik, as it turned out, was part of a remarkable plea agreement. In March and April 1983, Skalnik pleaded no contest to three charges of grand theft: one for defrauding the Garners, the older couple whose son had been incarcerated with him; one for swindling Robert Seidenberg, the man he met on the cruise to the Bahamas; and one for bilking Jackie Millner, the travel agent. In return, prosecutors cut Skalnik a sweetheart deal. He would not have to serve separate sentences for the Garner, Seidenberg, and Millner cases, each of which carried a maximum punishment of five years in prison. Instead, he would receive five years total, with credit for time he had already served. He would also pay no penalty for violating his probation. He would avoid any sentence enhancements, even though he was a repeat offender. And, in the luckiest break of all, he would face no consequences for molesting a child.

Why prosecutors would be willing to offer such a deal likely had to do with what they knew about Skalnik: He was useful. They would go on to request that he remain in the Pinellas County Jail rather than be sent to state prison, arguing that the men whom he had previously helped send to the penitentiary might seek retribution there. This concern for his safety masked a more urgent priority: Were he transferred out of the jail, he would no longer be an asset to the state attorney's office. Jail, where most people are awaiting trial (rather than prison, where they are held after they have been convicted), is where prosecutors needed eyes and ears. The plea deal ensured that Skalnik could continue to be an effective witness for the state in more ways than one. With the lewd-and-lascivious conduct charge out of the way, the state attorney's office could present him to jurors as a former police officer turned small-time scam artist, rather than a man who had molested a child.

Karen never knew about the state's deal with Skalnik, only that he was not punished for what he did to her. "No one ever said, 'That's wrong,'" she later remembered. "The message I got was that what he did was okay—that it wasn't serious, it wasn't a crime." In her father's eyes, she said, it was she who was to blame for what happened. "Everyone liked Paul, and they believed Paul, and I was seen as the troublemaker," she said. When the state attorney's office did not move forward with prosecution, her father's criticism of her escalated. He needled her about Skalnik, belittling and berating her. Karen ran away that year, when she was thirteen, and left home for good when she was fourteen, taking refuge at a runaway shelter. "I didn't trust anyone for a long, long time," she said.

The news that Skalnik was an informant spread quickly through the jail, and he was moved to a small cellblock where defendants with high-profile cases were kept apart from the general population. "It is no longer possible to house him in proximity to other inmates," one jailer wrote in his file, referencing concerns for his safety. Skalnik's notoriety would have made it all but impossible for him to win the trust of anyone held inside the jail, but in the summer of 1983 he got word to prosecutors that a twenty-four-year-old handyman on his cellblock who was charged with first-degree murder, Freddie Gaines, had confessed to him.

The confrontation that led to the killing for which Gaines was charged had unfolded on a busy night outside a St. Petersburg bar, and numerous onlookers gave conflicting accounts of the fatal struggle that erupted between him and his girlfriend's ex-boyfriend, Willie Frank Stewart. All that anyone could agree on was that by the end of it Stewart lay bleeding on the ground with a fatal knife wound. There was no consensus on which man had brought the knife to the bar, who first brandished it, or why. Gaines claimed that Stewart instigated the fight by pulling a knife, and that after wresting it away from his attacker, he had used it in self-defense.

Jurors might see, in the available evidence, a chance encounter that had turned violent, with Gaines acting in "a heat of passion," as Florida law defines voluntary manslaughter. But if prosecutors could show premeditation, they could secure a first-degree murder conviction. How jurors assessed Gaines's state of mind at the time of the killing would determine his fate. Manslaughter carried a maximum penalty of fifteen years in prison, while the punishment for first-degree murder was a sentence of either life or death. There was no question that prosecutors would go hard against Gaines; Russell, the state attorney, had built his office's reputation pursuing the harshest possible charges. To win a first-degree murder conviction, the state needed a clearer, more decisive narrative than the muddled eyewitness testimony they had—the kind of narrative an informant could supply.

The state attorney's office, under Russell's leadership, actively fostered a culture in which snitching was rewarded, and even encouraged. Prosecutors routinely visited the jail before their cases went to trial, offering tantalizing benefits to the men who were held there in exchange for information. Before Skalnik came forward, Gaines had himself received a visit from two assistant state attorneys who pressed him for details in another case: A former cellmate of his faced first-degree murder charges, and they wanted to know if the cellmate had ever discussed the killing. Gaines waved off the prosecutors, saying he had nothing to offer; the cellmate had never spoken about what happened. Undeterred, one prosecutor laid out the benefits of cooperating with the state attorney's office: He could get a reduced sentence if he helped them with their case. "I ain't got nothing to say," Gaines told them. "Y'all are wasting your time."

Gaines thought little of the exchange until he learned from his lawyer that Skalnik, whose reputation he knew well, had offered a story about him. At his trial that December, Skalnik testified for the state, extinguishing any notion that Gaines had acted spontaneously; according to him, Gaines had carried out a calculated, cold-blooded murder. Skalnik said Gaines had confessed during multiple conversations the two men had through a chain-link fence in the rec yard, admitting to everything: that he brought a knife to the Good Times Bar; that he sought out his old romantic rival, who he knew would be there; that he purposefully stabbed his victim in the heart. Skalnik said Gaines was unrepentant and had boasted that he should have been charged "with open-heart surgery." So proud was he of what he had done, Skalnik told the all-white jury, that Gaines, who is Black, "decorated the front of his cell with his indictment of first-degree murder."

Gaines sat at the defense table in the brown dress shirt and slacks his mother had bought for the occasion. He had remained poker-faced throughout the trial, exactly as his attorney had instructed him to do, but as he listened to Skalnik, he could no longer contain himself. "He's sitting right there telling lies," Gaines whispered to his lawyer. "Me and this man ain't never talked before!"

Skalnik assured the jury that he had come forward for no other reason than to preserve public safety, offering proof that he had not always been on the wrong side of the law. "I was a police officer," he said simply. His voice swelled, and for a moment he seemed to be on the verge of tears. "It is emotional for me, counselor," he explained before collecting himself.

The idea that Skalnik was acting only for the greater good and not because he stood to benefit from testifying against Gaines was emphasized by Assistant State Attorney Bruce Young. "It's your understanding," he asked Skalnik, "that nothing can be done for you as far as eliminating or reducing your sentence?"

"That's correct."

"Even if your lawyer wanted to go in front of a judge, the judge would have no jurisdiction to reduce the sentence, is that correct?"

"Yes, sir," Skalnik agreed. "That's correct."

Skalnik's testimony was a turning point in the case. When the verdict was read, declaring Gaines guilty of first-degree murder, his mother, Janette, screamed and fell to the floor, and two bailiffs carried her, wailing, from the courtroom. Jurors recommended that Gaines be sentenced to life, rather than death, but this act of grace came as cold comfort. Had they convicted him of the lesser charge of voluntary manslaughter, he would have walked free when he was in his late thirties, with enough time to make something of his life. Instead, as he stood before the judge at his sentencing hearing, thunderstruck, he understood that he might never see the outside world again.

6

THE CLOSER

By the time Gaines's trial concluded in the late winter of 1983, Skalnik had embarked on a new phase in his career as a snitch. That year and the next, prosecutors called him to testify against three more men, each of whom, if found guilty, faced a possible death sentence. All three of the defendants—Richard Cooper, Kenneth Gardner, and J. D. Walton—had been present at the scenes of the murders they stood accused of. But it was not clear that they represented the "worst of the worst," for whom the death penalty is supposed to be reserved. Several people were charged in connection to each crime, making the key question at their trials one of culpability: How much of a role did the accused play in the killing, and were his actions egregious enough to warrant the electric chair? Prosecutors used Skalnik to convince juries that each man was deserving of execution.

The confessions that Skalnik claimed were volunteered to him in these cases were lurid and dramatic, strewn with provocative details that brought each man's depravity into sudden, terrible focus. The truth is often messy and complicated, but his stories were simple. Gardner, who was charged alongside three others in the grisly stabbing death of an elderly hardware-store owner, reputedly bragged to Skalnik, "I killed him, but they'll never prove it." Cooper, accused of taking part in the killings of three men after a

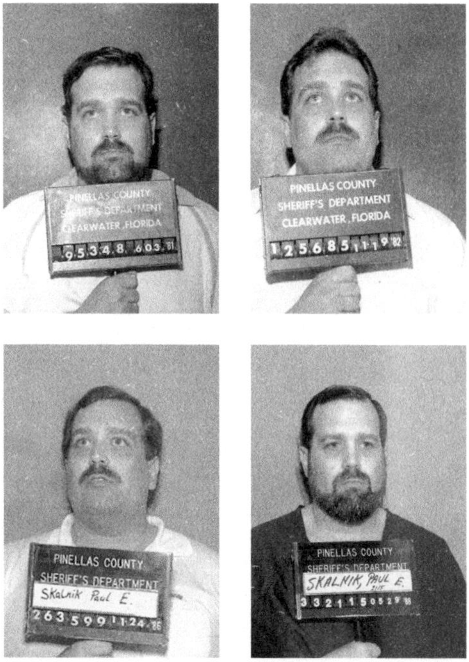

PAUL SKALNIK AT THE PINELLAS COUNTY JAIL IN CLEARWATER, FLORIDA, IN 1981, 1982, 1986, AND 1988

botched robbery, supposedly introduced himself to Skalnik with the brash declaration "I'm one of the men involved in the triple-murder slayings they thought was a Mafia gangland killing." And Walton, one of Cooper's co-defendants—whom Skalnik admitted he had never spoken to—considered the murders "a funny joke." Skalnik asserted that he was just repeating what Cooper had told him.

With the help of prosecutors, he also assured jurors that his motive for coming forward was purely altruistic. "I made a mistake in my life, and it was greed," he said when he took the stand at Gardner's trial, sketching out his redemption story. "I wanted to do something that I should have—I should have done it sooner in my life. This man next to me in my cell admitted to killing a man, showing no remorse and not caring. And I felt if the information I could give the state would assist, I wanted to give the information to the state. That is why I'm testifying." Under prompting from Bruce Young, the same prosecutor who tried Gaines, Skalnik agreed that he would not—and indeed could not—receive a reduced sentence for his testimony. "My time for reconsideration has long passed, and there is no hope for me whatsoever," he said.

Without Skalnik's testimony, jurors would likely still have recommended that all three men, at a minimum, be sentenced to life in prison. Skalnik's testimony allowed the state attorney's office to guarantee their executions. He was the state's closer, the witness whose words moved jurors to choose death. Where there was room for doubt, Skalnik erased it, as he did in Gardner's case, when his testimony put the murder weapon in Gardner's hands. Where jurors might consider leniency, as in Cooper's case, Skalnik told a story to harden their hearts. Cooper was still a teenager and looked even younger than his age—a potentially mitigating fact that could have earned the jury's mercy, until Skalnik turned it against him. "He said no jury would ever sentence him to the death chair," Skalnik testified, "because he's nineteen years old and because he's got that little baby face."

No one at the time realized the full measure of his influence, but Skalnik had become one of the most prolific, and most effective, jailhouse witnesses in American history. "I have placed 34 individuals in prison, including four on death row," he crowed in a letter he wrote on June 9, 1984, to Florida's senior senator, Lawton Chiles, requesting the lawmaker's help in winning him an early release. Though embellished, his numbers were not too far off. By then, he had testified against, or given information about, at least twenty-seven defendants in the Pinellas County Jail. Almost all had been convicted or taken plea deals. Three of them—Cooper, Gardner, and Walton—faced execution.

Skalnik seemed to project his own depravity onto these men, when arguably he was the coldest-blooded among them. Superficially, his transgressions lacked the brutality of their crimes; he did not use a sharp blade, or a gun, or his hands—just words and charm. But unlike these men, he was not high when he metaphorically twisted the knife, or acting impulsively, or reacting in a moment of fight-or-flight-induced panic. He had months to contemplate what he was going to say, refining his narrative as he met with investigators and prosecutors, sitting for pretrial depositions, and finally taking the stand. Nothing suggested that he felt remorse, or anything but indifference that his testimony might bring about someone's death. He displayed not the nervous energy of someone wrestling with a difficult moral choice but the calm confidence of someone who had made peace with trading lives for personal advantage. He testified with a strangely serene sangfroid.

That year, the *St. Petersburg Times* ran a story on the steep rise in death sentences in Pinellas County. The shift was dramatic: Throughout the entire 1970s, local judges had sentenced a total of two men to execution, but in the first nine months of 1984 alone they dispatched eight to death row. Defense attorneys reported having difficulty finding prospective jurors who had any reservations about capital punishment. They also noticed a shift in the mood at the state attorney's office. Though prosecutors had been willing to waive the death penalty in some first-degree murder cases just a few years earlier, they were no longer amenable to doing so. One lawyer told the paper, "They're going to have to build a separate wing on death row for Pinellas County."

With a witness like Skalnik in hand, prosecutors could afford to be aggressive. He had proven himself to be particularly valuable in the prosecution of the High Point murders—the killings that Cooper and Walton had carried out with a third man, Terry Van

Royal. The trio had broken into a Largo home looking for cash and cocaine, and the robbery had quickly gone awry; by the time they fled the scene, the three people inside the house had been forced to the ground, hands bound, and shot at close range with shotguns. The only one of the trio whom Skalnik did not testify against was Royal, who had protested when jailers tried to move Skalnik into his cell, ostensibly for the purpose of gathering information. "I told the guard I would not be in the same cell with him," Royal later wrote in an affidavit, "because I knew who he was, and what he did."

The lead detective in the case was a thirty-three-year-old rising star in the sheriff's department: John Halliday. Securing death sentences for the perpetrators of the High Point murders was the crowning achievement of his career at that point—one for which he had Skalnik, in part, to thank. In return, the detective called the parole commission to plead for leniency. "Mr. Halliday would like the commission to know the subject has been of great assistance to the sheriff's office in that he testified in 33 felony cases," reads an interoffice memo documenting the investigator's call. Halliday then wrote directly to a parole commissioner. "I have never done this for an inmate during my ten years in law enforcement." Halliday urged the commissioner to "consider Skalnik for parole at the earliest possible convenience." The investigator even vouched for Skalnik's contrition, adding, "He is truly sincere in that he has learned his lesson."

Despite the repeated assurances the prosecutor Bruce Young had made to jurors that Skalnik could not gain any favorable treatment by testifying for the state, Young himself advocated, behind the scenes, for leniency. "Mr. Skalnik has been a state witness in a number of very important cases, including several first-degree murder cases, and his testimony has been honest and truthful in all cases," Young wrote to the Florida Department of Corrections in the first of two letters he sent on behalf of the state attorney's office.

Expressing concern for Skalnik's continued safety, he asked that his star witness not be sent to state prison but remain in the jail; better yet, Young proposed, the State of Florida could simply release him. "If Mr. Skalnik is eligible for parole," he wrote, "I would urge that Mr. Skalnik be considered for parole."

But in the summer of 1984, as concerns about security mounted, Skalnik was abruptly transported out of the jail—and out of Florida entirely. Under an interstate compact between Florida and Arizona, he was moved to a penitentiary situated in the vast expanse of desert that lies southeast of Phoenix to serve the remainder of his sentence. Skalnik was apoplectic. "What the hell must I go through to be eligible for parole or at least work release?" he raged in a letter he sent to Young, haranguing the prosecutor for failing to negotiate his freedom. "Are the new guidelines for grand theft—death!"

Prisons typically perform detailed evaluations of the people they confine, subjecting new arrivals to a battery of tests and in-depth interviews to determine the security level they require—a process that revealed Skalnik to be a poor candidate for early release. In contrast to the testimonies of Halliday and Young, Florida prison officials characterized him shortly before his transfer to Arizona as a "con artist of the highest degree" who was "without any remorse," warning that his "post-release prognosis would be guarded." A counselor in the Arizona prison system subsequently concluded that Skalnik posed a "high risk of further unlawful behavior." Nevertheless, after a concerted effort by Pinellas County prosecutors and law enforcement to win his release, Skalnik was returned to Florida and paroled on March 19, 1985—two years, almost to the day, after his five-year sentence was imposed.

Skalnik was soon working out of a peach-stucco-and-Spanish-tile office plaza in Clearwater not far from the beach. His business, Enterprise Investigators, looked legitimate, with a secretary and official letterhead emblazoned in a handsome, swooping script. Despite its professional veneer, the true purpose of Enterprise Investigators was to perpetrate real estate fraud and a variety of other scams. Skalnik lent credibility to these deceptions with a flurry of official-looking papers: counterfeit receipts, fake bank statements, and forged documents. He occasionally served papers for Bruce Young, who, after prosecuting a number of high-profile cases, had gone into private practice. Young hired him, though he had previously handled Skalnik's theft cases and prosecuted him for crimes of dishonesty. Skalnik made the most of it. One of the forged, notarized contracts for his real estate venture was typed up on letterhead he swiped from Young's law office.

An elderly St. Petersburg widow named Viola Giovanniello was the first to report him to law enforcement, in the early summer of 1986. Giovanniello told investigators that Skalnik had befriended her after the death of her husband, then cheated her out of $35,000 by selling her two Lincoln Town Cars that he had financed but did not own. A Clearwater divorcée, Dolores Wengatz, also went to police that summer. She described paying Skalnik $37,000 for a property in Sarasota that he had persuaded her to buy sight unseen—an investment for which he assured her he was an equal investor and for which he had lined up an eager buyer. Only when she drove out to see the property had she learned that it did not actually exist. When she confronted Skalnik with this fact, she said he had paused for a moment and then gasped, "Oh my God, I've been taken!"

Both women had grown close to Skalnik and were stung by his betrayals. "He seemed to be so polite and so nice, and he treated me like I was his mother," Giovanniello later told prosecutors. "Of course he would be nice to me; he took all my money."

Skalnik's parole officer, Becky Anderson, spoke to three additional victims. One woman said she had hemorrhaged more than $100,000 since becoming entangled in a romantic relationship with

Skalnik that dated back to the early 1980s; another reported losing $60,000 to Skalnik in a real estate scam; and the third described taking out two separate bank loans for him, both of which he defaulted on. Skalnik had made off with hundreds of thousands of dollars, in Anderson's estimation, though where it had all gone remained a mystery. When he learned that he was being investigated, he skipped town, leaving behind nothing for his newest wife—a young woman he had married four days after his release from prison—or their baby daughter.

In Anderson's report, she noted that Skalnik's new crimes were "mirror images of the charges he is currently on parole for," and that he had failed to pay restitution to his prior victims. Citing the gravity of the allegations against him, she recommended that Skalnik be held without bond once he was arrested, and that he be sentenced to "the maximum time allowed [by] the sentencing guidelines to include habitual offender enhancement." She closed her report by exhorting the state attorney's office to take decisive action once he was apprehended:

> This man has been, is, and always will be a danger to society. He has perfected the role of con man and has left a trail of victims that have lost life savings and more as a result of his actions. These victims will never be able to recoup the financial loss or psychological well-being that they have suffered. They should at least be assured by the sentence imposed that this individual's destruction of lives [will] not be allowed to happen again for a long, long time.

Skalnik, it turned out, had left the state and fled to Austin, where he duped a jewelry-store clerk into taking a check from a defunct bank account for a $6,100 gold Rolex. After a warrant was issued for his arrest in Texas that fall, he returned to Clearwater, and on November 24, 1986, he turned himself in.

An unsigned, handwritten letter soon arrived at the state attorney's office, urging prosecutors to not let Skalnik slip through their fingers again. "I have recently been informed that Paul E. Skalnik has been found and arrested," its author wrote. "I would like to appeal to you on behalf of all his past victims, not to mention those in his future. Mr. Skalnik's deceitful nature knows no bounds. There is no limit to his lowly schemes or his unlawful actions. Mr. Skalnik has proven that he cannot be trusted, yet he is allowed to go free on bail even after repeated disappearing acts. Please consider putting an end to this circle now by being as harsh on him as the law allows. How many chances will this man be given? How many more people will he hurt and victimize?"

PART II

7

JIM

Before he was Jimmy D., he was Jim: a cheerful, long-limbed kid with a bright smile and an easy way about him. The second of four children born to John and Grace Dailey, a farm equipment salesman and a bank teller, Jim was raised in Manhattan, Kansas, where he stood out, from an early age, for his preternatural good humor. A formal portrait from 1957 shows Jim, then eleven, standing beside his straight-faced family wearing an unrestrained grin, as if laughing at a joke no one else can hear. He was the mirror opposite of his father, a rigid and at times merciless disciplinarian who was not afraid to use brute force to shape his sons into the men he wanted them to be. Jim, at least outwardly, appeared unfazed. "Happy-go-lucky" was how his friends and classmates described him before he went off to Vietnam.

He was sixteen when he met Mary Kay Koon, who worked the concession stand at the Campus Theater, the local cinema where he found a job as a ticket taker. Her family owned a popular burger joint, the In-Between, which sat halfway between the area's two major employers, Kansas State University and Fort Riley. Though they traveled in different circles—he went to Manhattan High, and she attended Catholic school—they shared an infatuation with movies, particularly musicals. Their favorite was *West Side Story,* and when a romance bloomed between them, they carried on as if they, too, were in a swooning Technicolor production. Sometimes after the theater emptied out, Mary Kay would run down the aisle toward Jim and leap into his open arms. At the end of their evenings together, they sang farewell to each other with such overwrought emotion that Mary Kay's mother would flicker the porch light until they stopped.

Jim's sidekick and near-constant companion, even on dates with Mary Kay, was his kid sister, Joan, who was six years his junior. Jim brought her along with them to the Putt-Putt course and the bowling alley, and when they parked at the drive-in, Joan took the back seat. Mary Kay, a devout Catholic who was determined to keep their relationship as virtuous as possible, voiced no objections. Joan did not tell her or Jim until many years later that their father—who served as the choir director at their Episcopalian church and played Santa Claus at the American Legion Hall every year—had been molesting her. Instinctively protective, Jim kept her close and did everything he could to shield her from their father. Often, he picked her up from school and took her to work with him. The Campus Theater was their refuge, a diversion from the chaos of home. Joan watched Vincent Price play a madman in *House of Usher* so many times that she could recite his lines by heart.

Unlike their father, Jim was slow to anger, and both Joan and Mary Kay were struck by his gentleness. Once, when he saw his sister's distress at finding a mouse writhing in a mousetrap, he freed it, telling her with a wink, "Don't tell Mom and Dad." Within his tight group of friends, he was the joker, the skinny kid on the football team who liked to make people laugh, but who could be counted on when the moment turned serious. During a high school graduation party in the spring of 1964, when a seventeen-year-old named Judy Specht nearly drowned at Tuttle Creek Lake, just north of town, it was Jim who sprang into motion. He grabbed a raft to transport her to dry land and then performed chest compressions.

After her release from the hospital, she credited him with saving her life.

Jim went on to attend Kansas State, but he dropped out during his second semester, after his father died of a heart attack at the age of forty-three. With money tight at home, he went to work as a housepainter, but he soon decided to enlist. The war in Vietnam was ramping up, leaving him with a choice: wait to be drafted, or sign up and join whichever branch of the military seemed to offer the best chances of survival. Like most of his friends, Jim picked the Air Force—a four-year commitment, but one that would keep him out of the Army, which would bear the war's heaviest casualties. After completing basic training in Texas, and additional training in Mississippi, he reported for duty at Davis-Monthan Air Force Base, in Tucson, in the late summer of 1966.

Mary Kay remained in Kansas, where she attended a women's college in Salina, an hour's drive from Manhattan. Jim had proposed to her after high school, but at her parents' urging, they decided to hold off on marrying so she could focus on college, and they saw each other when Jim was home on leave. Their reunion just before he left for Tucson was more ardent than most, and when he called her one day in the fall of 1966, she told him in a wobbly voice that she thought she was pregnant. "Don't worry—I'll be home as soon as I can," he reassured her. He returned to Manhattan for a hastily arranged church wedding, in which he wore his Air Force dress blues and his usual joyous expression. Afterward, he drove his bride with him back to Tucson. In just a little more than a week, Mary Kay had gone from being a college junior majoring in business to an airman's wife beset by morning sickness.

Despite the upheaval of the pregnancy, Jim and Mary Kay were elated to finally be together, and in May 1967 they welcomed their son into the world. But the war loomed; each night, they watched the stark, black-and-white TV news dispatches out of South Viet-

MARY KAY KOON AND JIM DAILEY IN MANHATTAN, KANSAS, ON THE NIGHT BEFORE THEIR WEDDING, OCTOBER 19, 1966

nam that showed the conflict's intensifying combat. Late that year, Jim received word that he was being deployed to an air base outside Saigon, to work on U-2 spy planes as an aircraft radio repairman. His time there would mark the beginning of a profound shift—one that his mother would later try to put into words. "I sent two lovely young men to the Air Force and Marines," she said of Jim and his younger brother, Joe, "and they came back, and they were different boys."

Jim stepped onto the tarmac at Bien Hoa Air Base on February 2, 1968, on the third day of the Tet Offensive: a surprise, large-scale assault by communist forces that marked the start of the bloodiest phase of the war. More than eighty thousand North Vietnamese and Vietcong led coordinated raids on cities and military installations across South Vietnam, including the air base in Bien Hoa, which came under attack on the first day of the offensive. The Air

Force, with assistance from an Army aviation battalion, secured the base by nightfall, but by then 4 Americans and 137 Vietcong fighters lay dead. Twenty-six airmen were wounded, and another suffered a fatal heart attack.

Nighttime rocket and mortar attacks on the base became routine in the weeks and months that followed Jim's arrival. The attacks were always sudden and unpredictable, a cacophony of explosions that ruptured the quiet of the evening, followed by the wail of air-raid sirens. For protection, there were only the flimsy shelters—hooches—where the men slept under corrugated-tin roofs. At the first sound of trouble, they would make a mad dash for the sandbag-fortified bunkers nearby. Jim was spared once when his bunker took a direct hit; he was spared again when he and several other airmen bolted from their hooch before it was strafed with shrapnel. He learned to leave his mouth open so the concussive force of the rockets and mortars did not blow out his eardrums.

The dread that gripped him in those early days in Bien Hoa was amplified by the grim work he had to carry out in the wake of each strike. Jim was assigned to a detail whose objective was to locate anyone killed in an attack and to help the injured, transporting them to the base dispensary for medical attention. Were he to come across any body parts, he was to retrieve those, too. Once, he came to the aid of a wounded airman, bleeding and in a severe state of shock, whose intestines were spilling from his abdomen. After another strike, he salvaged a severed foot, still encased in a combat boot. Jim moved through those nights in a blur, waiting for dawn to arrive. His pleas to be taken off the detail were denied.

Jim's upbeat letters home to Mary Kay made no mention of the attacks on the base, but when he returned home that summer at the end of his six-month tour, she could see the changes that had come over him. Jim drank every night back in Tucson, and when he finally drifted off to sleep, he was restless and agitated. Mary Kay was jolted awake more than once to find him thrashing beside her, tormented by night terrors. Once, when a fire truck raced by their house, sirens blaring, Jim leaped out of bed and stood blinking in the early morning light, unsure where he was.

Despite the hardships of his tour, Jim took pride in the work he was doing and excelled at it. He received outstanding evaluations from his superiors in Bien Hoa, who cited his integrity, work ethic, respect for authority, consideration for his fellow airmen, and "demand for excellence," giving him the highest marks possible for his job performance. He was well liked by the other aircraft radio repairmen, some of whom he had trained in Tucson; several looked up to him as a big brother figure. At least outwardly, Jim thrived in their reflected admiration. When the time came to decide if he would reenlist, he signed up for another four years.

Jim would serve a total of three tours in Vietnam, none as harrowing as the first. It was his initial pass through Bien Hoa that seemed to break open some part of him that could not easily be put back together. He spent his evenings drinking whatever he

JIM DAILEY AT BIEN HOA AIR BASE, IN BIEN HOA, VIETNAM, 1969

could procure at the base liquor store, slowly losing his ability to moderate. He was, perhaps, more susceptible than most. Alcoholism had bedeviled both of his parents, and his younger siblings, Joe and Joan, would endure long struggles with addiction. Between tours, Jim had difficulty reintegrating into the more sedate rhythm of family life. When he was back in Tucson, he often left Mary Kay at home with their son, Michael, and their baby daughter, Stacey, while he went out drinking with his fellow airmen, sometimes stumbling into the house just before dawn.

Mary Kay and the kids accompanied him overseas, in 1971, when he was assigned to Clark Air Base in the Philippines. Jim continued to earn praise from his superiors, and while stationed at Clark, he was entrusted to work on the Apollo program, maintaining the airborne radios that tracked the location of the command module as it reentered the earth's atmosphere. As the war wound down, he put in long hours assisting with Operation Homecoming, a two-month airlift mission that transported American prisoners of war to Clark Air Base and then repatriated them.

At home, though, Jim was devolving. Sometimes the kids awoke to find strangers passed out in the living room after a long night of drinking. Once, men they did not know muscled their way into the house to claim the family's console stereo system, which Jim had lost betting on a cockfight. Furious, Mary Kay did something she never imagined she was capable of, astonishing herself with the force of her anger: She slapped him, hard. Jim did not hit back or raise his voice. He touched his face, surprised.

Afterward, he resolved that he would get better, and he checked himself into the base hospital for a monthlong, inpatient program for substance abuse. He managed to stay sober for a short period, only to relapse—a pattern that continued when he, Mary Kay, and the kids returned to the States in 1973 and he was assigned to Fairchild Air Force Base, just outside Spokane, Washington. During his sober periods, he tried to prove to Mary Kay that he was a good husband and father, teaching Sunday school at the base chapel and singing with her in their church choir. These spells never lasted; he would start drinking again, often until he blacked out. Mary Kay once found him lying in the bathtub, unconscious, his face nearly submerged under the running water.

In the fall of 1974, Jim was reassigned to Osan Air Base, in South Korea, for a one-year unaccompanied tour. Mary Kay and the children had to stay behind, returning home to Kansas. Both alcohol and drugs were plentiful around the base, and without a family to anchor him, they became Jim's primary focus. Money troubles followed, as did the strained explanations he gave Mary Kay about why her portion of his paycheck seldom reached her. The compassionate man she had once known had stranded her and their children in an untenable situation, leaving them without any reliable means of support. After agonizing about how to move forward, she decided that she had no other choice than to seek a divorce.

The ferociousness of Jim's alcoholism quickly eroded what remained of his life. Shattered by the collapse of his marriage, he described his state of mind to a military doctor as "extreme depression," and he contemplated suicide. His excessive drinking and erratic behavior prompted the Air Force to present the thirty-one-year-old with a painful choice: He could take an honorable discharge and leave the service, or he could challenge that recommendation but risk a dishonorable discharge. Reluctantly, in 1978, Jim exited the Air Force, abandoning the world he had inhabited since he was nineteen.

When he returned to civilian life after his last assignment at Spangdahlem Air Base, in Germany, he was at loose ends. He had no obvious plan before him, nowhere to go, and an insatiable need to drink. His first stop was Dover Air Force Base in Delaware, where he went to see his children. Mary Kay was living at Dover with her new husband, Dick Dollar, a radar repairman who had been one of Jim's closest friends when he was stationed in Tucson. Few men in Jim's position could have walked into Dick's home with such equanimity—there was Mary Kay, and the children, and even the same furniture from their previous life together—but Jim, who looked fragile that day despite his six-foot-four frame, seemed grateful to see everyone, including his old friend.

The two men greeted each other warmly, and Stacey, then eight years old, threw her arms around Jim's neck. Ten-year-old Michael, whose memories of his father's absences stretched back further, was polite but hung back.

The mood was celebratory when they all went out to dinner that night, and Dick, who footed the bill, allowed the children to believe that their father was treating them. Jim kept looking around the table, marveling at the family they had created. "You have it all," he said to Mary Kay when they later found themselves alone for a moment. His tone was pained, but sincere, when he added, "I'm so happy for you."

After the kids went to bed, Mary Kay and Dick sat down with Jim in the living room, and broached a wrenching subject. Dick did the talking, first laying out the basic facts about how Jim's departure from the Air Force was going to affect the lives of his children. The kids would no longer be allowed to attend the base school with their friends, Dick reminded him, and they would lose their health insurance, along with a host of other benefits, big and small. Dick then arrived at his point with simple directness: He wanted to adopt the children. This would allow Michael and Stacey to have no interruption to their lives and provide them with the best possible future. Dick promised that he would raise them as if they were his own.

As Jim took in what Dick was saying, tears streamed down his face. He sat in silence for a long time, and when he finally spoke, his voice was thick with emotion. "I know you will take good care of my kids," he said. He thanked Dick for stepping up and providing what he, as their father, could not. In a nod to his own anguished state of mind, he said quietly, "I wish you would adopt *me*."

Jim caught a bus out of town the next day and headed west, embarking on a rootless existence that led him deeper and deeper into the crucible of his addiction. He lived off money he made doing construction work and carpentry, and in his off-hours he drank until he had dulled his senses. In Tucson, he was arrested for punching a man in the eye during a bar fight; he pleaded guilty to aggravated battery in the summer of 1979 and spent five months in jail. After his release, he made his way back to Kansas. Nothing he tried there lasted long: not a brief stretch of sobriety after another attempt at rehab; not a quick second marriage; and not the one good job he landed, at an aviation electronics company outside Kansas City, in Olathe.

His favorite bar in Olathe was a small beer joint with pool tables called Sue's Place, and it was there, around 1983, that he met a shaggy-haired burnout in his twenties named Jack Pearcy. They shared, if little else, a hunger for alcohol and the ability to consume staggering amounts of it. First, they became drinking buddies, and then they started doing drugs together. Jim was using whatever he could find by then—cocaine, speed, quaaludes—and the two men, with nearly a decade between them and wildly divergent life experiences, found common purpose. To differentiate him from the other regulars named Jim, Jack christened his friend Jimmy D., and the nickname stuck.

Jim had trouble finding steady work, and his prospects looked bleak; he moved in with his younger brother, who was on his own long, post-Vietnam slide downward, wrestling with a heroin habit. When Jim learned, in the spring of 1985, that Jack was leaving town and heading to Florida with a girlfriend, he decided that he wanted in. Jack's longtime friend Dwain Shaw, whose marriage was on the rocks, followed close behind.

They arrived at the white sugar–sand beaches of Pinellas County, where the living was cheap, construction jobs were plentiful, and the easy pace along its bar-studded coastline felt like a never-ending party. For Jim, the area exerted a particular gravitational pull. Less than an hour's drive from Seminole, where Jack had secured a two-bedroom rental, was MacDill Air Force Base, in Tampa, where Dick Dollar, Mary Kay, and the kids were living. They were hardly kids anymore—Michael was seventeen and Stacey fifteen—and Jim had not seen them since they had visited him in Kansas four years earlier. With his arrival in Seminole, he was once again near them, but he could not work up the nerve to pick up the phone. Ashamed of what he had become, he never told them he was right there, on the other side of Tampa Bay.

8

SHELLY

A bridge tender first noticed her from his post atop the Walsingham Road bridge, a hulking steel drawbridge in Indian Rocks Beach, eight miles south of Clearwater. His discovery came not long after dawn, as the sun crested over the Intracoastal Waterway, an inland channel that skirts the western edge of Pinellas County. The air was already thick and humid; seagulls screeched and canted overhead. The bridge tender put down his newspaper and squinted into his binoculars. In the shimmering water, he noticed a human figure—a mannequin, he first thought—facing skyward.

In the shadow of the drawbridge was a secluded strip of land where couples sometimes came to park. Every so often, the long, low rumble of a car crossing the bridge reverberated overhead. Below, the marshy banks were thick with cordgrass, buffeted by the near-constant wind. Mangroves lined the channel, their roots protruding, half above the waterline, half unseen.

The tide was coming in when the police arrived. Detectives dressed in white shirtsleeves, dark slacks, and ties swarmed the rocky shore, trying to preserve the scene before it was subsumed by the rising water. A pair of jeans lay tangled nearby; blood stained the rocks.

The still figure in the water was carried to dry land. She was

INVESTIGATORS IN INDIAN ROCKS BEACH, FLORIDA, EXAMINING THE CRIME SCENE ON MAY 6, 1985

slight and sandy-haired, her age indeterminate, though she appeared to be a teenager or young woman. Her death, it was immediately evident, had been singular in its violence. Thirty-one stab wounds pierced her body. Her right jugular vein was severed, her left lung punctured, her face slashed. She was unclothed, with a welter of bruises across her upper body. Deep gashes gouged her hands, as if she had tried to shield herself from the ferocity of the attack. Water had lodged in her lungs, suggesting that she had still been alive when her head went under the water.

A massive search ensued, as investigators combed the area for evidence and mapped out the crime scene. Dive teams plumbed the Intracoastal, dragging the channel's sandy bottom. Officers fanned out across the adjacent land, sweeping the ground with metal detectors as they strode through the tall grass. A pair of crumpled black panties was found by two puddles of blood. Nearby sat a pool of vomit. Otherwise, the crime scene yielded little: No knife or blade was found; no fingerprints or semen were

Nude body identified as young, troubled girl

By CHRISTINA K. COSDON
and ELIZABETH MAUER
St. Petersburg Times Staff Writers

Shelly Boggio was often in trouble. She refused to attend school, and police say it wasn't unusual for her to stay away from home overnight, even though she was only 14.

She didn't come home Sunday night, either. The next morning, her nude body was found floating in the Intracoastal Waterway at Indian Rocks Beach.

After two days of trying, police were able to identify her body Wednesday when three of her relatives came forward.

"It was the ring and the scars that confirmed it," said Indian Rocks Beach Police Chief Sam Heath.

SHELLY BOGGIO

Shelly was wearing a small silver ring with a turquoise in the shape of an eagle when she was killed. A large burn scar covered the lower part of her abdomen, and there was another on her left thigh.

After police released that description, Heath said, Frank Boggio contacted police Tuesday night and said he had a bad feeling that the victim was his daughter Shelly Elizabeth.

Heath said Boggio told detectives that he and his daughters — Shelly's identical twin sister Stacy and 18-year-old Sherry — were not concerned when the teen-ager did not come home Sunday night. She frequently did not come home on nights when she was partying with friends, Heath related.

SUNDAY NIGHT, Shelly and Stacy were out with friends near their home near Kenneth City, said Heath. At some point, the sisters separated. Heath declined to comment how the teen-ager came to be in Indian Rocks Beach or if she had been seen that

Please see GIRL, 11-B

NEWS COVERAGE OF SHELLY BOGGIO'S DEATH, IN 1985, IN THE *ST. PETERSBURG TIMES*

recovered. Clues that might have helped investigators—shoe prints still visible in the sand or tire tracks that led away from the water—would have been quickly washed away by the rising tide.

Officers canvassed the surrounding area, but no one had seen or heard anything. There were no immediate leads, and the victim's identity remained unknown. Appealing to the public for help, the Indian Rocks Beach Police Department released a description of her: five feet seven, approximately 110 pounds, tanned skin, green eyes.

Investigators got their first good lead the following day—May 7, 1985—when a seventeen-year-old named Sherry Boggio, who lived half an hour's drive away, called to say that the victim sounded like one of her younger sisters. Shelly was fourteen, the caller explained, and had not come home for two days. A detective asked Sherry to come to the police station, where he showed her photos of the victim, taken postmortem. The makeup applied to the girl's face to camouflage her injuries was so heavy that Sherry was only able to identify her sister by the silver ring, eagle shaped and inset with turquoise, that Shelly wore on her left hand.

Detectives now had that much: her name. It was not uncommon for Shelly to stay out all night, they learned, so her failure to come home had not triggered any frantic phone calls. Nor had her absence from school raised an alarm; she had stopped showing up at school long before she went missing. Until becoming the focus of an urgent homicide investigation, Shelly had passed through the world almost unnoticed.

The first big break in the case came two days later, on May 9, when a young woman driving a white Toyota Corolla with Kansas plates turned in to the driveway of a single-story stucco house in Seminole. It was just before midnight, and the house, in a Pinellas County subdivision called Pine Grove Estates, was quiet and dark. Detectives were conducting round-the-clock surveillance of the residence, which Shelly's twin, Stacy, had identified as the home of a man named Jack.

That past weekend, she remembered, she, her twin sister, and a friend had been trying to thumb a ride when Jack and two of his buddies picked them up. Jack brought them back to the house, where the group smoked joints Jack rolled and watched *Alfred Hitchcock Presents.*

Later that evening, Stacy said, her sister went out dancing with Jack, his girlfriend, and one of the men at the house. Stacy and her friend went home. It was the last time she ever saw her sister.

Jack, investigators learned, was a recent newcomer to Florida—a Kansan named Jack Pearcy. The other men at the house were Kansans, too: Dwain Shaw and James Dailey, known as Jimmy D.

A detective, who sat in an unmarked car across the street from the stucco house, watched as a woman stepped out from behind the wheel of the Toyota and let herself into the house. She matched the description of Jack's girlfriend, Gayle Bailey. The detective alerted the lead investigator in the case, John Halliday, to her arrival.

Halliday, who worked homicides and sex crimes for the Pinellas County Sheriff's Office, had made a name for himself several years earlier cracking the case of the High Point murders, in which two men were sentenced to death with the help of Paul Skalnik's testimony. By 3:30 a.m., he was seated in an interrogation room across from Gayle, the young woman in the Toyota. The twenty-one-year-old looked slightly dazed, her feathered hair falling into her blue eyes, as Halliday informed her that she had the right to remain silent. She was pregnant, about five months along.

In that first, halting conversation, which stretched past dawn, Gayle added to what the investigator had already learned about the day of May 5. Tensions were running high, Gayle explained, when Jack brought the girls back to the house. "He told me it was bothering him, wondering if this baby was his or not," she said. "We weren't getting along." She remembered him openly pursuing Shelly in front of her, telling her that he was taking the teenager out dancing; she said she tagged along with them to Jerry's Rock 'n' Disco, and that Jimmy D. came too. She pretended not to care when her boyfriend asked Shelly to dance—she even lent Shelly her own shoes to dance in, seeing that the teenager's moccasins were worn through with holes—but she grew angrier as the night wore on. "They took me home because I got mad," she said. "I went to my bedroom, and I closed the door."

Gayle remembered being so upset that she was not aware of what time it was when she climbed into bed. "I wasn't paying no attention," she said. "I was crying." That left Shelly behind in the living room with the three men in the house: Jack, Jimmy D., and the friend visiting from Kansas, Dwain Shaw. The other girls had gone their separate ways by then. Gayle told the detective that was the last time she saw Shelly.

In Halliday's experience, it was not unusual for witnesses to hold back information at the very beginning. To get at the truth, he later said, he interviewed Gayle "five, six, seven times."

With Gayle, the facts were hard to pin down. On the first night of questioning, she told Halliday three different stories about her whereabouts in the days following Shelly's visit. First, she claimed Jack had packed a suitcase the next morning, declaring that he needed to go away for a while to clear his head and instructing her to drop him off, along with the other two men in the house, in Tampa. She told Halliday that she did so, and that in her despair afterward, she drove straight to Kansas and back. When the detective easily debunked her story by calling the friend she claimed to have stayed with there, Gayle confessed that she had actually headed east to the Atlantic shoreline, to Daytona. Unable to name the highways she took there, she offered a third story: "I just cruised on up the coast, just piddled around and slept in the car a couple of nights." She swore she did not know where Jack went or how to find him. "I felt abandoned," she added. "I did and I still do."

Skeptical, Halliday had officers continue to surveil the house in Seminole, and trail Gayle if she strayed from it. Hours after that first interview, an officer followed her to a gas station pay phone. "I don't know what to do," the officer overheard her saying. "They have already taken a statement from me. I don't know if they believe me."

Detectives subsequently searched her Toyota and found a room key from a motel in the ocean-side city of Hollywood, north of Miami. Informed of this discovery, Gayle told the fourth, and final, story about where she had gone. She explained that on the morning of May 6 she found Shelly's moccasins, along with an earring and a sash the teenager had been wearing, in her car. Certain that Jack had been unfaithful, she was, she said, "screaming and throwing a fit." The men in the house went for a drive, she remembered, and when they returned, Jack was in a hurry: "He said, 'Come on, we're going to Miami.' I said, 'Why?' And he said, 'Just don't worry about it.'" Soon everyone in the house piled into her Toyota, and the foursome headed out of town.

Gayle also revised what she had told Halliday about the last time she saw Shelly. While there are partial recordings and transcripts of her early conversations with the detective, there are no recordings of these follow-up interviews—no documentation of the questions the detective asked, or how Gayle's answers changed over time. There is only a final audio recording in which she delivered a largely uninterrupted, stream-of-consciousness account of the evening. In this version, she did not hole up in her bedroom crying after they came home from Jerry's Rock 'n' Disco. Instead, she retreated to the bathroom, and when she returned to the living room, she found Dwain there, alone. At that moment, she realized that Jack had used her brief absence to steal away with Shelly. She said she caught sight of them sitting in the car outside, engine running, along with Jimmy D.

"I asked Dwain—he was laying on the couch—I said, 'Well, am I supposed to go, or what?'" she recalled. "And as I said that, the car was pulling out of the driveway."

Who was in the car that slid into the muggy darkness was a question of singular importance to the investigation, and Halliday, in the end, had obtained what appeared to be an eyewitness account. Gayle's recollection advanced the idea that Shelly was not alone with Jack in the hours leading up to the murder; rather, she was with him and Jimmy D.

9

JACK

Before striking out for Florida earlier that year, Jack Pearcy had worked as a roofer and lived in Olathe, Kansas, with his longtime girlfriend, Lori Cupp, and their young son. Intensely possessive and volatile, Jack was prone to sudden eruptions of anger at Lori, and the police were often called out to the couple's house. When officers responded to a 1982 domestic disturbance call, Lori accused Jack of repeatedly kicking her in the stomach. ("I may be carrying your child!" she cried out. "Why don't you kick me again?") Refusing to comply with the responding officers' orders, Jack shoved one of the cops against the wall and then punched the wall with both fists. In the spring of 1984, police were dispatched after he dragged Lori out of a car and threw her to the ground. That November, he threatened her while wielding a shotgun.

At a time when men were rarely held to account for the violence they visited upon their wives and girlfriends, Jack did not face any meaningful consequences. He was handed a no-contact order for the first incident, in 1982, and a year of probation for dragging her from the car. Lori declined to cooperate with prosecutors after Jack threatened her with a shotgun—"He scared me real bad," she told police—and the charge against him, "threat to commit violence with the intent to terrorize another," was dismissed. Lori would later tell investigators that Jack raped her, but he was never prosecuted. Then, early in 1985, he left her, heading out for Florida with another woman.

Three months later, on a morning in late May, Lori received a cryptic phone call from Jack, from a pay phone outside Kansas City. He did not say what had brought him back home, but he told her that he needed to see their son. Lori agreed to pick him up, and she drove him and their five-year-old to a nearby park, where he played with the boy. Jack looked worn out, as if he had not slept for days, and he seemed on edge. He said little, except that there had been some trouble in Florida. Lori assumed that he had been mixed up in something drug related, but she did not press him, knowing better than to ask too many questions.

Jack persuaded her to spend the night with him at a local motel and, in the morning, told her that he wanted to visit his family. Lori took him to see his sister, and then they stopped by his grandmother's house. Afterward, they drove around Olathe while Jack downed three one-quart bottles of beer. That afternoon, they went to see his mother.

They didn't know that two police officers were surveilling his mother's house. The officers tailed the couple when they left, pulling Lori over several blocks away. Guns drawn, the officers ordered Jack out of the car.

Jack had been on the move for more than two weeks when he was brought into the Olathe police station and led into a small interrogation room. Clad in tight blue jeans and a tank top that hugged his torso, he was a physically imposing presence. At thirty, he was wiry and well built, his arms coiled with muscle. A tattoo of a peacock decorated his right shoulder, and a scar, the remnant of an accident he'd had while razing trees with a chain saw, marked his left forearm. He took a seat in a gray plastic chair. Wearily, he pressed his fingers to his forehead and closed his eyes.

Joe Pruett, a voluble Olathe police detective, entered the room and pulled up another chair. The investigator had first encountered Jack in the late 1970s when he responded to a one-vehicle accident on U.S. 56, where he found the young man, drunk and incoherent, circling an overturned car. It would be the first of roughly a dozen times Pruett was called out to handle a situation involving Jack, a familiarity he sought to capitalize on as they sat facing each other. "You know me, you know Roger," Pruett said, referring to another investigator, Roger LaRue, who had stepped out of the room for a moment. "All I'm asking for is your cooperation."

But Jack had first come to the attention of the Olathe police before Pruett joined the force, when, as a teenager, he spun out his car on a busy thoroughfare. Soon after, Jack was dispatched to the Lookout Mountain School for Boys, a state reform school outside Denver, not far from where his father, an electrical engineer who had divorced Jack's mother four years earlier, was living. The institution, which had a long history of harsh treatment for so-called incorrigibles, could not contain the seventeen-year-old: He soon staged an escape and disappeared. After he was arrested for stealing a cache of guns from his father's house in Colorado Springs, he broke out of the county jail by sawing through the bars on a window. The remainder of his adolescence was spent confined to the Colorado State Reformatory, an adult prison where he was locked up with men more than twice his age. He was freed in 1975, at the age of twenty.

Jack returned to Olathe, where he managed to hold down jobs as a meat cutter and a bouncer at a local bar, but his erratic behavior often attracted the attention of police. He threatened one man with a gun and punched another man in the mouth during an argument over a dollar. He kicked a police officer in the stomach. He raced a friend's Camaro at high speed through a parking lot, nearly striking a child. All told, Jack was arrested on eight different criminal charges in the late 1970s, including aggravated assault, attempted burglary, larceny, and drug possession. In 1980, he served a short stint in county jail for battery. Later that year, he and a friend, Detroy Williams, agreed to carry out the killing of a wealthy Missouri physician in exchange for money and drugs. They had been told both would be in plentiful supply at the doctor's sprawling ranch. The two men traveled to the tiny Ozarks town of Climax Springs, Missouri, armed with two guns and a hunting knife.

Several days later, Dr. Duncan Danforth's body was found on a rutted gravel road outside Climax Springs, where the elderly doctor had been shot, point-blank, in the back of the head. Investigators learned that a week before his murder Danforth had wed a twenty-two-year-old woman, more than fifty years his junior, to whom he had left much of his estate. They soon zeroed in on her boyfriend, an Olathe native named Michael Stith, who told investigators he had hired Jack and Detroy to do the killing.

Stith was tried, convicted, and handed a life sentence, while his co-conspirators fared far better: In exchange for their cooperation, Jack and Detroy were granted total immunity from prosecution. At trial, they told jurors they had set out to shoot the doctor, lying in wait for him on two different occasions, before getting cold feet and returning to Kansas. The real killer, they said, was the man who hired them. Inconsistencies in their story abounded; Jack's alibi for the night of the killing never checked out, and the state's own forensic pathologist testified that Danforth had been shot with a .45, the same caliber of gun that Jack carried while stalking him. But prosecutors, in service to their theory of the case, seemed to gloss over these contradictions.

"Soon as Roger gets back here, I'm going to advise you of your rights," Detective Pruett said, watching Jack closely. "What you're charged with, at this point, is delivering a controlled substance to a person under the age of eighteen."

Jack understood that the drug charge was just a pretext to take him into custody. When he had called his mother the previous week, she'd told him that Pruett had paid her a visit and that he was wanted for questioning in connection with a murder in Florida.

Now Pruett laid it out for him: Two investigators from Florida were already en route to Olathe.

"Do you know when they're going to be here?" Jack asked, nonchalant.

"The flight gets in at 6:45 p.m.," Pruett said.

Jack looked at his watch. It was still the middle of the afternoon.

"They'll be here at eight," the detective added, rapping his knuckles against his chair with a little too much anticipation. He knew Jack had been involved in a murder-for-hire case years before, and had been a star witness for the prosecution. Now he hoped for the same kind of willingness to work with investigators. "I'm going to need your cooperation all the way, because when they show tonight, I want to be able to say that Jack cooperated."

A less conscientious detective might have sat back until the Florida investigators arrived, but Pruett felt certain that he could get their suspect talking. He believed Jack would be more likely to open up to him than to strangers. Still, for as many times as the two men had crossed paths over the years, Pruett never understood what made Jack tick. There was something off-kilter about him, a detachment that people who encountered Jack found unnerving. He spoke with a curiously flat affect, his deep voice a near monotone. His gaze, by contrast, was intense, his eyes a startling, bracing blue. Back in Missouri, a state witness in the murder-for-hire case had made a point during her testimony to describe how unsettling she found him, even though he was not the one on trial. "He had very—to me—very cold eyes," she told jurors.

Pruett had been drawn into the Florida case about two weeks

earlier, on May 9, when a detective from Clearwater called, saying he was investigating the homicide of a fourteen-year-old girl. The detective needed help locating Jack, who'd been seen with the girl on the night she went missing. He was also looking for information on the Kansans whom Jack lived with in Florida, all of whom appeared to have ties to Olathe. Pruett had decided to pay Jack's mother a visit, and she urged her son to surrender. Jack returned to Kansas, then hesitated. When he failed to turn himself in, Pruett ordered the stakeout of his mother's house.

Five years had passed since the murder-for-hire killing in Missouri. Neither Pruett nor the Florida investigators who later interviewed him would look back at that investigation to see what they could learn from it. So they were unaware that Jack, in his conversations with Missouri law enforcement and his sworn testimony in the case, had repeatedly returned to the subject of his hunting knife. The knife had been incidental to the Missouri investigation. The victim had been shot, not stabbed. But Jack had taken his blade with him when he set out to kill the doctor, and it clearly meant something to him. "Regular hunting knife, about six or seven inches long," as he described it to a detective a few weeks after the physician's slaying. "Just the kind you carry in a fishing box." He added, "I carry a knife like that all the time."

Pruett turned on the video camera behind the two-way mirror that spanned one wall of the interrogation room, then took a seat beside Detective LaRue. Jack waived his *Miranda* rights and agreed to answer questions without a lawyer present.

He told the detectives that he had crossed paths with Shelly Boggio on the afternoon of May 5, when she, her twin sister, and a third teenage girl whose name he could not remember flagged him down. The day was warm and balmy, and Jack was behind the wheel of his new girlfriend's white Toyota Corolla, cruising around

St. Petersburg with two friends he had been drinking with since the morning. Jimmy D. was renting a bedroom from him, and Dwain, who was taking a break from a troubled marriage, was sleeping on his couch. The girls were dashing across the street when Jack spotted them. "They yelled at us," he said, "and we stopped and gave them a ride."

Jack said he had hung out with the twins and their older sister before, but he swore that he never grasped just how young Shelly was. "I didn't know she was fourteen," he insisted, shaking his head. "Her sisters, they hang around all the bars down there. That's how I learned which bars to go to, the bands and everything like that, you know? So there's no way I knew that they were that young, because I've met them in the bars down on the beach. The Driftwood Bar is where I first got to know them."

That night, Jack said, the group returned to his house in Seminole.

"What time did you arrive there?" Pruett asked.

"I can't tell you," Jack said. "We hit so many bars."

After drinking and smoking weed at the house, some of them went out dancing at a place called Jerry's Rock 'n' Disco. Later that night, the impromptu gathering dwindled down to just him and Shelly, and he drove her to a beachside bar.

"So it was just you and Shelly at that point?" Pruett asked.

Jack was quiet. "Mm-hmm," he said, nodding.

Pruett moved his chair closer, leaning forward in his seat. "Now what I want to know is this," the detective said. "Did you have sex with that little girl that day?"

"No."

"Did you ever have sex with her?"

"No, sure haven't."

"You willing to take a lie detector test to that?"

Jack tapped his cigarette against the rim of an ashtray and nodded. "You betcha."

Shelly, he said, had wanted to keep partying, but he could not keep up. "I was ready to crash," he explained. "I was getting tired, so she said, 'Well, let's go back and get Jimmy D.' "

Jim was the old man of the group. A thirty-eight-year-old veteran, already ground down by years of hard living, was not an obvious person for a teenage girl to seek out in the middle of the night. But Jack said that he drove Shelly, at her request, back to the house in Seminole, nine miles away, to rouse Jimmy D.

The three of them headed out into the night, Jack said, and made one last stop at a bar. Then "Jimmy drove for a while and I passed out."

Jack said he remembered little of what happened from that point forward, except that they ended up somewhere near the beach, beside a bridge. The next thing he could recall was Jimmy D. shaking him awake: "He was pushing on me, waking me up, telling me to drive." Jack said he drove himself and Jimmy D. home, before passing out. He made no mention of Shelly again; she simply vanished from the narrative.

Detective Pruett, who had listened with careful attention, exhaled when Jack was done. "Now I want to believe you," the detective said, "and I think the majority of what you told me is true. But I'm having a little trouble with this, okay?"

"Where'd I lose you?" Jack said.

For the better part of an hour, the detective went around and around with him. Had Jack really not seen or heard anything?

"I heard them arguing or something, but, you know, I was half conscious," Jack said with a shrug. "I was drinking all day long."

"You didn't see any blood on his shirt when you got home?"

"I seen blood on my shoes the next morning. That's when I snapped—something's wrong, when I seen I had blood on my shoes."

"How did you get blood on your shoes?"

"When he woke me up, I imagine I walked in it."

When the detectives stepped out of the room, Jack eyed his reflection in the two-way mirror, running his fingers through his shaggy brown hair. He seemed untroubled, even bored. He blew smoke rings into the air. He fidgeted with a $20 bill and some change, which he had placed on the table in front of him at the start of the interview. Every so often, he turned a small pocketknife over in his hands.

When the detectives came back and took their seats, Jack made a strange admission: He had returned to Indian Rocks Beach the following morning, and he had ordered Jimmy D. to come with him. "We drove across that bridge and I seen everything going on," he said, referring to the crowd of police officers and investigators at the scene. "He didn't even have to tell me; I knew something bad had happened." When Pruett pressed him to explain why he had not demanded answers from Jimmy D., he shook his head. "I guess I really didn't even want to know," he said. "I was just scared. I just wanted to get out of the area. I went back home and I packed my suitcase and hit the road."

Pruett knew that the crime scene had yielded a single piece of physical evidence that seemed to point back to a perpetrator: a pool of vomit, found alongside the water, that did not match the contents of Shelly's stomach. Pruett had held back this fact as he tried to elicit information. When the detective finally arrived at the question of who threw up there that night, Jack acknowledged that it was, in fact, him. Drinking often aggravated an ulcer he had, he said. "I was just sick as hell, throwing up," he said.

Emboldened, the detective asked about another piece of evidence—one that law enforcement had not been able to find. "Who had the buck knife that night when you went to the beach?" Pruett asked.

"Wasn't really a buck knife," Jack said.

"Can you describe it for me? Be specific."

Jack gamely fielded dozens of questions from both detectives about the knife, providing a vivid picture. He recalled its carved leather handle; its leather sheath, tipped with brass; its sharpening stone holder; the single hole that pierced its blade. "It was a military bayonet-type knife," he explained. Gesturing with his hands, he demonstrated the length of the blade (roughly six or seven inches long), as well as the entire knife (closer to a foot in length). He recalled the deep groove that ran lengthwise along the blade's spine. Almost as an afterthought, he asserted that the knife was Jimmy D.'s.

The detectives asked him to sketch the knife on a legal pad, and Jack obliged. "At no time did Jimmy tell you that he did it?" Pruett asked.

"No, he didn't happen to say, you know, 'I did this,'" Jack muttered. He was bent over the legal pad, his face fixed in concentration.

"Is there any doubt in your mind he did it?"

"No, how could there be?" he said.

Jack stopped every now and then to correct an errant line. When he was done, Detective LaRue had him initial the drawing. Satisfied, Jack sat back and reached for another cigarette. Before him lay a life-sized rendering of the murder weapon.

The detectives questioned him into the evening. He spoke elliptically about his role, but he kept talking. Only as the arrival of the Florida investigators grew nearer did he seem to grasp the severity of the situation he was in. Abruptly, he wondered aloud, "What they got, the electric chair down there?"

By the time Detective Halliday and another, less seasoned investigator, Detective Terry Buchaus, arrived from Florida that night,

JOHN HALLIDAY ESCORTING A DEFENDANT PAST REPORTERS DURING A 1992 MURDER TRIAL

their picture of the crime had begun to take shape. That it was the work of two people had been Buchaus's hunch all along. The detective, who had only joined the Indian Rocks Beach force six months earlier, had formed this opinion on the very first day of the investigation while photographing and documenting the crime scene. When he was later asked in court to explain what led him to believe that two people perpetrated the killing, he could not point to anything specific. Buchaus said he had a second sense about it, an instinct. "I just had that feeling," he testified. "Sometimes you just have a feeling."

Halliday stood six feet four, with a crown of thick blond hair, a tan mustache, and a powerful build, the sheer scale of him commanding attention as he stepped inside the cramped police station in Olathe. The son of an FBI agent, he hailed from upstate New York, and though he had spent more than a decade policing the sun-dazed sprawl of west-central Florida, he delivered his words with a New Yorker's directness. His approach to any interrogation was part persistence, part force of personality. He was, in the words of one man whom Halliday had questioned, "intimidating, to say the least."

Halliday and Buchaus had started working the case the morning Shelly's body was found. They pieced together that Jack and the three other people staying at his house in Seminole—his new girlfriend, Gayle Bailey, his longtime friend Dwain Shaw, and Jim—had driven to Miami the day after the murder and checked into a hotel. Then, one by one, they had gone their separate ways. Jack's girlfriend returned to Seminole. Dwain took a bus up the east coast of Florida, bought a Thunderbird, and drove back to Olathe. Jack took a bus to Colorado and then headed east to Kansas. Jack told the Olathe detectives that he last saw Jim walking away from their hotel in Miami, a guitar and suitcase in hand. Of the four housemates, only Jim remained unaccounted for.

Jack had taken away an important lesson from the Missouri murder-for-hire case: It was best to be the first one to tell the story. And useful stories—the kind that offered detectives a clear path forward, and prosecutors a winnable case—had a way of sticking. In Jim's absence, Jack could tell the story that served him best.

Pruett brought the Florida investigators up to speed, explaining that Jack had admitted to being present at the scene of the murder, but that he claimed to have been unconscious at the time of the crime. The visiting detectives then made what seemed, to Pruett, to be an unusual request: They asked him to turn off any recording devices in the interrogation room. Documenting interviews with suspects was standard operating procedure in Olathe, and it was especially important in a high-stakes murder case. Preserving every word a suspect said—including details that sometimes made more sense once all the evidence was in place—only strengthened an investigation. It also headed off any questions that might arise later about the conduct of the interrogators. But recording interviews, the two visitors from Florida explained, was not how they did things in Pinellas County. Pruett turned off the video camera and stepped out of the room, leaving behind a tape recorder in case they changed their minds.

The investigators sat down in that same small interrogation room with Jack at nine o'clock that evening. While Pruett had taken pains to build a rapport with Jack, trying to draw him out with a polite but firm midwestern diplomacy, Halliday got right to the point. He established how much he already knew, down to the name of the Miami hotel where Jack fled after the murder. Halliday's presence, however, spoke louder than anything he said. That he and Buchaus had traveled halfway across the country on a moment's notice reflected not only the gravity of the crime but also their certainty that they had a likely suspect.

By the time it was Jack's turn to speak, he'd had hours to reflect on what law enforcement knew about the murder and to reconsider his approach. He told them that he had left out some details in the statement he'd given to the Olathe detectives.

Jack now said that he hadn't passed out in the car at Indian Rocks Beach. Instead, he told them, he witnessed the horror that unfolded. He looked on helplessly as Jim, for reasons he left unexplained, flew into a rage. "I got out of the car to try to stop Jimmy D. from stabbing her but I puked when I saw what he was doing to her," Jack said, according to Halliday's brief summary of the interrogation. The conversation was brief, fourteen minutes in all. But by the time Jack was done, he had provided what he said was an eyewitness account of the killing, one in which he had clearly identified Shelly's killer. "I last remember her running into the water," he said, "with Jimmy D. running after her."

10

DARK WATERS

This idea—that the killing was a two-person crime—was front of mind for the investigators as they sat down at the Olathe police station with Dwain Shaw, one day after they interviewed Jack. Like Gayle, he claimed to know nothing about what happened to Shelly. The twenty-eight-year-old roofer, who had worked construction jobs with Jack since they were in their early twenties, told the investigators that he did not learn of the murder until a detective contacted his girlfriend. He did remember, though, that Jack was acting strangely the morning after the teenager's visit to the house and had announced that they were all taking an impromptu trip to Miami. "He seemed like he was thinking serious about something, just staring," Dwain told investigators of the long drive to South Florida that followed. "I said, 'What the hell is wrong with you? Talk to me.' And the way he looked at me and started talking, I said, 'No, no, no, don't tell me. I don't want to know.'"

Dwain's recollection of events echoed Gayle's, except in one fundamental way. Like her, he remembered Jack slipping out of the house with Shelly. But he said that he, not Jimmy D., went with them.

Dwain had no doubt about this. He explained that he had wanted to talk to his girlfriend in Kansas, so he asked Jack for a ride to a nearby pay phone. Jack agreed to drop him off, initially waiting for him in the car with Shelly. But they grew restless as his conversation with his girlfriend stretched on. "They got impatient and was honking," Dwain said. "I told them to leave me, so they left." He remembered placing the call around 1:00 a.m. and seeing Jack and Shelly peel off soon afterward.

Based on the condition of Shelly's body when she was found the next morning, the medical examiner estimated that she was killed sometime between 2:00 and 4:00 a.m. The investigators did not share this information with Dwain, but they asked what else he could remember about those early morning hours.

Dwain said he remembered talking on the phone to his girlfriend for at least half an hour, maybe as long as forty-five minutes. "Then I called my wife and talked to her for the same, or longer," he said. "Got mad at her and walked home." Gayle was up waiting, and she was fuming over the fact that Jack had snuck out on her. Dwain said he spent the next two hours counseling her and trying to calm her down before he dozed off on the couch.

"Where was Jimmy?" Buchaus asked.

"He wasn't in the living room," Dwain said. "I think he was in bed, in the bedroom."

The investigators pressed Dwain, who admitted that he had been drinking heavily on the night in question. "Are you sure he wasn't with them?" one asked.

"Could he have been out—out in the car with Shelly?" asked the other.

This was the opposite of what Dwain had said. But under their scrutiny, he grew equivocal, offering a more qualified answer. "He could have been," Dwain replied.

Dwain went on to say that Jack returned home late that night, without the teenager. Halliday, instead, remained focused on the sequence of events as he understood it. "Jack and Jimmy was out with the girl, and they came back without her," the detective said, inaccurately summarizing Dwain's comments. Later, he misrepresented Dwain's story again: "Jimmy and Jack go out to the car. Shelly is with them, or out in the car. And then they come back in, by themselves." Dwain didn't correct him.

Dwain's original account of Jack having driven off with Shelly alone was corroborated by his girlfriend, Betty Mingus, whom the investigators also spoke to at the Olathe police station. She remembered Dwain calling her collect from the pay phone that night. Someone kept honking a car horn in the background, she recalled, and she asked Dwain who was there with him. "He said, 'Jack and some girl.' He was telling them, 'Go on, I'll just walk home.'" Her recollection mirrored what Dwain told the investigators: Jimmy D. was not there.

But if Jim was in his bedroom during the window of time when the murder likely occurred, as Dwain's account suggested, he did not stay there the whole night. Soon after Jack returned home, Dwain saw the two men leave the house together.

Jack and Jimmy D. returned home early that morning, Dwain said, and when they did, he noticed an odd detail: Jimmy D.'s pants were wet. This fit with something Gayle had said to the detectives, about catching sight of Jimmy D. walking into the bathroom in wet pants early that morning. Neither she nor Dwain reported thinking much of it, at the time. Dwain said he rolled over on the couch and went back to sleep.

Throughout the investigation, Shelly remained a ghost in her own narrative: a girl reduced to her name, her age, and the awful circumstances of her death. The most comprehensive record of her existence was a 119-page report by the Pinellas County medical examiner documenting the condition of her body postmortem. If the detectives learned more about her, they did not include their findings in their reports. They made no mention of interviewing her father, even though he was her legal guardian. In the official records of the case, the particulars of her life were left vague.

Shelly remained an abstraction, in no small part because the reality of her was complicated; she did not conform to the expectations that are imposed, even in death, on women and girls. "Shelly Boggio was often in trouble," began an article that ran in the *St. Petersburg Times* days after she was found, under the headline "Nude Body Identified as Young, Troubled Girl." "She refused to attend school, and it wasn't unusual for her to stay away from home at night, even though she was only fourteen. . . . She frequently didn't come home on nights when she was partying with friends." Presenting her murder as a cautionary tale, the article focused on her transgressions: that she had missed sixty-seven days of school in a single semester; that she was a grade behind her twin sister; that she smoked. A truant officer who was familiar with Shelly and her twin offered up the only positive words in the story. "They were both really attractive," he said of the fourteen-year-olds.

A more nuanced picture emerges from the court filings that chronicle her parents' contentious divorce. Shelly was still a toddler when her mother, Cheri, walked out on her father, Frank, leaving him alone to care for the couple's three young children. At the time, the family lived in Battle Creek, Michigan, where Frank owned and operated a small beauty salon called Mr. Frank's Hairstyles. After alleging in court proceedings that Cheri had shown little interest in their daughters—"by her conduct and actions," read the complaint, she "has not demonstrated any love, affection, nor interest in the welfare and well-being of said children"—Frank won custody of the twins. While Cheri was granted custody of their eldest, all three girls aligned themselves with Frank in their teenage years. And, in 1984, when he abruptly sold the hair salon and left Michigan behind for a new life in the Sunshine State, the twins and their older sister, Sherry, went with him.

The move proved to be ill-fated. Frank later told authorities that he gave the proceeds from the sale of his salon to his girlfriend, who was supposed to meet him in Florida, but that she ran off with the money instead. He was nearly penniless when he and his daughters arrived in Kenneth City, an inexpensive suburb of St. Petersburg, and moved into a faded, nine-hundred-square-foot rental house. Although Frank would eventually find work at a local salon, he and the girls largely lived hand to mouth. They did not always have enough to eat, and when it was cold, they warmed the house by leaving the stove door open. Shelly's middle school, located in a notoriously rough neighborhood, behind a fortress-like entrance crowned in barbed wire, provided no refuge. During the time she was enrolled there, five teachers were dismissed for sexual misconduct; three of them were charged with producing child pornography.

As Frank's dream of an easier life remained elusory, Shelly struggled to cut her own path. With her fifteenth birthday approaching, she remained stuck in junior high, out of step with her peers, even as she attracted the attention of men who saw her—or who chose to see her—as older than she really was. The local drinking age was nineteen, but she got waved into beachside bars anyway. With her deep tan and her feathered, sandy-blond hair that she parted down the middle, she looked like many other Florida girls, yet she was her own person, too: soft-spoken but fearless. When a carful of teenagers once pulled over to ask her and her twin sister if they knew where they could score some weed, Shelly assured them that she did. She told them to give her $30 and to drop her and her sister off at an apartment where she could make the purchase for them. When the car reached the apartment complex, the girls slipped out the back and ran, pocketing the money.

Shelly was often unaccounted for, coming and going as she

pleased; even by the laissez-faire standards of the day, her father's parenting was unconventional at best. But Frank did make one rule clear: He did not want her anywhere near Jack Pearcy. The Kansan had stopped by their house one day in the spring of 1985, and his interest in Shelly was obvious enough to elicit a warning from Frank. "My dad just sort of let him know that he was a little too old to be hanging around a fourteen-year-old," Shelly's twin, Stacy, later testified. "So, he never came over again."

On May 24, three days after their arrival in Olathe, the Florida investigators boarded a commercial flight back to Tampa with Jack shackled beside them. They later booked him into the Pinellas County Jail in Clearwater, and though he was still only charged with delivering a controlled substance to a minor, his bond was set at $150,000, ensuring that he would remain behind bars while the investigation continued. The detectives hoped that Jack might agree to talk to them again, since he had continued to make incriminating admissions: Back in Kansas, after their interview had concluded, he mentioned that he threw out the shoes he wore on the night of the murder, tossing them into a dumpster in Colorado, "because they had blood all over them."

JACK PEARCY AT THE PINELLAS COUNTY JAIL IN CLEARWATER, FLORIDA, ON MAY 25, 1985

Several weeks later, on June 19, Jack and his public defender met with a prosecutor at the state attorney's office. Jack was vying for a deal; the statement he would make that day was a "proffer," a preview of testimony he could provide as a cooperating witness. Prosecutors would then evaluate whether his statement was valuable enough to warrant entering into an agreement with him. If so, they would negotiate a plea deal, offering him some leniency in exchange for his testimony against Jim. It was the same kind of arrangement he had used to his advantage five years earlier, during the investigation into the doctor's killing in Missouri.

Jack admitted to the prosecutor that he'd taken the teenager out on his own after they returned from Jerry's Rock 'n' Disco. He made no mention of stopping at a pay phone on the way, saying only that he and Shelly headed to a beachside bar called Hank's Seabreeze Lounge. There, he recalled, the Toyota got stuck in the sand, and when he was unable to dig the car out, several men helped him free it. Afterward, he said, Shelly insisted on returning to the house to pick up Jim: "She still wanted to party, so she said, 'Get Jimmy D.' "

From that point forward, Jimmy D. was the central character of Jack's narrative. Jack cast himself as a disinterested onlooker, peripheral to the unfolding events. He said Jimmy D. started "necking" with Shelly in the back seat after the trio visited a bar, then directed Jack to take them down to a secluded area in Indian Rocks Beach. Offhandedly, Jack added that he was familiar with the deserted inlet: It was one of his favorite fishing spots. "I have caught some pretty good fish off there a few times," he said.

Jack said he stayed in the car while Jimmy D. lay down with Shelly by the water. "I wasn't paying any attention to what they were doing," he said. "I just sat there drinking a wine cooler and kicked my seat back and was listening to the radio."

He said he idled away as much as an hour before he heard a noise and looked out into the darkness. That was when he saw Jimmy D. straddling Shelly, who was lying face down on the ground with her jeans around her knees. "I could see him making a stabbing motion," Jack said. "I could see the knife in his hand." Jack said he ran over to help Shelly, but he lost his footing and fell, and when he caught sight of her face, he began vomiting. He admitted being in such proximity to her that he heard her labored breathing: "gurgling noises," in his words. He said he watched helplessly as Jimmy D. dragged her by her feet into the water and left her there for dead.

Eager to seal a deal with the state attorney's office, he offered up more information: He said he knew where they could find the murder weapon. That afternoon, he led them to an overgrown reservoir near Indian Rocks Beach, where police divers would recover a knife sheath, though no knife. This was more evidence of Jimmy D.'s guilt, he said: It was Jimmy D. who had the idea to pull over at the reservoir and Jimmy D. who tossed the knife in.

When Jack took a polygraph the following day, he became agitated and was forced to acknowledge that he had not been completely forthcoming. In a series of convoluted statements, he conceded that he used the knife to hurt Shelly, though he insisted Jimmy D. was the actual killer. "I think I cut her, though I don't think I stabbed her," he said. "I'm blocking it out. I don't want to remember. I don't remember stabbing her in the head. I don't know how many times I might have cut her." Eventually, he became so distraught that he said he might need to speak to a priest. He had a recurring nightmare in which he observed the murder unfolding, he said. In it, the killer turned to look at him, and he saw that the killer's face was in fact his own.

In Jim Dailey's absence, suspicions about him deepened. The strange story about his returning home in wet pants, followed by his disappearance, only reinforced the idea that he had played some part in the killing. Though Jack had failed to convince prosecutors that he was only a reluctant onlooker, the substance of his story—that he was not alone with Shelly at Indian Rocks Beach—stuck. His statement to the state attorney's office, which he gave six weeks after Shelly's body was found, marked the de facto end of the investigation. On June 27, a little more than a week after Jack gave his statement claiming to have watched Jim Dailey stab Shelly, investigators obtained a first-degree murder warrant for Jim.

Finding him remained Halliday's focus as summer turned to fall. The detective notified police departments in cities where Jim had previously lived or where he had relatives—Manhattan, Kansas; Tucson, Arizona; Spokane, Washington; Coeur d'Alene, Idaho—but turned up nothing.

Then, in November, law enforcement tracked him down to the Central Coast of California, where he was working as a carpenter near the towns of Monterey and Carmel. Both before and after his extradition to Florida, the thirty-nine-year-old declined to talk, turning Halliday away when the detective came to see him. Jim did not peddle a story, or angle for a deal, or offer his version of the truth. He said only that he wanted to speak with an attorney, and with that he fell silent.

11

SNITCH

Jim was booked into the Pinellas County Jail on February 13, 1986, and held without bond. In the mug shot taken that day, he looks hard into the camera. Gone is his easy confidence and broad grin. A horseshoe mustache droops over his lips, which are pressed tightly into a straight line. His shoulders are slumped, his expression somber. A grand jury had indicted both him and Jack for first-degree murder, and prosecutors intended to seek the death penalty.

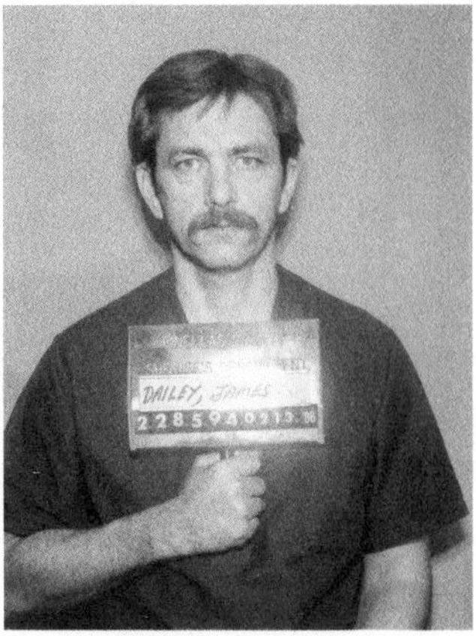

JIM DAILEY AT THE PINELLAS COUNTY JAIL IN CLEARWATER, FLORIDA, ON FEBRUARY 13, 1986

Because he could not afford to hire an attorney, the court appointed him one: a congenial former prosecutor named Henry Andringa. In conversations with his new lawyer, he was emphatic that he knew nothing about the killing. He remembered going to sleep when Jack left the house with Shelly, and being awoken some time later by Jack, who was alone and wanted to get high. He said that he went with Jack to a nearby causeway, where they smoked weed and drank. There, Jack told him that Gayle wanted him to move out, to make room for the baby, and Jim agreed that he would leave. Jack was itching to get out of town the next day, but that had not seemed unusual; the group often took road trips on a whim, at Jack's direction. After they all went to Miami, Jim said, he knew it was time to move on, and he struck out on his own.

Andringa learned that in Miami detectives had turned up hotel records showing that Jim checked in under his real name, while Jack provided a fake one. It was a small detail, but the lawyer would later make the most of it when the case went to trial, using it to argue that his client had no knowledge of the murder. Not all the facts, however, made this argument easy. Jim explained that he had gotten his jeans wet that night while he and Jack were at the causeway getting wasted; they had tossed a Frisbee around, and he had retrieved the Frisbee when it fell in the water. It was a peculiar story, and not one that Andringa readily believed. In the face of his lawyer's skepticism, Jim did not offer a tidier explanation or a more favorable version of events. "If I was going to make up a story," he would later say, "I'd make up a better story than that, but that's the truth. That's exactly what happened."

To mount a vigorous defense, it would be essential to uncover as much as possible about the hours leading up to the murder. What had the state's investigators missed, and what else could be learned about what happened that night? In a case as ambiguous and high stakes as Jim's, having a private investigator conduct a fresh probe of the evidence would allow the defense to build a fuller picture—one that reached beyond the limits of Halliday's interviews and reports.

Yet Andringa, who was juggling other cases, would proceed on his own, and his approach would be marked by caution and incuriousness. Although he had spent three years as a prosecutor in the state attorney's office before going into private practice, he was not a courtroom pugilist; he had a more restrained, deliberative style. By failing to enlist anyone to help him reexamine the events of that night—to track down witnesses, challenge the state's timeline, uncover details that law enforcement had overlooked—he effectively limited the defense to the facts that the state had already assembled, which worked against his client.

The most favorable evidence the defense had was Dwain's recollection of catching a ride with Jack and Shelly to a pay phone, where he said he began making calls around 1:00 a.m. According to Dwain, Jim was not with them. This placed Jim at home—not in the car with Shelly—just before the window of time in which she was believed to have been killed. Moreover, Dwain remembered Jack and Shelly leaving him at the pay phone and driving on without him, heading into the night on their own. Dwain's recollection matched with something Jack had said in his sworn statement, in which he admitted to being alone with Shelly for part of the evening, when he took her to Hank's Seabreeze Lounge, which was a straight shot to Indian Rocks Beach, up the two-lane highway that ran along the coastline. Jack, however, claimed he took her to the bar earlier in the night. Dwain's memory challenged this, putting Jack alone with Shelly much later, and therefore much closer to the estimated time of her death. This time frame lined up with another witness's memory of the evening: An acquaintance of Shelly's named Deborah North had reported seeing her at the Seabreeze before the bar closed at 1:45 a.m. North had arrived there around midnight and did not spot Shelly until some time later.

North—who was on the state's witness list, but whom prosecutors would never call to testify—was an obvious person for Andringa to seek out. An attorney who represented Jack did just that, obtaining sworn testimony from her in the summer of 1986, as both defendants awaited trial. The disturbing story she told, of the last time she saw Shelly, began with the teenager entering the

Seabreeze barefoot. "She looked real high," North said. "Her hair was all a mess, and she was just looking around. She was sweating, and she was asking just about anybody to help her get a car out of the sand." Shelly was with a man who was not familiar to North, who was trying to dig the car out with a shovel—a memory that matched Jack's description of their visit to the bar.

North remembered seeing them outside the Seabreeze for between half an hour and an hour. The last time North saw Shelly, the teenager had sunk down so low in the back seat of the car that only the top of her head was visible. "A minute later," North said, "I didn't see her at all, like maybe she laid down or something." This was a radically different picture from the one Jack had sketched, of a girl so eager to keep partying that she had him drive back to the house to pick up Jim.

Several people had pushed the car out of the sand that night, something bar patrons might have later remembered. Any one of them might have helped pinpoint when Jack drove away from the bar with Shelly, and which direction the two headed in. They might have illuminated Jack's state of mind, and the plausibility of his claim that Shelly wanted to keep partying. But Andringa never tried to interview North or any of the other eyewitnesses who had been at the Seabreeze. Who they were, and what they recalled of that night, would remain unknown.

Jack was the first to stand trial for Shelly's murder that November, having failed to persuade the state attorney's office that he was a helpless bystander to the crime. Again and again over the course of the weeklong trial, prosecutors used his own words against him, playing the video of his first interrogation in Kansas and calling investigators to the stand to describe his bizarre and self-incriminating declarations. "None of his stories make sense," the assistant state attorney Beverly Andrews told the jury, mimicking the way Jack offered ever-shifting accounts of the last hours of Shelly's life: "*Yes, I will definitely tell the truth. I have not told it yet, but I'll tell it this time.*"

Andrews had a reputation as a fierce advocate for crime victims. At thirty-three, she was already a formidable trial lawyer and the first woman to head one of the four trial divisions within the state attorney's office. She was at her most animated when she stood before jurors and exhorted them to do justice. Andrews asked for—and won—long sentences. She prosecuted Jack alongside a more junior but no less hard-charging prosecutor named Robert Heyman, who, four years out of law school, already had the polish of a seasoned litigator. Like Andrews, he was adept at winning over a jury. In another first-degree murder case they tried together, jurors gave them a rose after handing down a guilty verdict.

Prosecutors rarely start with a blank slate; they inherit the investigation that preceded their entrance into a case, along with the subjective decisions and judgment calls that shaped detectives' theory of the crime. Absent are the alternate hypotheses that the detectives rejected, the details they dismissed as insignificant, the inconsistencies they explained away. Prosecutors are meant to serve as a check on that process: to stress test the investigation, question its assumptions, and ensure the evidence supports the charges. But that early framing often exerts a powerful gravitational pull, shaping a case long before it reaches a courtroom, and Jack's account was a useful one, furnishing the state attorney's office with a purported eyewitness to the murder.

"A prosecutor should approach the preparation of a case with a healthy skepticism," wrote the law professor Bennett L. Gershman in a 2001 article in *The Georgetown Journal of Legal Ethics*, which underscored prosecutors' duty to pursue the fairest outcome in a case, not simply to win a conviction. "He should not assume that his witnesses are telling the truth, the forensic evidence is accurate, and the defendant is guilty. Only by maintaining the attitude of a true skeptic can a prosecutor ensure the validity of the hypothesis of guilt and be able to exclude reasonable hypotheses of innocence." The adversarial system, however, does not lend itself to this approach, writes Gershman, himself a former prosecutor. DAs and state attorneys "driven by conviction statistics" and "focused on projecting a tough law-and-order image" fail to foster such skepticism.

Nothing suggests that the state attorney's office—dominated by a prosecutor who measured success in wins—ever confronted the central logic problem of the investigation: Why was Jack considered not credible, except when he said Jim was the killer? Even as prosecutors demonstrated that Jack was not a reliable narrator, they stuck with the basic conceit of his story: that he was not alone with Shelly at Indian Rocks Beach. Halliday turned again and again to the evidence that supported the two-man theory while minimizing information that cut against it. His report summarizing his interview with Dwain made no mention of Jack coming home alone late on the night of Shelly's murder and then leaving with Jim. It was this omission that fundamentally changed the substance of Dwain's account, leaving the impression that Jim had been at Jack's side all night long. And nowhere, in the nearly two hundred pages of reports that Halliday and Buchaus generated, did they make any mention of Deborah North, or her encounter with Shelly at the Seabreeze, though North had been interviewed by an Indian Rocks Beach police officer.

When Halliday's turn came to testify in Jack's trial, he described what Jack had said in his sworn statement to prosecutors. "He said that Dailey was on top of Shelly and he saw what looked to be like motions of stabbing," the detective said. "He said that he had helped to drag her body to the water, and that he had stabbed her one time in the hand, and that he did it because Dailey made him do it." As prosecutors summoned to the stand a succession of investigators and pathologists, they continued to advance the idea that the murder was the work of both Jack and Jim. "She was fighting off two men," Andrews told the jury, "and two men carried her to her death in the Intracoastal."

At the time of Jack's trial, Florida outpaced all other states in the nation in the number of people it sentenced to death. The Sunshine State was part of the so-called Death Belt: the band of southern states, stretching from Florida to Texas, that accounted for more than 90 percent of executions carried out in the late twentieth century. By the mid-1980s, one out of every six condemned prisoners in America was on Florida's death row. But even by Florida's standards, Pinellas County stood out. Prosecutors sought the death penalty in nearly every first-degree murder case that came before the state attorney's office, and for three years in a row, from 1982 to 1984, its judges and juries sent more people to death row than any other county in Florida.

The state attorney James T. Russell understood that an unsparingly punitive approach resonated with voters, and the merciless reputation he cultivated for his office helped him get elected again and again. Appearing too soft was perilous for any elected official, a lesson the Florida governor Bob Graham, a mild-mannered centrist, learned the hard way when he was tarred early in his first term with the nickname Governor Jell-O. Graham reinvented himself by signing death warrants, accelerating the number of condemned men he cleared for Florida's electric chair in 1982, when he ran for reelection, and again in 1986, when he ran for U.S. Senate. All told, he signed 153 death warrants, 16 of which were carried out during his tenure. The resulting boost in popularity helped Graham—admiringly rechristened Governor Death—win both elections by wide margins. Despite the unseemliness of what one critic called his "crass political calculus," he emerged as a national political force who would make a run for the White House.

Russell sought the death penalty in nearly every first-degree murder case his office prosecuted. His lock-'em-up ideology was hardly unique to Florida; it was the animating force in legislatures, courtrooms, and district attorney's offices across the country—so much so that over the 1980s and 1990s America's prison population would quadruple. But Russell took the zeitgeist to its furthest extreme, creating a high-octane workplace culture that offered no incentive to exercise restraint. His approach appealed to his constituents, who were disproportionately older and overwhelmingly white, and who did not balk at his opinion that the drug-fueled turf wars in Miami could be stemmed by sending more people to the electric chair. "They'd find that little bit of difference in their murder rate," he said in 1984, "if Dade County started burning some people."

On November 23, the jury in *The State of Florida v. Jack Pearcy* reached a unanimous verdict: guilty of murder in the first degree. Then came the thornier question of whether to recommend the death penalty. Halliday's testimony had depicted Jim as the crime's driving force, complicating the state's efforts to persuade jurors that Jack deserved the electric chair. Two days before Thanksgiving, they recommended a life sentence.

Andrews and Heyman urged the judge to override the jury's recommendation, arguing in a forceful sentencing memo that "no evidence exists that Pearcy was not the main actor in this child's brutal murder." But the judge, Thomas E. Penick Jr., was unmoved. Mindful that the Florida Supreme Court had begun reversing the rulings of judges who overrode the will of jurors in capital cases, he elected to follow the jury's recommendation. Jack would get life, with the possibility of parole.

For the state attorney's office, the failure to win a death sentence was a monumental blow. Jack had dodged the electric chair after participating in, and most likely carrying out, one of the county's most monstrous crimes. Shelly Boggio's older sister, Sherry, told reporters that she had only one hope for him. "I wish he were dead," she said.

Jim's upcoming trial—set for the following spring, with Judge Penick—was still half a year away, but the challenges of the prosecution's case were now in sharper focus. When trying Jack, the state had been able to tie him to the crime scene using statements he had made to law enforcement and a solitary piece of physical evidence that confirmed his presence there that night: the vomit he admitted throwing up by the water's edge. In Jim's case, there was no hard evidence. Still, prosecutors moved forward with plans to try him for first-degree murder. For James Russell's office, Jim's trial would be the last opportunity in the Boggio case to secure a death sentence.

Nine days after the conclusion of Jack's trial, on December 4, 1986, Halliday strode into a small room deep inside the hulking concrete-and-steel complex that made up the Pinellas County Jail. The detective's work on the case was nearly done; a year and a half had passed since he had obtained arrest warrants for Jack and Jim, and his investigation, for all practical purposes, had concluded. Nevertheless, at his direction, jailers began pulling men who were housed with Jim out of their cellblock. One by one, fifteen men were brought, in handcuffs, to the interrogation room where Halliday waited. There was an urgency to his voice as he questioned them. Had Jim ever discussed the case before? Ever admitted to anything?

Halliday was skilled at finding men in the jail who would talk. During his seven years as a homicide detective, he had used jailhouse witnesses in his investigations more than thirty different times. Skalnik had been the most effective of them, helping to deliver death sentences for two of the perpetrators in the High Point murders, and as luck would have it, he was back in the Pinellas County Jail. Just before Thanksgiving, he had returned to face the grand theft charges stemming from the phony car sales he had made to the Giovanniello and Wengatz families.

Skalnik, however, was housed in a different cellblock from Jim. Halliday would have to see who else might be willing to work with him.

Among the men questioned that day was a twenty-year-old named Michael Sorrentino. The normally chatty and extroverted South Florida native—who, like most men in the jail, was waiting for his case to go to trial—grew quiet when he was led into the windowless interrogation room. Lying before him were articles from local newspapers about Shelly's murder: articles that provided the who, what, where, and when of the crime. "I got a very uneasy feeling looking at the newspaper articles," Sorrentino later said. "Had I wanted to say something, or fabricate something, all the tools were there to give them whatever they might be looking for."

Halliday would later deny that there were any newspapers in the interrogation room, but to Sorrentino there was no question about what he saw when he entered the room or what was being asked of him. He declined to sit down, telling the detective he had no information to offer.

When it became clear that Sorrentino was not going to be helpful, he was taken back to his cell. "I hope you don't try this in my case," Sorrentino muttered on the way out.

Fifteen men, in all, were brought out of the cellblock where Jim was confined. In a slender, lined notebook, Halliday recorded what each of them told him. "Nothing," he jotted down after one interview. After others, he wrote,

Said Dailey denies charge
doesn't know a thing
Nothing
Knows nothing. Didn't even know Dailey.
stays to himself. Knows nothing.
Refused to come to be interviewed.
"Wish I could have helped you but its a little outa my league."

Halliday came up empty. But in the jail, the word was out: Jim Dailey's case needed a snitch.

During the nearly ten months that Jim had spent in the jail before Halliday came looking for informants, no one reported hearing him talk about the Boggio murder. In the weeks that followed the detective's visit, three different men stepped forward, each claiming to have overheard Jim say he was involved in the killing.

The detective also heard from Skalnik, who did not mention Jim, at first. But Skalnik made clear that he wanted to help the detective gather information on the men in his cellblock. In a handwritten note that Skalnik managed to get passed along to Halliday, he included a few details about another case the detective was investigating and indicated he had been speaking with the defendant. "Murder, assault," it read. "Girl stored in tank. Wants to talk more about case." At the bottom, Skalnik scrawled, "Should I continue or not?"

In the months that followed, Skalnik told Halliday that the men around him were, once again, confessing their crimes to him. Although Skalnik was in a single-man isolation cell, he said one man leaned close to the bars and calmly described killing his former girlfriend—who was five months pregnant—and showing her body to hitchhikers. And, according to Skalnik, two other men each admitted to killing friends. All of these men faced first-degree murder charges, which made his accounts of their confessions especially valuable to the state attorney's office—though the evidence in one case was so weak that the presiding judge acknowledged there was "a reasonable hypothesis of innocence."

Prosecutors added Skalnik to the witness list in all three upcoming trials. This time they did not let him loose. That he would have to remain behind bars while awaiting his own trial, for grand theft, left him seething. He pleaded with the judge who presided over his case to turn him free, drafting a legal petition in which he argued that he was being unlawfully detained, and that his notoriety in jail as an informant had put his life in "extreme jeopardy." He tried to fire his public defenders. He turned his fury on the parole commission, threatening to expose corruption within its ranks. ("With the assistance of a local reporter, I intend to share with the public the *true* workings of this system," he warned.) In a frantic, overwrought letter, he appealed to Florida's new governor, Bob Martinez, for help, copying the Massachusetts senator Ted Kennedy and the Ohio senator John Glenn.

His efforts led nowhere. That March, during a phone call with Halliday, Skalnik sounded so despairing that the detective alerted the jail that the thirty-seven-year-old might be a danger to himself. Skalnik was sent to the jail's medical wing that night, but the following day he was returned to the solitude of his cell.

And then, on May 1, 1987, came opportunity: A new prisoner, Jim Dailey, was moved onto his floor. The timing was uncanny; the Dailey trial, which would eventually be pushed off to the summer, was slated to begin in just eighteen days. Two days after Jim was moved from the lower G Wing of the jail to the upper G Wing, where Skalnik was held, Skalnik got word to Halliday: Jim had confessed to him.

12

A SIMPLE LIE

The State of Florida v. James Dailey got under way on June 24, 1987, during a hot and unusually dry stretch of summer. The courtroom's balky air-conditioning system eventually gave out, and when it did, Judge Penick—usually a stickler for protocol—made one small concession, allowing men to remove their jackets so long as they kept their ties on. Shelly Boggio's father, Frank, paced the hallway outside the courtroom. Inside, the hard wooden benches behind the defense table were sparsely filled. Jim's mother, Grace, had come all the way from Kansas, and though she was usually a steadying presence, she looked fragile. Mary Kay was there too, and she stared straight ahead, dumbfounded by the circumstances her ex-husband found himself in. Jim, expressionless, wore a dark suit that accentuated the trial's somber mood, occasionally scribbling notes in a yellow legal pad as he listened to witnesses.

Mary Kay was accompanied to court each day by their eighteen-year-old daughter, Stacey, who had seen her father's name in the news when he was arrested. Quietly, on her own, she had gone to the jail to see him. Unlike her older brother, who would remain estranged, Stacey felt a deep connection to their father despite his long absences, and her visit to the jail—the first of many—was warm and familiar. She urged him to call her mother and stepfather, a promise he made good on, and afterward Mary Kay and Dick had gone to see him too. The relief Mary Kay felt upon learning that Jim was close by was tempered by her grief. Her ex-husband, once so self-assured, looked sallow and sunken-eyed, and as he sought to explain himself, insisting over and over that he had nothing to do with the killing, she mourned for what might have been. Had he just called her when he got to Florida, maybe she could have freed him from Jack's grip.

"Why didn't you reach out to us?" she asked him, uncomprehending. "If you had just called, everything might be different now."

The trial lasted just three and a half days. The prosecutors in Jack's case, Beverly Andrews and Robert Heyman, reprised their roles, and as representatives of the state attorney's office they evinced an unshakable certainty in Jim's guilt. But to make a first-degree murder charge stick, they would have to overcome a narrative challenge: Jack Pearcy was the only witness who could place Jim at the scene of the crime, and with his conviction and sentence behind him he had no incentive to help the state. Nor did he seem eager to recount his version of the murder in front of Jim; he avoided looking at his old friend when the state called him to the stand in the hope that he would testify, mumbling over and over again, "I invoke my right to remain silent."

The prosecution would have to rely on Gayle Bailey and Dwain Shaw, but they could not agree on a vital piece of evidence: who had accompanied Jack and Shelly when they left the house shortly before she was killed.

In the two years that had passed since the killing, Gayle had given birth to the child she shared with Jack and settled in Jacksonville, less than an hour's drive from the maximum-security prison where he was incarcerated. She visited him often, bringing their son to see him. Her allegiance to him was evident as she took the stand and described her confusion about an important moment in the hours leading up to Shelly's murder: Jack's decision to drive home, and briefly stop at the house, after they went dancing at Jerry's Rock 'n' Disco. That he might have been trying to get rid of her so that he could make a move on Shelly was not an idea she had allowed herself to entertain. "Don't know why, to this day, we stopped back there," Gayle testified, seemingly at a loss. "I was under the impression that we were going to take Shelly home. When I went into the restroom and came back out, they were gone."

In the car with Jack and Shelly, she testified, was Jim. She was certain of this, she said; Dwain was the one who stayed behind at the house.

When Dwain was called to testify, he was wearing a jail jumpsuit, his hair neatly shorn. He explained that his current residence was the federal penitentiary in El Reno, Oklahoma, where he was serving time for armed robbery. His voice barely above a whisper, he offered a different version of events from Gayle, explaining that he, not Jim, had caught a ride with Jack and Shelly, and that they had dropped him off at a pay phone. He had last seen them driving off together. Jim was not with them.

His story directly contradicted Gayle's—a fact that prosecutors explained by casting doubt on his memory. "Sir, you stated that you were just separated and were drinking pretty heavily," Andrews said, referring to his estrangement from his wife. "Isn't that correct?"

"Yes," Dwain agreed.

"In fact, you were the only one so drunk that you passed out, as you put it, when you got back to the house in Seminole?"

"Yes."

As Andrews guided him through the night's events, no mention was made of Jack's solo return home, hours after driving off with Shelly—a crucial detail Dwain had shared with Halliday early in the investigation. Halliday had not included this fact in his report, and that omission had become part of the state's official narrative of that night. Andrews's line of questioning mirrored this storyline, and the defense, which did not have its own robust investigation to draw from, did not correct the error on cross-examination. As a result, Dwain never clarified that Jack had returned to the house alone before going back out with Jim; Dwain offered only that he had seen the two men come home together, much later. Like Gayle, he recalled that Jim's pants were wet.

While the housemates' testimony cast a shadow of doubt over Jim, it fell woefully short of the evidence required to win a capital case. To close the distance between suspicion and a first-degree murder conviction, the state attorney's office turned to a different set of witnesses: men inside the jail who claimed to have heard Jim talk about the murder. A prosecutor's decision to lean on a jailhouse witness is usually a red flag, a tacit admission that the state's evidence is wobblier than it should be. *Florida v. Dailey* would feature three.

The first jailhouse witness to take the stand was a plainspoken prisoner named James Leitner who worked in the jail's law library. His job brought him into contact with men from all over the institution, he told the jury, and when Jack asked him to give a note to Jim the prior December, he had briefly served as a go-between for the two men. That same month, he said, Jim came to the law library and asked that a message be relayed back: If Jack were ever afforded the opportunity of a retrial, he promised he would come clean and clear Jack's name. "He said, 'Tell him that I will come back and tell them what really happened—that really, *I'm* the one that did it,'" Leitner testified.

Leitner claimed that he was not the only witness to Jim's admission. Another man who worked in the law library, Pablo DeJesus, had been sitting nearby. "Pablo looked over at Mr. Dailey and said, 'Why did you have to kill the girl?'" Leitner told the jury. "Dailey

JIM DAILEY AT HIS 1987 MURDER TRIAL IN CLEARWATER, FLORIDA

looked at Pablo and said, 'Man, I just lost it.'" DeJesus then took the stand and repeated the same story.

Both Leitner and DeJesus had a strong incentive to help the prosecution; they were awaiting sentencing on charges of cocaine trafficking and faced substantial time in prison. Leitner had already shaved two years off a sentence for kidnapping and assault in Colorado by testifying for prosecutors there. When Jim's defense attorney, Henry Andringa, tried to pin him down on cross-examination, Leitner would not admit to vying for a deal. Andringa had no better luck when he grilled DeJesus, who insisted that he was cooperating because his conscience had moved him to do so. Staying silent "was against my morals as a father and a human," he said.

Jim's lawyer continued to press him, but DeJesus would not abandon his position that his intentions were noble. "All right," Judge Penick finally said. "Sir, thank you for coming and testifying. Call your next witness, State."

Andrews rose from her seat. "State would call Paul Skalnik," she said.

. . .

It was late in the morning on a Friday, June 26, when Skalnik settled into the witness box and turned to acknowledge the jury with a nod and a sober half smile. He was no longer the dashing figure in a three-piece suit that he had once been; he had grown stockier over the years, and that afternoon his new girth strained against his jail jumpsuit.

To the main players in the courtroom, he was a familiar figure. "I met Mr. Skalnik back in 1980, '81, somewhere way back there," Judge Penick murmured to the attorneys outside the earshot of the jury. It was Penick who had signed off on Skalnik's original plea deal in 1981, allowing his sentencing to be postponed while he went to work in the jail as a snitch. And it was Penick who had agreed to give him probation the following year, releasing him into the world weeks before he molested Karen Parker. Andrews also shared a history with her witness. In 1983, Skalnik had provided crucial testimony against Kenneth Gardner, whom she prosecuted for first-degree murder in the stabbing death of an elderly hardware-store owner. Skalnik had, by the time of the Dailey trial, been a fixture around the courthouse for six years, but to the jurors the man in the witness box was an unknown.

Andrews began her examination with a few brisk questions that helped Skalnik establish himself as someone who had landed in jail for committing a series of regrettable, but relatively low-stakes, crimes. He explained that he faced up to twenty years in prison on four grand theft charges, and that he had been convicted of other felonies in the past. "Five or six, if I am not mistaken," he said.

Skalnik said nothing about having been charged with molesting a twelve-year-old girl—and why would he? The state attorney's office had dropped the lewd-and-lascivious case.

"Has anyone from law enforcement offered you—that includes

the state attorney's office—anything to induce you to testify here today?" Andrews asked.

"No, ma'am, they have not."

"Have you testified as a witness in other criminal cases?"

"Yes, ma'am, I have," he said.

"Approximately how many times would you say you have testified in criminal cases?"

"Approximately six to eight," he said, his breezy tone suggesting he might be using "approximately" loosely.

"And for that testimony, do you think you received any consideration on your sentence?"

Skalnik grinned. "No, ma'am. I was probably treated worse than if I hadn't testified."

"Are you currently in an isolation cell now in the jail?"

"Yes, ma'am, I am."

"Is that because it is known in the jail that you have testified in other criminal cases?"

"Yes, ma'am—and that I am a former police officer."

That this was a point of pride for Skalnik was evident by the way he straightened in his seat. Quick to cast himself as one of the good guys, he added, "I still do have law enforcement inside of me."

He looked eager to say more, but Andrews did not give him the chance. "Do you know James Dailey?" she asked.

"Yes, ma'am," he said. "I do."

"Do you see him in the courtroom?"

"Yes, ma'am."

"Can you please point to him and state what he is wearing?"

"He is the gentleman sitting in the center of the table to the left, wearing a striped shirt and striped tie and dark suit."

Skalnik asserted that he was on friendly terms with Jim and the other men who were held in his cellblock, who had bought Skalnik's cover story about why he was being held in protective custody. "I told them I was embezzling and was caught out of the country," he said. "That was the reason that I was in isolation, was because they were afraid I would escape." Such a lie was necessary, he explained, to ensure his own safety.

As he went on to describe how he had come to hear what he said was a confession to the murder, he painted a scenario that was, almost word for word, what he had testified in previous cases, going all the way back to the Moody Park Three trial in Houston, eight years earlier. Skalnik said he was passing by Jim's cell early one morning when Jim struck up a conversation. "He met me at the bars of his cell," Skalnik said. Andrews did not ask her witness to explain how such a face-to-face meeting was possible, given that prisoners who are held in isolation cannot stroll around freely, conversing with whomever they like.

Skalnik said Jim quickly steered the conversation to the murder. "He talked about how he and Mr. Pearcy had been together in a car; that it involved a young teenage girl; that Mr. Pearcy had actually held the young girl 'under,'" Skalnik said. That the victim in question had been found, drowned, in a large body of water had been all over the news, but Skalnik gave the jury the impression that he knew nothing about the case. He expressed befuddlement. "I did not know what 'under' was," he said.

Then, according to Skalnik, Jim proceeded to reveal what he had not said to anyone else—not to investigators, not to the other men in the jail, not to Mary Kay, not to his own lawyer. Skalnik delivered each word slowly and deliberately, his blue-gray eyes widening as he spoke: "He said the young girl kept staring at him, screaming, and would not die. And he stabbed her. And threw the knife away."

To hear such an admission "was so hard to comprehend and to accept," Skalnik continued, shaking his head in disbelief. "I had seen this gentleman walking in the hallways, laughing and kidding with other inmates. And all of a sudden, to see a man's eyes, and to describe how he can stab a young girl—and she was screaming and staring at him and would not die."

"Were those Mr. Dailey's words as best you can remember?" Andrews asked.

"As best I can recall," Skalnik said gravely. "'She is screaming, staring at me, and would not die.'"

13

CONVICTION

"A defendant's confession is like no other evidence," wrote the U.S. Supreme Court justice Byron White in the 1991 majority decision in *Arizona v. Fulminante,* a capital case that rested on a confession furnished by a jailhouse witness. "It is probably the most probative and damaging evidence that can be admitted against him, and, if it is a full confession, a jury may be tempted to rely on it alone in reaching its decision."

Skalnik's brief but lurid account of Jim's supposed confession was critical to the state's case. So potent is the power of a confession, researchers have found, that its potency does not diminish if the defendant's alleged admission of guilt is narrated by a third party rather than the defendant himself. Skalnik's testimony not only implicated Jim in the stabbing; it also conveniently provided the evidence of premeditation prosecutors needed to win a first-degree murder conviction: Seeing that a victim "would not die," and then deciding to stab her to death, was sufficient to prove forethought under Florida law. Before the trial, when Jim learned that Skalnik would be testifying against him, he was disgusted but not surprised. He had seen it coming. "This is a damn setup," he'd protested when he was first moved near Skalnik. He had never spoken to the man before, he told Andringa, and the idea that he would talk to someone like Skalnik was laughable. Jim was well

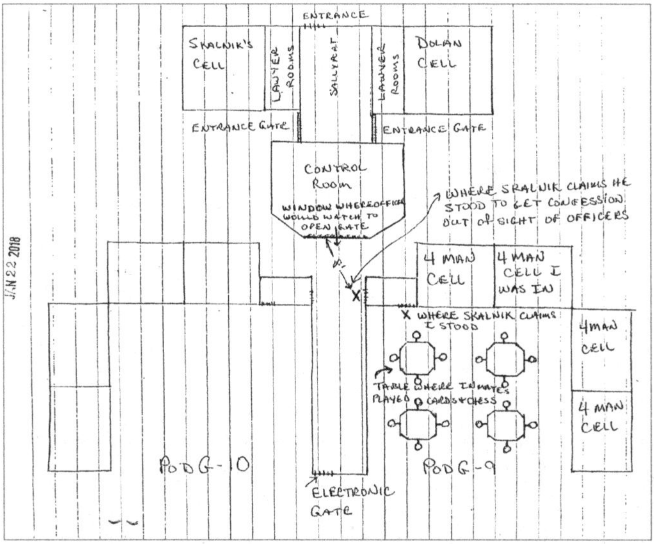

THIS DRAWING BY JIM DAILEY, A RE-CREATION OF HIS ORIGINAL DIAGRAM, WAS SUBMITTED AS PART OF HIS POSTCONVICTION LITIGATION.

aware that law enforcement had been scouring the jail for anyone willing to testify against him and had already been warned that Skalnik was a snitch.

Besides, the jail's layout made Skalnik's account implausible. Jim drew a detailed diagram of his cellblock for his lawyer. The sketch, carefully rendered on a sheet of lined paper, showed that any conversation which might have occurred between them would have taken place in full view of correctional officers and inmates, at enough of a distance that Jim would have been forced to raise his voice.

When the time came to cross-examine Skalnik, however, the defense failed to share this improbable choreography. Andringa relegated the job of interrogating Skalnik to his law partner, James Denhardt, who was new to the case, and Denhardt did not challenge Skalnik to explain how an in-depth conversation with another inmate could have occurred given the restrictions of protective custody. Nor did he confront Skalnik with testimony he had given just weeks earlier; in a pretrial deposition, Skalnik admitted that his reputation in the jail as a snitch was so widespread that he feared for his life—sworn statements that contradicted his trial testimony that the men in the jail trusted him. Instead, the cross-examination, which devolved into a tortuous back-and-forth about whether a court reporter had accurately transcribed the deposition, left several jurors dozing in their seats.

In the end, it did not matter that Skalnik had little information about the murder itself, or that the few details he provided—*Jack Pearcy, car, young girl, knife*—had been repeated in local media coverage of the case. Any questions as to his truthfulness were put to rest when Andrews called Halliday to the stand as the state's final witness. The detective vouched for Skalnik, testifying that the inmate had supplied him with credible information in a number of cases he had investigated in the past. Skalnik's prior assistance, he added, had yielded "extremely positive results."

On the morning of June 27, 1987, after three days of testimony, Judge Penick addressed the assembled lawyers. "The state has rested," he said. "Defense, your case."

Throughout the trial, Andringa had chipped away at details of the state's case through cross-examination, highlighting inconsistencies and sowing doubt. But to win, he would have to do more. He would have to present an alternative to the prosecution's theory of the crime, and he would have to challenge Skalnik's account of Jim's jailhouse confession. He could have asked jail officials to describe the cellblock's layout and the protocols that govern inmates in protective custody. He could have summoned men held in nearby cells to speak to whether they had seen Jim talking to Skalnik. He could have called Deborah North, who had seen Jack alone with Shelly outside Hank's Seabreeze Lounge on the night of the murder, or the bar's patrons. But Andringa didn't call any witnesses at all. He rose from his seat, stood before the court, and said just five words: "The defense rests, Your Honor."

Behind the scenes, a debate had raged over whether Jim should testify. The conventional wisdom is that a defendant who takes the stand at his own trial often risks more than he stands to gain. Even the most truthful defendant lacks the legal savvy of the prosecutors who will interrogate him, making him vulnerable to a potentially disastrous cross-examination. When Jim insisted on testifying, Andringa cautioned that doing so was not in his best interests; his account of how he got his jeans wet sounded so far-fetched, the lawyer warned, that he would lose any credibility he had with jurors if he recounted it under oath. Only when his mother and Mary Kay were called in to implore him to listen did he agree not to take the stand. Andringa's advice was sound, but it only deepened the defense's narrative problem. Jim would never have the chance to tell the jury that back in Kansas, Jack had routinely shown up on his doorstep at odd hours of the night wanting to get wasted, just as he did on the night of the murder. The wet jeans went unexplained.

Andrews, who delivered the state's summation, started by acknowledging the many weaknesses of her case. "You may ask, 'Well, if Jack Pearcy has already been convicted, why are we here?,' " she said as she addressed the jury. "We are here because *two* men committed that murder, *two* men assisted each other in committing that murder, and *both* men are legally and morally responsible for her death." She admitted that she did not know, and had not proven, Jim's motive for taking part in the crime, but she explained that the state was not obligated to do so under the law. Conceding that the evidence was at times incomplete, she argued that this only pointed to how well Jack and Jim had covered their tracks. "There is a lack of evidence—physical evidence and eyewitnesses—because they did their best to hide and conceal this crime," she said.

What Andrews returned to over and over again was the testimony of the jailhouse witnesses, and Skalnik in particular. "The three prisoners that were brought in from the Pinellas County Jail are thieves and drug dealers," she said. "We never told you that they would be anything different. They came in their jail clothes. I am not asking you people to like them. I'm not asking you to take them home to dinner with you. But I am asking you to *believe* them." Halliday, she pointed out, believed them. "You heard about Detective Halliday's experiences, and what unit he is with, and the types of crimes he investigates," she said. "If these men are cons, they would not con Detective Halliday."

Andrews assured the jury that the jailhouse witnesses did not receive any favorable treatment in exchange for their cooperation. She reminded the jury of Skalnik's testimony: "Skalnik said, so far, nothing's been offered to him. He is facing twenty—the maximum."

Finally, she turned to the defendant:

> Mr. Dailey sits there in front of you, clean-shaven, coat and tie on, looking sort of like a stockbroker.
>
> I ask you to think about what he looked like on the night of May 5th, the early morning hours of May 6th, 1985, on that strip of land north of the Indian Rocks Bridge, with a knife in his hand, Shelly Boggio's blood on him. Standing over there, probably after that girl had been sexually assaulted, after 31 stab wounds, 17 cutting wounds. The child wouldn't die, so he drowned her and left her naked body to float—maybe to sink so it wouldn't be found for a while, give him even more time—in the dark waters of the Intracoastal in this county. And then he drifted out of town, drifted into Miami, and drifted away.

Quoting Leitner and DeJesus, and then Skalnik, she concluded with the words of the jailhouse witnesses: "He said he 'lost it' to two witnesses, and as a result of that, Shelly Boggio lost her life. *She stared at him and she would not die,* so he killed her."

The jurors deliberated for less than two hours before finding Jim guilty of murder in the first degree.

Mary Kay had attended every day of the trial, waiting to see the evidence or hear the testimony that would help her grasp why the full weight of the State of Florida had been brought to bear against her ex-husband. She remembered Halliday coming to her house during the investigation and telling her, as they sat at her dining room table, "When you hear all the evidence, there won't be any question in your mind." But that moment never came. Jim had made terrible decisions in his life, she knew, and he had engaged in willful self-destruction, but to her the state's case lacked common sense. It takes a unique personality to stab a teenage girl thirty-one times. Given the two possible candidates, which man seemed more capable of such an extraordinary act of violence?

The most agonizing part of the trial, as far as Mary Kay was concerned, was still to come. A guilty verdict in a capital case is followed by a penalty phase: a separate mini-trial in which the jury weighs whether to recommend a sentence of life or death. The penalty phase presents an opportunity for the defense to provide the full biography of the defendant who has been convicted, and to explain what experiences shaped him, including factors like childhood abuse, a brain injury, or mental illness, in the hope of persuading jurors to spare his life. But as was true in many capital cases in the 1980s, Jim's lawyers gave short shrift to the trauma that had shaped their client. The jury would never hear about his searing experience at Bien Hoa, or his dysfunctional childhood, or the extent to which he struggled with addiction. His "drinking problem" was mentioned just twice.

Andringa's strategy was simply to humanize his client, and to make the case for mercy, he called four witnesses. Jim's mother, Grace, spoke haltingly, her words weighted by grief, as she told the jury that her son was "so sweet and loving and kind-hearted," and that he "had a good singing voice and always sang in our church choir." He had served as her primary emotional support, she explained, after her husband died. His daughter, Stacey, read aloud from hand-drawn birthday cards he had sent her over the years, and told the jury of a time after her parents divorced when he wrote her a song, which he played for her on the guitar, in which he assured her that he would always love her. Mary Kay emphasized the kindness he had always shown her, even during heated arguments, and spoke of his protective instincts, telling the story of him saving her high school classmate from drowning. Her husband, Dick, recalled the man he had served beside overseas. "We went to Vietnam twice," he said. "He was a billboard-type GI. He was a recruiter's dream."

Like most of Jim's trial, the tone was calm and restrained, lending a civilized air to the crude question at hand: whether the State of Florida should one day execute him. None of the defense witnesses broke down, or pleaded for the jurors to spare his life. Perhaps they understood it wouldn't matter. Within the staid structure of a criminal trial, they tried instead to politely arouse the jury's sympathies with details that suggested Jim's life was worth saving.

The prosecution argued that the totality of Jim's life did not outweigh the horror of the crime. "There can be no doubt," Andrews's co-counsel, Robert Heyman, told the jury at the conclusion of the penalty phase. "There can be no doubt when you look at those photographs, the type of suffering, the type of realization Shelly Boggio had of her impending death. As Paul Skalnik said the defendant indicated, 'No matter how many times I stabbed her, she just wouldn't die.'"

The jury wasted little time in recommending that Jim be executed by electric chair. The decision, the court clerk announced, was unanimous.

Jim's turn to speak came on August 7, at his sentencing hearing, after Judge Penick followed the jury's recommendation and formally sentenced him to death. Wearing a long, mournful expression, Jim stood in front of the judge, glancing down at a handwritten statement as he spoke. He began by recognizing the "terrible kind of pain" Shelly's murder had caused her twin sister, and the anguish felt by her family members, who sat in the courtroom, weeping. "I say these things as a caring human being and as a person wrongfully convicted of this heinous crime," he said.

"I am not afraid of death," he continued. "What I do fear is waking up, every morning, in prison, for the rest of my life, for a crime I did not commit." As he addressed the judge, he explained that he had visited twenty-six different countries during his time in the service, and that the experience of seeing the world had only reinforced his belief that America was the greatest nation on earth—a belief now fundamentally shaken. "At least in other countries you know ahead of time to expect that state witnesses will be brought against you, and that lies will be told," he said bitterly. "At least they don't hide behind the facade of 'truth and justice for all.'" The disillusionment that his death sentence had brought about, he suggested, was almost as agonizing as the sentence itself. In Pinellas County, the quest for convictions "has been turned into a win-at-all-costs game," he said, his voice rising as he spoke. "Truth is allowed to be manipulated and paid liars are allowed to testify." His trial, he added before he was led away in shackles, had been a "mockery of justice."

. . .

Five days later, Skalnik walked out of the Pinellas County Jail. There is little question as to why; a Florida Parole and Probation Commission memo states that his release was "due to his cooperation with the state attorney's office in the first-degree murder trial."

Skalnik had assured prosecutors that he would stay in the area for his own trial, which was scheduled for that October, and for the three upcoming murder trials that he was slated to testify in, but that summer day anything felt possible. He strode out of the jail, leaving behind its sour air and incessant din. Outside, past the fences topped with razor wire, the air was fresh and clean, the taste of salt on the wind. The sun shone brightly overhead. Passenger planes departing the nearby airport angled upward and away, until they skimmed the blue sky above, heading to places unknown.

PART III

14

STARKE

What Jim first noticed was the heat. His cell at Florida State Prison was built of solid concrete, which retained and intensified the summer swelter. There were no reprieves, as there had been on many scorching afternoons on the Gulf Coast, when sudden downpours cooled the air and lightning cracked open the sky. Here, the summer pressed down, windless and still. Jim now found himself in an entirely different Florida, in a penitentiary on the outskirts of the town of Starke, about thirty miles south of the Georgia state line. Hemmed in by the stately pine forests and timberlands of north-central Florida, Starke was a place rooted not in the coast's easygoing rhythms but in the Deep South's long embrace of capital punishment.

Jim had arrived at the prison on August 10, 1987, under armed guard, escorted in a three-car convoy. His hair was freshly shorn and his face clean-shaven, his upper lip bare where his mustache had once been. The landscape around the prison had been similarly denuded, leaving nowhere for a prisoner to run. Where the dense pine forest once stood, there was instead a vast, unbroken expanse of St. Augustine grass, mowed down to the nub. Barbed-wire fencing, buttressed by looping coils of razor wire and picketed by watchtowers, encircled the penitentiary's cheerless white exterior. Inside, on the first floor of Q Wing, sat Florida's electric chair:

a sturdy, straight-backed slab of red oak, laced with thick leather restraints, known as Old Sparky.

Jim was led in handcuffs through a series of heavy metal gates to nearby S Wing, where condemned men were housed. Just a few years earlier, Florida's death row had been a lawless place racked by violence; in the span of four days in 1980, one prisoner used the sharpened end of a spoon handle to fatally stab a correctional officer, another speared an officer in the chest with a filed-down welding rod, and a third burned an officer with a bucketful of scalding water. Since then, prisoners' movements had been severely restricted; except for two trips to the rec yard each week, Jim would remain confined to his six-by-nine-foot cell. He would live like this, in near-total isolation, for as long as his appeals moved through the courts—a process that could take years, or even decades. The state could not slate him for execution until he had exhausted every last avenue of appeal.

The air in his cell seemed to stand still. Slick with the residual grime of its previous inhabitants, the cell reeked of sweat and cigarettes and excrement. Jim was given some rags and bleach, and he began scouring the walls, the floor, the metal toilet. He scrubbed until his arms ached. When he was done, he lay down on the thin mattress that covered his steel bunk and listened to the alien acoustics of the place. Every so often, the piercing screech of metal scraping against concrete echoed through the three-tiered cellblock—the sound, he later learned, of men slamming their lockers against the wall to kill rats as they scuttled by. All night long, in the dark, he lay awake.

Like Jim, many of the men who were sent to Florida State Prison in the 1980s to await their executions had been tried by big-city prosecutors who were riding the wave of tough-on-crime sentiment that was sweeping the nation during the Reagan era. Some of the condemned were still teenagers. Sentenced to death in Miami, Fort Lauderdale, Orlando, Jacksonville, Tampa, and Clearwater, they were dispatched to Starke, where the way the state meted out justice had not changed since Old Sparky was built by prisoners in 1923. That year, the state legislature made electrocution the official manner of execution; before then, counties carried out judicial executions themselves, usually by hanging. Unlike a noose—which could leave a man to suffer an agonizingly slow asphyxiation or work too efficiently and decapitate them—the electric chair was seen as a modern advancement: a more civilized, efficient solution to the messy work of killing.

The first person whom jailers tied down to Old Sparky was a Black thirteen-year-old boy named Fortune Ferguson who had been arrested, tried, and convicted in a single day for the rape of a white eight-year-old girl. He won a last-second reprieve, leaving Frank Johnson, a Black man who had been convicted of shooting a white locomotive engineer, to take his place. On October 7, 1924, Johnson was led to the chair and strapped in. "The current was applied," read one newspaper dispatch, "and four minutes and twenty seconds later, the negro was pronounced dead." Florida put 195 men to death in the forty years that followed; more than two-thirds of them were Black. Fortune Ferguson was one of them—sent back to the chair in 1927, when he was sixteen years old.

Florida embraced capital punishment for as long as it could, but public support for the death penalty steadily declined during the civil rights era, and by 1967 legal challenges over its constitutionality brought executions to a halt around the country. Five years later, in *Furman v. Georgia,* the U.S. Supreme Court struck down existing death-penalty laws, ruling that they violated the Eighth Amendment's protection against cruel and unusual punishment. The death penalty was so randomly and capriciously imposed, wrote Justice Potter Stewart, that it was akin to "being struck by lightning." The landmark decision voided states' capital punishment statutes, nullifying existing death sentences.

The ninety-five men and one woman on Florida's death row—the nation's largest—rejoiced. "We laughed, we whooped, we hollered, and shook the doors," one prisoner told reporters. Their sentences were automatically commuted to life without parole.

As death rows around the country emptied, Florida called its legislature into special session and passed the first death-penalty statute in the country that attempted to address the Supreme Court's objections. The Florida statute, along with new laws in Georgia and Texas, was upheld by the Supreme Court in 1976. Capital punishment was once again the law of the land.

The first man in America to be executed in the wake of this decision was a white man named John Spenkelink, condemned for fatally bludgeoning and shooting a fellow drifter in a Tallahassee motel. Just one person had been put to death in the United States in the previous twelve years—another white man, Gary Gilmore, who waived his right to appeal his murder conviction in Utah and invited the state to kill him, in 1977, by firing squad. Unlike Gilmore, Spenkelink fought his death sentence—and with it, the anticipated crush of executions that would follow if the courts allowed it to move forward.

A reprieve never came. On the morning of May 25, 1979, the warden poured Spenkelink two shots of whiskey, and the machinery of death kicked into gear. Some other states had turned away from the electric chair by then, passing laws that changed their method of execution to lethal injection; the then-untested protocol—a three-drug cocktail—promised a "gentle, humane" death, as a Texas prison chaplain explained at the time, not unlike "laying down and going to sleep." But Florida, proudly hidebound, had stuck with Old Sparky. Correctional officers shaved Spenkelink's head and right calf, contact points for the electrodes that would connect him to the electric chair. "You motherfuckers really think you're tough, don't you?" Spenkelink spat when the warden came to tell him that it was time.

A team of officers led the thirty-year-old, handcuffed, down a corridor to the electric chair, where they worked quickly to restrain him, immobilizing his chest, waist, and limbs with leather straps, and tightening another strap over his chin and mouth to hold his head in place. Spenkelink, who could move only his eyes, settled into a wide, terrified stare. Finally, a black hood was lowered over his face and the signal was given. At 10:12 a.m., the executioner, who was also cloaked in black, flipped the switch.

Spenkelink's body lurched forward, straining against the 2,500-volt surge, and his hands, which turned blue, clenched into fists. When his heart did not give out, he was given a second jolt, and then a third. He was pronounced dead six minutes later, at 10:18 a.m. The black hood was pulled back to reveal a swollen, purplish face. Smoke rose from his leg, where the electrode had seared his skin. The chamber smelled of burnt flesh.

The gruesome spectacle of Spenkelink's electrocution—which took place in front of thirty-two witnesses, including lawmakers, prosecutors, and reporters from across the state—did nothing to dampen Florida's enthusiasm for capital punishment. The number of people sent to death row swelled in the years that followed. By the time Jim arrived at Florida State Prison, he was one of nearly three hundred prisoners whom Florida judges had sentenced to death. When one of them, a Black man from Miami named Beauford White, was led down the long corridor to the execution chamber later that August and strapped to the electric chair, the specter of an excruciating death at the hands of the state ceased to be an abstraction to Jim. That day, as he sat alone in his cell, he could hear the mounting whine of the generators that powered Old Sparky.

Months passed, a year, then two. Jim learned to tune out the cacophony that came with living alongside so many other men, who blared their black-and-white TVs at top volume and called out to each other over the dull roar: an incessant, rumbling chorus of jangling alarms, barked orders from correctional officers, squeaking rubber soles on concrete, the clang of metal gates slamming shut. In the summers, Jim slept with his head beneath his sheet to deter the legions of mosquitoes from feasting on him; he jury-rigged makeshift fans, using the lids of sherbet cartons for blades and fashioning a fan belt from thread spools and dental floss. In the winters, when his cell was so frigid that he could see his breath, he figured out that if he rolled up a newspaper and lit one end, he could warm his stainless steel toilet enough to make it tolerable to sit on. Just before executions, he and the other men on his wing turned their transistor radios to the same station—part protest, part show of solidarity—and cranked them up to drown out the noise.

All of this time, Jim's appeals slowly advanced through the courts. The first step, his direct appeal, led the Florida Supreme Court to uphold his conviction but overturn his death sentence in 1991, finding that Judge Penick had ignored mitigating factors that might have warranted a less severe punishment. Penick nevertheless reimposed the death sentence—a decision the high court ultimately upheld in 1995. Jim had not yet come close to exhausting his appeals, however; defendants who are sentenced to death are entitled to additional rounds of review, first in state court and then in federal court. These cases demand extra scrutiny, the U.S. Supreme Court established in 1976, because the irrevocable nature of an execution sets it apart from all other punishments. "Death," the court declared, "is different."

One January day in 1998, a correctional officer who held a bundle of mail approached Jim's cell and handed him an envelope. The neat handwriting in green ink that decorated the outside was unfamiliar, as was the return address, in the Netherlands. Mystified, Jim reached into the envelope, pulled out several sheets of lined paper, and began to read.

In near-perfect English, the letter writer—a twenty-two-year-old college graduate named Marieke Jansen—introduced herself and asked if Jim would like to correspond with her. She had been moved by the story of another Dutch woman, Gea Knol, who had written a book about her years-long correspondence with a man on Florida's death row. Like most Dutch citizens, Marieke opposed capital punishment—the Netherlands abolished the practice in 1870—and she longed to find a meaningful way to protest America's embrace of what she saw as an archaic and morally bankrupt institution. Supporting one person who faced a death sentence felt less abstract than other forms of political activism, and Marieke asked Knol if there was another death-row prisoner who might benefit from hearing from someone halfway around the world. Knol conferred with her pen pal on death row, and several months later Marieke received Jim's name and mailing address. The internet, which did not yet hold a seemingly infinite wealth of data, yielded little other information.

Before Marieke wrote to him, she forced herself to think of the most heinous crimes imaginable, and to contemplate whether she could have an authentic conversation—maybe even a friendship—with someone who had caused tremendous suffering. She hoped to see some goodness in the stranger whose name she had been given, no matter what crime he had committed, but she decided ahead of time not to commit herself blindly; if he turned out to be a sociopath or if he were incapable of self-reflection, she promised herself

MARIEKE JANSEN IN VELP, NETHERLANDS, IN 1995

that she would end the correspondence. Her goal was to try to see the whole person, an approach that stood in contrast, in her mind, to the way that the American criminal justice system froze defendants in time at the precise moment they committed their crimes, disregarding everything that came before and after.

Jim wrote back immediately. "I was surprised and very happy to receive my letter from you," he replied. He described himself as fifty-one years old with brown hair "that is turning silver at an alarming rate," and added that, despite his circumstances, he was an optimist at heart. "Even where I find myself, at this time, I manage to stay upbeat and in good spirits." He sought to find common ground by telling her about his travel overseas with the Air Force, which had included a brief stay in her country—"I was very lucky to get to see the world at Uncle Sam's expense"—and he told her about his ex-wife Mary Kay, with whom he remained close, as well as his two grown children and five grandchildren. "I'm one of the lucky ones whose family didn't desert them under these circumstances," he wrote. The word "lucky" appeared in his letter over and over. For the family and friends who had stuck by him, "I can thank my lucky stars for that."

Jim told her that he would like to exchange letters, even if writing to a stranger might feel awkward at first. "I'm sure it will get easier to talk to each other as we go along," he wrote. "You can ask me any questions you like and I'll answer as honestly as I am able. I didn't want to get started on how bad it is in here, in this letter." He signed off: "I sure hope you write back. Sincerely, Jim."

In the first few months of their correspondence, Jim seemed acutely aware of how a stranger might perceive him, and he worked hard to show Marieke that he had good intentions. "I'm not looking for anything but friendship," he assured her. He also promised her that he would never ask her for money. With family and friends who deposited funds in his commissary account, he explained, he was able to buy items like instant coffee and art supplies, which made prison slightly more tolerable. He had taken up painting, despite having never been an artist, and it now occupied the time that writing songs on his guitar or woodworking had before he was incarcerated. "My old Air Force buddy, Larry Rasmussen, sends me $50 a month and has done that for me since I've been locked up," he wrote. "Now that's a true-blue friend." With his commissary money, Jim helped another man on death row, a Korean War veteran who had no support in the outside world.

He ended each letter with a nod to the longtime boyfriend Marieke had mentioned she lived with—"Please give Wouter my best wishes and highest regards"—and as if to further emphasize the platonic nature of their correspondence, he often wrote to her about Mary Kay. He told Marieke that he had never fallen out of love with his ex-wife, who he said made regular treks up to Starke, with her husband, to visit him. "We had a wonderful life together until Vietnam screwed with my head," he wrote.

In return, Marieke tried to show him what lay beyond his prison cell. She sent photos of her Munsterlander puppy, definitions of idiosyncratic Dutch words, and reports on the progress of the roses and delphiniums she had planted in her garden. To help counteract the sensory deprivation of prison, she made it a point to always provide him with accounts of the natural world—the smell of rain; the sensation of warm sand beneath her feet; the muffled silence of a snowfall—and she sent her letters in colorful envelopes, adding a shock of fuchsia or turquoise to the prison mailbag. Jim wrote back about the magpies he heard chirping and squawking at sunrise; the hurricanes that bore down on north-central Florida; the humidity that made him sweat so much that he soaked his sheets at night. In between the advice he offered her about the everyday problems she shared with him, he described the smallness of his life. Except for the twice-per-week visits to the rec yard, he wrote, he remained confined to his cell. "We call it 24/7," he wrote. "Locked down 24 hours, seven days a week."

Jim did not dwell on the isolation of his existence, but his letters brimmed with frustration over the bureaucratic folly of Florida Department of Corrections regulations. Any violation could result in a disciplinary report, he explained, as well as a stint in solitary confinement, where he would be deprived of his visits to the rec yard and the thirteen-inch, black-and-white TV that served as his tether to the outside world. "George Porter is in solitary for sixty days," Jim wrote of a fellow prisoner, one summer day. "Man, I feel so bad for him. They came at 3:45 a.m. and gave him a drug test and he couldn't make his bladder work. Heck, he's 66 years old and the old plumbing just doesn't work like it used to. Well, they have a zero-tolerance policy here and if you can't piss on command they give you sixty days in the hole. Pretty barbaric, isn't it? This is just a taste of the stuff we have to put up with around here. Everybody knows George doesn't use drugs, but that doesn't make one bit of difference. Rules are rules."

For as much as Jim shared, he also left much unsaid. Only rarely did he refer to the sword of Damocles that hung over him and all the other men there. "Depression and heartache," he wrote on April 4, 1998. "The state of Florida took the life of a very good friend, plus three more people, in the short time period of eight days. I met Leo Jones the first day I arrived on the row. He took me under his wing and shared his canteen with me until I could get on my feet. He was a kind and very gentle person." Jim did not believe that Jones, who had been convicted of the sniper killing of a Jacksonville police officer, was guilty. Two Florida Supreme Court justices had voted to grant Jones a new trial, citing evidence that they believed cast serious doubt on whether he ever committed the crime, but they had been overruled by the majority. "Now we'll never know the truth," Jim wrote. "As soon as the state executes someone, all their files are closed, so there will be no more investigations, and all the questions will remain unanswered."

15

THE ART OF THE DEAL

Skalnik had been released after Jim's trial in the summer of 1987 on the condition that he stay in the area for his own trial, which was scheduled for that October. Instead, he drove a rented Lincoln Town Car across the state line, breaking every promise he had made to prosecutors in Clearwater. He left behind a fiancée, whom he had led to believe that he was an FBI agent. They were to be married that fall at a church in Palm Harbor, followed by a reception for 350 guests at a nearby country club. Though the invitations had already gone out and the bridesmaids' dresses had been ordered, he disappeared without explanation. The Lincoln Town Car, which he never returned, was later reported stolen.

He surfaced that fall in Austin, Texas, the city that had always preoccupied his imagination. Passing himself off as J. Paul Bourne, a high roller flush with oil money, he accessorized his three-piece suits with a diamond ring and diamond-studded oil well pendant. His timing was conspicuously off—the price of oil had collapsed the previous year, and Texas was in the middle of a punishing bust—but in Austin, a sleepy college town that lacked ties to the petroleum industry, no one seemed to notice. In his guise as Bourne, he opened multiple checking accounts on the promise that millions would be wired in. He talked a single jewelry store out of $29,941 in bracelets, rings, and baubles through a scheme that ensnared his first wife. Skalnik had managed to rekindle a romance with the registered nurse and brought her to the jewelry store to shop for wedding rings. He persuaded the store to extend him a line of credit, then later returned alone with her checkbook, claiming they had just married and that she had not yet changed her name on the account.

Back in Clearwater, prosecutors were left in the lurch; their star witness, who was slated to testify in three upcoming murder trials, was suddenly a fugitive from justice. His failure to appear for his own trial for grand theft was an embarrassment for the state attorney's office, which had allowed him to walk free without having to post bond, even though he had violated every period of probation and parole ever afforded him. The frustration felt by Viola Giovanniello, the widow whom Skalnik had defrauded the previous year, was noted in prosecutors' files: "Mrs. Giovanniello has totally gone to pieces over the many continuances of this case, and feels that the defendant is in control of the system and not that the system is in control of the defendant."

Sergeant Robert Bowers, a detective in the Austin Police Department's forgery department who investigated the jewelry store swindle, learned that J. Paul Bourne claimed to have once been an Austin police officer—a detail that stirred his memory. Bowers recalled a cop who was on the force in the early 1970s who had gotten in trouble for passing bad checks and who fit the suspect's physical description. He began to investigate and discovered that the man he was thinking of, Paul Skalnik, had recently renewed his Texas driver's license, listing his home address as that of the woman whose checks he had passed off as his own. And the detective quickly uncovered the outstanding warrant for grand theft, for the $6,100 Rolex Skalnik had picked up on a previous foray through Austin.

When Skalnik was arrested on February 2, 1988, he was wearing some of his spoils, including a gold rope necklace, a gold chain bracelet, and a diamond-encrusted ring. He was quickly bailed out by a prosperous real estate agent he had befriended at a church softball game who believed Skalnik to be a fellow follower of Christ. When Skalnik failed to appear for his court date that spring, forfeiting the $7,500 his friend had posted for his bond, Skalnik was charged with bail jumping. He was arrested again on April 27 and returned to the Travis County Jail.

From his cell, Skalnik made a direct appeal to the local district attorney, Ronnie Earle. "I'm not certain you remember me, but during the early 1970s, I was an Austin police officer and spoke with you numerous times at the municipal court," he wrote in longhand on sheets torn from a yellow legal pad. "Since leaving APD, I have worked for numerous government agencies, having assisted in placing eleven people on death row in Florida, one in Texas, and a total of more than 64 people in prison in numerous states." A detective in Florida named John Halliday, he said, could attest to his track record.

Skalnik then arrived at the purpose of his letter: He had provided the DA's office with information on three men, all of whom faced serious charges, and in return he hoped Earle would go easy on him. "Mr. Earle, I'm engaged to a lovely woman here in Austin," he wrote. "I wish to settle down, return to the University of Texas, and start a new life. Please attempt to understand. I would appreciate any consideration you could afford me."

Before he could reprise his role as a snitch, however, an assistant district attorney in Earle's office saw what should have been obvious to any prosecutor. Skalnik, she warned in an interoffice memo, "is a BIG con artist." She made clear that the DA's office would not be cutting any deals. With no good options left, Skalnik pleaded guilty to theft and bail jumping and was sentenced to four years in prison. He was not sent to the Texas Department of Corrections right away, though. First, he was extradited back to Florida.

. . .

By then, Skalnik's relationship with the state attorney's office in Clearwater had soured, thanks to his decision to bolt to Texas. Prosecutors went ahead with the first-degree murder cases he had given information in, but without the benefit of his testimony. The shakiest of the three, *The State of Florida v. David James McPartland,* fell apart in his absence. The state's case, which lacked any physical or forensic evidence, featured Skalnik's allegation that the defendant had confessed to him. (McPartland was adamant that he had never spoken to Skalnik and offered to take a polygraph exam to prove it.) The judge overseeing the case took the rare step of throwing out the charge in the middle of McPartland's trial, determining that the state attorney's office had not presented enough evidence to warrant sending the case to a jury. It was a sharp rebuke to the case's prosecutor, Beverly Andrews, coming less than a year after her win in the Dailey case.

Skalnik, who was booked into the Pinellas County Jail on May 26, 1988, was furious to find himself back where he started, and he grew emboldened as he stewed in his cell that summer. He asked his public defender to go to the state attorney's office with the terms of a deal: He wanted to be returned to Texas, where he would be permitted to serve time on both his Texas and his Florida charges concurrently, for a period of no more than four years. For a recently captured fugitive who faced up to twenty years in prison on his grand theft charges alone—and who had committed a string of other crimes for which he had yet to be charged—this was a laughable proposition.

But he warned that if the state attorney's office did not meet his conditions, he would go public with an incendiary allegation: He would say that prosecutors had, for years, knowingly elicited false testimony from him.

When prosecutors balked at his demands, he turned on them. On August 7, Skalnik filed a motion with the judge presiding over his case in which he claimed to have been a party to extensive prosecutorial misconduct. He alleged that in numerous cases he was "coached in testimony, wherein alleged facts were supplied, instructions given, and answers supplied to refute any assertions that any agreement for a deal was made by the state." This testimony gave jurors the false impression that he was "acting alone, had actually heard all these 'confessions,' and had no agreement with the state for a reward for his testimony." Prosecutors "knew of the potential questionability of said confessions," the motion charged, but nevertheless made an "effort to convince juries that the defendant was at all times telling the absolute truth."

Just like the men whom Skalnik had leveled outrageous claims against over the years, prosecutors found themselves on the defensive, scrambling to discredit him. Skalnik had not just accused them of serious ethical violations; he had also thrown their hard-won convictions into jeopardy, claiming to have tainted more than fifty cases with unreliable information. In formal responses submitted to the court, the state attorney's office categorically denied his assertions, dismissing them as "falsehoods, ranging in degree from gross exaggeration to preposterous fabrication."

The irony was exquisite. The same office that had previously instructed judges and juries to take Skalnik at his word, that had spent years defending his incredible stories as gospel truth, was now asking the court to treat his accusations as fantasy. It dismissed his allegations as "innuendos rather than specific factual assertions" and "the fabrications of a frustrated criminal."

Still, the state attorney's office refused to reckon with what this meant for the men Skalnik had testified against. If he could fabricate stories about prosecutors with such apparent ease, what did this say about the truthfulness of his prior testimony? Prosecutors had a ready answer: nothing at all. Skalnik remained a reliable witness, they insisted—but only when his testimony concerned criminal defendants, not them. His testimony against these men, they argued, "was credible, was often independently substantiated, and withstood extensive cross-examination."

In fact, behind the scenes, an investigator with the state attorney's office was having difficulty verifying that Skalnik had provided information that could be independently corroborated. Just two examples were provided, both by Detective Halliday. He said Skalnik's tips had led law enforcement to a ski mask that a defendant wore during the commission of a murder as well as a gun used in another killing. (Of the gun, the investigator wrote, "This information is incorrect. The information from Skalnik was accurate; however it came months after the gun was retrieved.") Rather than dig deeper, the state attorney's office undertook a campaign to prove that Skalnik's previous testimony was trustworthy. One prosecutor proposed in an internal memo that "each assistant state attorney who took testimony from Skalnik in a case, or who used Skalnik as a witness in a case, would testify to having no reason to disbelieve Skalnik. Additionally, Halliday and any other police officers we find to have had contact with Skalnik would testify in the same manner."

In the end, his allegations turned out to be merely leverage for himself—leverage that he used to negotiate a better deal. In return for his withdrawal of his motion, with the claim that it had been the sole work of his ambitious public defender, and that he had simply signed the last page without reviewing it, he and the state attorney's office arrived at a mutually beneficial arrangement. For a total of six felonies—four counts of grand theft and two counts of failure to appear in court—he would receive a five-year sentence. (The state never charged him for making off with his fiancée's rental car or defrauding wedding vendors or asked the court to lengthen his sentence using a habitual offender enhancement.) The deal also ensured that Skalnik would be sent far away from Pinellas County, a win for both parties. He entered his plea on the condition that his sentence be served in Texas.

Skalnik evaded even that relatively meager punishment. In November 1989, after he had completed seven months in prison in Huntsville, Texas, on his bail-jumping charge, the Texas Department of Corrections—which had never agreed to allow him to serve his Florida sentence there—released him, giving him a one-way bus ticket out of town. The Florida Parole Commission, which initially sought to correct the error, would eventually abandon its efforts to extradite him.

Skalnik, all told, had gotten everything he wanted. As the 1980s drew to a close, he put Florida behind him, but not before adding his gloss to the near decade he had spent in Pinellas County. "The state attorney's office has always characterized me as an honest, forthright witness," he wrote to a judge before his release, "and together, we never lost a case."

Skalnik returned to his hometown of League City, southeast of Houston—where, as a boy, he had watched the flat expanse of coastal plain give way to the rising ambitions of the space age. He had been in junior high when NASA broke ground on the Manned Spacecraft Center (later renamed the Lyndon B. Johnson Space Center), a short drive from League City. Practically overnight, the area's oyster-shell roads were paved, its cow pastures bulldozed into cul-de-sacs. Schools filled with clean-cut overachievers, the sons and daughters of NASA's engineers and astronauts, whose brand-new homes came outfitted with swimming pools and central air.

After their arrival, Skalnik erased everything about himself that marked him as small-town. He dropped his y'alls, clipped the long vowels that betrayed him as a native son of southeast Texas, and mimicked the crisp diction of his new suburban neighbors. He began wearing a dark blazer, just like his favorite character on TV: the clever criminal defense attorney Perry Mason. It was around this time that he told his first big lie, confiding to others—as he would throughout his life—that he had been adopted. In truth, he was his parents' biological son, but this fantasy hinted at a deeper longing, a sense that he was meant for something bigger than the life he'd been born into.

The Skalnik family occupied a dilapidated frame house with just one bedroom that Skalnik shared with his parents, Emile and Gina. The shabby dwelling and unkempt yard stood out in their otherwise orderly, middle-class neighborhood. Inside, life was defined by his father, a refinery worker with a fearsome temper, whom Skalnik once watched beat a man unconscious. Emile expected nothing less than greatness out of his only child, and he did not hold back when he felt that Skalnik fell short. At one high school baseball game, Emile showed up drunk and berated him in front of his teammates for his lackluster performance. Some nights, long after the neighbors' houses went dark, Emile would order him into the yard, where the teenager would swing a bat again and again beneath the porch light, his father barking commands from the shadows.

At Clear Creek High School, Skalnik threw himself into the performance of success. He lettered in baseball, served on the student council, played clarinet in the marching band, sang in the choir, landed a bit role in *Bye Bye Birdie,* and joined the Future Business Leaders of America, of which he was later elected chapter president. Outside school, he was a Boy Scout, an acolyte at St. Christopher Episcopal, and a campaign volunteer for President Lyndon Johnson. Hungry to be seen as exceptional, he started taking flying lessons when he was fifteen. Years later, his father would write to a Florida judge, insisting that his son had enjoyed "a good home life, good education, and worked hard at many activities." Emile attached thirty-eight pages of documentation: certificates, recommendation letters, awards—proof, on paper at least, that his son had always shown promise.

But Skalnik never lived up to his father's expectations; as he got older, he failed at everything he tried. He trained for, but never earned, his pilot's license. He lasted one month in Marine Corps Officer Candidates School. He flunked out of the University of Texas after three semesters. And though he made it through the Austin Police Academy, his time in law enforcement was a brief and resounding failure. When he was a rookie, he and other officers were involved in a high-speed chase that ended with him striking a Mexican American man in the head with the butt of his gun, causing serious injuries. The incident triggered a federal civil rights investigation, but—as would become a pattern—Skalnik wasn't punished. Federal prosecutors accepted the officers' version of the encounter and declined to press charges.

A shape-shifter, he made himself into what others wanted. Years under a brutal, demanding father had attuned him to people's weaknesses and desires; his ruthless opportunism, unbound by principle or empathy, allowed him to manipulate people and situations so deftly that he rarely had to pay the price others would. This proved to be Skalnik's gift: a preternatural ability to avoid consequences. When he was caught writing a string of bad checks while employed by the police department, nothing happened to him; in exchange for tendering his resignation, he was never indicted. All told, his career in law enforcement lasted just thirteen months.

After a failed stint as a life insurance agent, he surfaced in Florida, posing as a salesman for a Scandinavian furniture company: a scam that allowed him to pocket high-dollar preorders for goods that did not exist. When he was arrested in 1976, police found evidence in his car suggesting he was running yet another scheme; he had a stash of checks, IDs, and stationery bearing the seal of the Texas State House of Representatives, where he had briefly worked as an administrative aide. But Skalnik—who had no prior criminal record—walked away with probation. The next time he was arrested, in Houston in 1978, he knew just how to exploit the system: He started snitching.

Skalnik spent most of the next eleven years either behind bars or evading the law. He returned to his hometown in late 1989, just in time for Christmas. "Paul blew out of League City in the late '60s, and when he came back, he was a high roller—or so he told everybody," remembered one of his high school classmates. The source of his newfound wealth would later fuel speculation: He operated a Ponzi scheme, went one story. He defrauded his own parents, selling their house out from under them, went another. Whatever the truth, Skalnik dressed like a man of means, favoring crisp polo shirts, slacks, a Rolex, and tasseled loafers. Ready to stake his claim for respectability, he leased a Cadillac and an office in nearby Friendswood.

In 1991, Misty Anderson was living with her mother and two younger sisters in Friendswood—a place that had grown dramatically since Skalnik's first stint there in the late 1970s, living with Lisa and Penny and posing as an airline executive. It was no longer a small town, but a burgeoning Houston suburb. Misty's mother, Brenda, had been one of the most beautiful and sought-after girls at Clear Creek High School when Skalnik was a student there, and now, pretending to be a successful real estate developer, he pursued her. He lavished Brenda with gifts: big bouquets of roses, jewelry, even a used Jaguar. After a brief courtship, she wed him—having no idea he was already married. (The previous year, he'd had a short-lived marriage to another woman but never filed for divorce.) Unknowingly, Brenda became his eighth wife.

Misty often second-guessed herself, her self-doubt magnified by the insecurity of adolescence, but at fifteen she was certain of one thing: She didn't like Skalnik. Holding out hope that her divorced parents might reconcile, she saw him as an unwelcome intruder in their family—and a calculating and unctuous one at that. When he gave her and her sisters gold bracelets early in his courtship of their mother, it struck her as a transparent attempt to buy their affection. Failing to win her over, he shifted tactics once he and Brenda were married. He would casually tell Brenda how difficult teenagers could be, how they often acted out when their mothers found happiness. Gradually, his observations became more pointed: Misty was trying to sabotage Brenda's chance at love.

It wasn't long before Skalnik accused Misty of stealing the engagement ring he had given her mother—a ring he claimed held a 7-carat diamond. Misty suspected it was really just a cubic zirconia and that he had pocketed the ring to make her look like a thief.

As punishment, Skalnik grounded her, insisting that she could be reformed only through a punishing regimen that he ordered her to carry out over her summer vacation, when temperatures soared into the nineties. "Every day I had to dig holes in the ground along our fence line, under the hot sun, with no water," Misty later remembered. "I was not allowed to shower, not allowed to brush my teeth. I was only allowed to eat once a day. I would get so faint that I would see stars." When Skalnik permitted her to come inside, she had to stay in her room, forbidden to call friends and cut off from the outside world. Only after a month of isolation, when she was at her most desperate and vulnerable, did Skalnik offer her a way out. "He came in my bedroom and said, 'I have an idea that's going to make things better between us,'" she said.

MISTY ANDERSON AT HER HIGH SCHOOL'S HOMECOMING DANCE IN 1992, IN FRIENDSWOOD, TEXAS

At first, Misty did not speak a

word about the sexual abuse that followed. "I didn't think anyone would believe me," she said. But later that summer, Misty summoned the courage to confide in a family friend, who urged her to tell her mother. When she did, Skalnik's spell over Brenda was, in an instant, broken. Brenda called the police, and Skalnik was arrested and charged with sexual assault of a child.

Neither Brenda nor Misty had any way of knowing that Skalnik had been charged with an almost identical crime less than a decade earlier in Florida. Nor did Texas prosecutors. At the time of Skalnik's arrest, he was seen, in the eyes of the law, as a first-time sex offender.

"With a prior conviction for sexual assault of a child, he would have been looking at twenty-five years to life," said Margaret Hindman, the assistant district attorney in Galveston County who prosecuted him. Instead, he faced two to twenty years. Still, Hindman pursued him with a vigor that Pinellas County prosecutors had not. She was astonished when she learned about Skalnik's long run as a state witness. "This guy clearly was grandiose, delusional, and had narcissistic-personality disorder," she said. "He boasted that he was with the FBI, that he was with the CIA, and none of it checked out. It's hard to believe prosecutors relied on him."

Skalnik professed his innocence but ended up pleading no contest in exchange for a ten-year prison sentence. Misty had hoped for harsher punishment, but the deal, at least, spared her from having to endure a trial.

Years later, when she found out what had happened to Karen Parker, she was floored and bedeviled by questions. Why would prosecutors not have fought to protect a girl just like her—a girl who was not yet even a teenager? Perhaps most painful of all, she had to consider: Would Skalnik have had the opportunity to abuse her had Florida prosecutors held him to account the first time?

16

AN UNREAL DREAM

My attorney situation is the pits," Jim wrote to Marieke on March 19, 1998. More than a decade had passed since his arrival on death row, and he was still fighting the conviction that delivered him there. On the long and often tortuous journey that capital appeals take through the courts, he had reached the next, and most critical, phase: state post-conviction proceedings. During his direct appeal, the courts had been limited to reviewing only what was already in the trial record, but in state post-conviction proceedings his attorneys could widen the aperture and introduce new evidence the courts had not previously heard.

To determine what new evidence there might be in a capital case typically requires conducting a wholesale reinvestigation. Yet Jim, like most death-row prisoners, did not have the money to hire a lawyer. He had to rely on a state agency, the Capital Collateral Regional Counsel, that represents indigent prisoners facing death sentences. His case was one of scores that demanded the attention of the CCRC, where attorneys had few resources and crushing caseloads.

The agency was a frequent target for Florida politicians who were eager to prove they were tough on crime. The previous year, Governor Lawton Chiles had appointed John Moser, a career prosecutor who had never handled a death-penalty appeal, to head the

Tampa office, which was in charge of Jim's case. Moser promised to make the office ruthlessly efficient. Lawyers were to curtail the practice of subpoenaing all of a case's public records, even though those records could contain evidence that was key to a defendant's appeal. Investigators were to conduct interviews by phone, rather than in person, even though a good number of the witnesses they needed to speak with were reluctant to talk, did not have a fixed address, or needed the reassurance of a face-to-face introduction. Many attorneys at the Tampa office worried that the rules weakened their ability to effectively represent their clients.

"[Moser] has fired or run off all the experienced attorneys and investigators," Jim wrote. "Last week he fired my investigator and she was my best hope of getting my conviction overturned. She believed in my innocence and was working very hard to prove it. Now I'm having to start all over with two green-behind-the-ears attorneys and an investigator with less than a year's experience."

It was true that Jim's attorneys weren't seasoned post-conviction lawyers. Harry Brody was a gruff civil litigator who was new to capital appeals, and Jeff Hazen, seventeen years Brody's junior, had just passed the bar. But Jim would soon realize that having them on his case was a lucky break.

The two attorneys were a perfectly mismatched pair: Brody, intense and cynical, favored denim shirts he rolled up to the elbows, while Hazen, disarmingly sincere, stuck to button-downs and a tie. Brody was a published poet who had gone to law school to support his family; he used such extravagant and lofty language in his legal writing that it earned him Hazen's occasional ribbing. ("That's beautiful, Harry, but it's not getting anybody off of death row.") Hazen, who had served in the Army before becoming the first person in his family to go to college, made up for feeling like an outsider in the status-conscious world of lawyers by overpreparing, and what he lacked in real-world experience, he made up for with his unflagging work ethic. Both lawyers, upon reviewing the record, were appalled by the anemic legal defense Jim had received during his trial. They were also struck by the incongruity between the genial man they met in Starke and the crime of which he stood convicted. Privately, Hazen took to calling him "Gentleman Jim."

Determined to give their client the zealous advocacy he had never received, they threw themselves into the case. Jim, too, put in long hours rereading his trial transcripts and drafting handwritten memos that outlined new avenues of inquiry. "The state is so stingy with money on the defense side," he wrote to Marieke. "Of course, the state prosecutors have almost unlimited funds and they can afford all the expert witnesses, lab analysis, and bought-and-paid-for snitches. There is absolutely nothing fair about this judicial system and there never will be as long as the funding is so lopsided."

Early in their investigation, Brody and Hazen reached out to Henry Andringa, Jim's original defense attorney, hoping to gain insights into the case. Andringa's life had taken several remarkable turns since the trial: He had become a circuit court judge, and he had married Beverly Andrews, one of Jim's prosecutors. Andrews would later testify that their relationship did not begin until seven months after Jim's sentencing—a timeline that effectively ruled out any claim Jim could make that their relationship created a conflict of interest or deprived him of a fair trial. But Andringa, an elected judge married to the case's prosecutor, remained guarded around the two CCRC lawyers.

With limited cooperation from Jim's original counsel, Brody and Hazen turned to the work of other attorneys who had preceded them. They were floored to learn that, five years before, Jack Pearcy had made a series of bombshell admissions to one of Jim's appellate lawyers. Under oath, before a court reporter, Jack confirmed that Jim had not left the house with him when he and Shelly drove away in the early morning of May 6, 1985. As Dwain Shaw had told

Halliday years earlier, it had been Dwain, not Jim, who went with them. Jack said he dropped Dwain off at a pay phone and then left with Shelly.

This placed Jack alone with Shelly around the time of her death, making him the last known person to see her alive. He refused to say what happened to Shelly after that point, only that he returned home, by himself, roughly ninety minutes later.

Back at the house, he said, he roused Jim. "I went in, got Jim up," Jack said. "I told him, 'Come on, let's go smoke a couple joints, drink a beer or something.'" He and Jim then drove to a nearby causeway, he said, and began tossing a Frisbee around. "He ended up going out in the water," Jack said, "while we was playing Frisbee. We drank beer, we smoked a couple of joints." His account corroborated Jim's explanation for why his jeans were wet when the two men returned home—the explanation Jim's lead trial attorney, Henry Andringa, warned him sounded too far-fetched to repeat to a jury.

Jack went on to say that he had told law enforcement, falsely, that Jim left the house with him and Shelly because he had hoped to avoid punishment. "It was just a self-serving statement to exonerate myself," Jack said. "At that time, Jim wasn't even in custody. I was in custody, and they were going to charge me, and I was just trying to get around it, that's all. Lay the blame somewhere else." Jack, who would become eligible for parole as soon as 2010, had little to gain by coming forward with a story in which he placed himself alone with the murder victim around the time of her death. Brody and Hazen thought it had the ring of truth to it; his account matched Dwain's account to investigators.

Because Jack made these admissions during Jim's direct appeal, which narrowly focuses on the trial record, they were of no help to Jim's previous lawyers. But for Brody and Hazen, they were a godsend—precisely the kind of new evidence that a motion for post-conviction relief is designed to bring to light. They would be a godsend, that is, if the lawyers could get Jack to appear in court and confirm what he had said in 1993.

When Brody and Hazen contacted Jack, he was incarcerated at Century Correctional Institution, in the westernmost reaches of Florida, along the Alabama state line. He had spent the years since his trial racking up disciplinary violations, beginning with a failed escape attempt from the Pinellas County Jail in 1987, in which he tried to tunnel out of his cell using razor blades and a salvaged piece of metal. The following year, he was found concealing a handcuff key inside the lining of his sneaker. In state prison, he was repeatedly placed in solitary confinement for using and possessing drugs.

Jack agreed to have an initial phone conversation with the lawyers, but when they got on the phone, it quickly became clear that he had experienced a change of heart since he had given his sworn statement. In his low, flat voice, he explained that he had decided to proceed with his appeals, and that he did not want to say anything that might jeopardize his chances of winning a new trial. Hazen felt heartsick as he listened. "Jim wasn't involved," he remembered Jack saying. "I'll testify to that when my case is over. But I can't help you right now."

Brody and Hazen were just starting to make headway on their investigation when they had to turn to a more urgent matter. Florida's new governor, Jeb Bush, who had initially taken a more restrained approach to capital punishment than some of his predecessors, signed two death warrants on June 9, 1999. Both of the condemned men, Allen Lee Davis and Thomas Provenzano, were clients of the CCRC's Tampa office, and it would fall to Brody and Hazen to seek, against long odds, reprieves for them before their execution dates arrived just a month later.

One of their central arguments was that Old Sparky's antiquated electrical parts were at risk of malfunctioning, and that such a failure could cause prolonged suffering. Questions about the chair's integrity dated back nearly a decade, to the May 4, 1990, execution of a man named Jesse Tafero, whose head had caught on fire at the first jolt of electricity. "For four eternal minutes, Tafero continued to breathe and slowly nod his head as his executioners repeatedly turned the current on and off," the *Miami Herald*'s Ellen McGarrahan wrote hours after witnessing the execution. "Each time they turned the switch back on, flames shot out and smoke rose from under the black mask covering the condemned man's face."

By the time Governor Bush signed death warrants for Davis and Provenzano, only three other states used the electric chair as their sole method of execution. Davis, who weighed 344 pounds and was in poor health, was the first scheduled to die. On the morning of July 8, 1999, officers rolled him into the execution chamber in a wheelchair, lifted him into Old Sparky, and secured thick leather straps over his torso, limbs, and mouth. The executioner, whose identity was concealed beneath a black hood, turned on the current at 7:05 a.m., and the low hum of electricity filled the room. Davis stiffened, his hands balling into fists. Then blood trickled from his mask. It ran over his mouth strap and spilled onto his white shirt, a bright red stain blossoming across his chest. After the last burst of electricity, his chest heaved, rising and falling nearly a dozen times before he was declared dead.

Brody and Hazen, who had sat vigil with Davis until midnight before retiring to a Starke motel with a bottle of bourbon, were spared the sight of watching their client die; their office's director had gone in their place. But that day, the ghastly nature of the execution spurred the Florida Supreme Court to set a hearing to examine whether the electric chair violated the Eighth Amendment's ban on cruel and unusual punishment, and the lawyers rushed to document Davis's suffering. They won the right to conduct an independent autopsy, which Hazen attended, and obtained graphic color photographs taken by state inspectors moments after the execution, showing Davis's bloodied, purpled face, grotesquely contorted by the mouth strap, his eyes clenched shut in apparent agony.

Though the court narrowly upheld the legality of the electric chair that September, one justice—Leander J. Shaw Jr.—issued a stinging dissent, to which he appended three of the photos Brody and Hazen had obtained. In doing so, the judge made the images available to the public. The disclosure, which coincided with the new ability, via the internet, to rapidly disseminate information around the world, turned the gruesome execution into an international news story, and brought intense scrutiny to how the state carried out executions. The U.S. Supreme Court agreed that fall to hear the appeal of a Florida death-row inmate who challenged the constitutionality of the electric chair. It was a signal that the court—which had last considered the issue in 1890, when it upheld the practice as a humane alternative to hanging—was troubled by what happened in Starke.

Rather than risk the humiliation of losing in the nation's highest court, Governor Bush would summon the state legislature into special session and advance a bill that made lethal injection the primary method of execution. Lawmakers passed the bill into law, and in Starke prison officials replaced Old Sparky with a gurney. The chair itself, however, was never removed from Florida State Prison. It remains there, maintained for any condemned inmate who opts to die by electrocution.

When Brody and Hazen turned their attention back to Jim's case, they zeroed in on Skalnik—in particular, the sworn statement he had filed a year after the trial, in which he accused the state attorney's office of misconduct. Although Skalnik did not identify Jim or any defendants by name, he had admitted to perjury in numerous cases, saying he manufactured stories about other men's confessions and falsely testified that he received no leniency in return. But Skalnik's admissions were worthless unless he was willing to repeat them in open court, under oath, and submit to cross-examination. The odds of him doing so seemed slim; he had disavowed his claims when the state attorney's office agreed to reduce his sentence. Until he testified otherwise, his original trial testimony would stand. It didn't matter how questionable Skalnik's story now seemed; in the eyes of the courts, testimony given under oath and challenged through cross-examination is presumed to have been properly scrutinized, so it carries more weight—whether or not the process actually reveals the truth.

One of the CCRC's investigators tracked Skalnik down to a minimum-security penitentiary in a remote stretch of the Texas Panhandle, where he was nearing the end of his ten-year sentence for sexual assault. Skalnik was noncommittal when Brody and Hazen first reached him by phone. He would have to review the trial transcripts to refresh his memory of Jim's case, he said—a remark that was either a dodge or a window into how cavalier he was about the role he had played in determining Jim's fate.

The attorneys sent him a transcript of his testimony, then reached out to him again. This time, he sounded more amenable, going so far as to say that he wanted to apologize for what he had done in Jim's case. He stopped there, explaining that he could not speak candidly on the phone but promising to say more if the lawyers came to see him. Hazen followed up with a letter, telling Skalnik that he would make the trip to Texas, but that he only wanted the truth, whether it proved to be helpful to his client or not.

On September 29, 1999, Hazen flew to Amarillo, in the Texas Panhandle. His meeting with Skalnik was not until the following day, but he was determined not to flub what he knew could be a decisive interview, and he immediately made the hundred-mile drive to the prison to scope out where he'd need to be the next morning. Industrial feedlots and faded railroad towns dotted the treeless landscape, which stretched in all directions. It was a sunny, placid afternoon, and as he drove beneath the enormous West Texas sky and considered his upcoming conversation with Skalnik, he felt a spark of hope. Before he settled in at his hotel room that night to review Skalnik's previous statements, he wandered into a boot shop and, on a whim, bought a pair of cowboy boots.

The next day, Hazen took a seat across from Skalnik, in a room reserved for attorney-client meetings. Skalnik had just turned fifty, and his seven years in prison had not been kind to him. His thinning hair was turning gray, and his complexion was sallow; his now colossal belly gave him a round, swollen appearance. Yet he seemed unbowed, his jaunty confidence still intact as he sized up the young lawyer. Skalnik began by airing his grievances with the state attorney's office but stopped short of offering anything new about his testimony. When Hazen pointedly asked him whether prosecutors had made him any promises before he testified against Jim, Skalnik denied that there had been a deal. He spent most of their time together skating around Hazen's questions, offering nothing of substance. But if he sensed that he was losing Hazen, he tried to reel the lawyer back in. "I can help you," Skalnik said obliquely, "but the timing has to be right."

For nearly four hours, Hazen tried to elicit something new, but Skalnik talked in circles, and it soon became clear that Skalnik had never intended to tell him anything; luring him out to the farthest reaches of West Texas had only been for sport. Hazen had to shake his head at the irony: The death-row prisoners he represented, many of whom had committed horrendous acts of violence, were people in whom he could almost always find some small measure of humanity. He did not, however, see any redeeming qualities in Skalnik. As he made the long drive back to Amarillo, Hazen felt pained that he had wasted two precious days on what had turned out to be a fool's errand. All he had to show for his time was a stiff new pair of cowboy boots.

Before the advent of DNA analysis, wrongful convictions were believed to be exceedingly rare; the notion that someone could be found guilty of a crime he did not commit, and that the appeals process would not correct the error, was roundly dismissed as fantasy. "The accused has every advantage," the federal judge Learned Hand, one of the most revered jurists of his time, wrote in 1923. "Our dangers do not lie in too little tenderness to the accused. Our procedure has always been haunted by the ghost of the innocent man convicted. It is an unreal dream. What we need to fear is the archaic formalism and watery sentiment that obstructs, delays, and defeats the prosecution of crime."

Hand's pronouncement summed up the outlook of many judges who followed him: The American criminal justice system is virtually infallible. When a capital case came before the U.S. Supreme Court in 1993 in which a Texas man who faced execution argued that he should be given a chance to present new evidence that he said would exonerate him, but which had come to light late in his appeals, Justice Sandra Day O'Connor joined the majority in rejecting his argument. "Our society has a high degree of confidence in its criminal trials, in no small part because the Constitution offers unparalleled protections against convicting the innocent," she wrote in a concurring opinion in the case, *Herrera v. Collins*. In a separate concurring opinion, Justice Antonin Scalia echoed the idea that the defendant had received due process, and that federal courts are not obligated to consider a state prisoner's claim of innocence so late in his appeals, even if the evidence of his innocence did not arise until then. "With any luck," Scalia wrote, "we shall avoid ever having to face this embarrassing question again."

That same year, DNA analysis cleared a Maryland man named Kirk Bloodsworth of the rape and murder of a nine-year-old girl—the first time the technology exonerated someone of a crime for which he had been sentenced to death. The odds of securing a DNA exoneration are vanishingly small; the vast majority of criminal cases do not have biological material that can be tested, and even if such evidence exists—and even if it was properly collected and preserved—defendants still must persuade a court to allow the testing to go forward, often over prosecutors' objections. Yet between 1994 and 1999, DNA testing exonerated eight men who had faced death sentences. They joined a growing number of condemned prisoners whose convictions were overturned without the benefit of DNA evidence, suggesting that capital convictions, even with their extra layers of scrutiny, were fraught with error.

Jim was painfully aware that the greatest scientific breakthrough in modern forensics did him no good. "I have one of the hardest kind of cases to overturn," he wrote to Marieke. "There is no DNA." Without the benefit of DNA, or a recantation from Jack Pearcy, or an admission from Skalnik that he lied on the stand, Jim's lawyers needed to find other ways to dismantle the state's case. As they continued to pore over the record, trying to find the best avenues to pursue, they kept returning to the testimony of the jailhouse witnesses.

Brody and Hazen wondered if the two men who claimed to have heard Jim confess in the jail's law library, Pablo DeJesus and James Leitner, still stood by their testimony. And what would they say, so many years after the fact, about whether the state attorney's office promised them a deal before they took the stand? Like Skalnik, both men had been amply rewarded after the trial. DeJesus received seven years, and Leitner five years, for drug-trafficking charges that normally carried much lengthier penalties. Their sentences were also allowed to run concurrently with prison terms the men already had to serve in Maryland and Colorado, respectively.

In the end, they had served the same amount of time as if prosecutors had dropped the Florida charges altogether.

DeJesus, who lived south of Tampa in Bradenton, refused to talk to Brody and Hazen, so the lawyers turned their attention to Leitner instead. Leitner had also returned to the Tampa area after his release from prison; he worked at an RV dealership in nearby Plant City, where the two lawyers stopped by one afternoon. Business was slow that day, and Leitner—who, at forty-six, had settled into a quiet life—agreed to sit and talk. According to the attorneys, Leitner made a stunning admission: He conceded that he never heard Jim confess to the murder, and that he only testified for the prosecution because he hoped to win a reduced sentence. He seemed remorseful, but also uneasy, and he expressed his reluctance to say or do more. Brody and Hazen hoped to be able to persuade him to come forward and recant his testimony in court, on the record. But first they had to convince a judge that Jim's conviction deserved a second look.

17

SIX BY NINE FEET

While Jim's attorneys asked the court for more time to interview witnesses and prepare the evidence they hoped would win him a new trial, a victims' advocate with the Florida Attorney General's Office contacted Shelly Boggio's family to ready them for what was to come. Fourteen years—the span of Shelly's entire life—had passed since her murder. In that time, her family had endured two trials and a lengthy appeals process, and each court date, with its accompanying delays and postponements, had forced them to revisit their pain. By the time the attorney general's office reached out in the summer of 1999, they were exhausted.

Late that summer, Shelly's older sister, Sherry, wrote to Governor Jeb Bush, pleading for intercession. She told him what she believed to be true: that two men, James Dailey and Jack Pearcy, had raped her little sister, stabbed her fifty times, and drowned her. "Shelly was only a baby, sir, and there's not a day that goes by that I don't still miss her."

There was no doubt in Sherry's mind that Jim had confessed to participating in the murder. She had heard Skalnik's testimony, and the words that he swore Jim spoke: *She is screaming, staring at me, and would not die.* She had listened as two more jailhouse witnesses testified that Jim admitted to the killing. She had watched as prosecutors made their case that Jim stabbed Shelly, and as twelve

SHELLY BOGGIO'S OLDER SISTER, SHERRY (RIGHT), AT JIM DAILEY'S RESENTENCING HEARING ON DECEMBER 10, 1993

jurors unanimously voted to convict him, and as a judge handed down his death sentence. The question for the Boggios, by 1999, was not whether Jim killed Shelly but why, so many years after he was sent to death row, he was still alive. As her older sister saw it, Jim wanted to prolong their family's anguish.

Her father, she explained to the governor, had passed away six years earlier. While he was dying of cancer, he'd worried about whether "this monster"—Jim—would ever receive the punishment he deserved. She'd promised her father that she would see to it that Jim paid with his life. "But all of these years later, there isn't even a death warrant," she wrote.

The reply she received, from a Florida Department of Corrections employee to whom the governor's office had forwarded her email, matter-of-factly explained that the governor could not set an execution date until Jim had exhausted his appeals. Except for a perfunctory nod to the family's suffering ("Please accept my deepest condolences"), the email's author struck a bland and bureaucratic tone. "Each person is entitled to appellate review that is thorough, fair, and affords the individual his right to due process," it read. "To deny this right to anyone, no matter what they have done, would be a threat to us all. Before the governor signs a death warrant, he must assure—to the people of Florida, and to himself—that all the above objectives have been met."

To Sherry, the governor's duty to uphold the abstract ideals of American jurisprudence did not bear any relevance to her family's pain. "You are telling me that he has to worry about this murderer's rights," she wrote back. "What about Shelly's rights? What about our rights?!!!" She expressed her disgust that no one at the governor's office appeared to have bothered to look up her sister's case. "Shelly lost her right to live in 1985," she wrote. "These men took that right from her. What rights should they still have?!!!!!! Fourteen years later they still have rights? I don't think so!!!!!!"

The motion for post-conviction relief that Brody and Hazen filed in state court on November 12, 1999, was the culmination of more than a year of work, and despite its sober and lawyerly language, it was a searing rebuke of the prosecution's case. The attorneys argued that the state never had any solid evidence that Jim committed the murder, and that it instead rested on the dubious testimony of three jailhouse witnesses, the self-serving statements of a co-defendant who sought to avoid the electric chair, and the false testimony of the co-defendant's girlfriend, whose claims could be disproven with evidence—namely, phone records—that had been sitting in the case file the whole time.

It was while poring through bankers' boxes at the CCRC marked "Dailey" that Hazen had stumbled across a Southwestern Bell telephone bill for Dwain Shaw's girlfriend, showing that she had received a collect call in Kansas in the early morning hours of May 6, 1985. The call had originated at a pay phone in St. Petersburg, Florida, at 1:15 a.m. This was hard, temporal evidence that corroborated Dwain's account: that he, not Jim, had left the house with Jack and Shelly, and caught a ride with them to a nearby pay phone, where they had dropped him off, before driving away to be on their own. Though prosecutors had cast doubt on his memory at trial, the phone bill backed up Dwain's timeline of the night, calling both the state's theory of the case and Gayle Bailey's testimony into serious doubt. The prosecution's narrative had never made sense to Hazen. Why would Jack, who had spent the whole evening trying to get Shelly alone, want Jim to come along?

Brody and Hazen pointed to the phone records as proof that Jim had received an inadequate defense. Though the Southwestern Bell bill sat among other papers in the file, Jim's lead attorney, Henry Andringa, had not used it. Brody and Hazen's motion also highlighted the defense's failure to do rudimentary investigative work, like trying to track down witnesses who, on the night of the murder, had visited Hank's Seabreeze Lounge, where Shelly was seen with Jack. And Brody and Hazen laid out what was lost when the defense did not call to the stand other men who were held in jail at the same time as Jim. These witnesses could have told the jury that Detective Halliday pressed them for information about Jim before Skalnik stepped forward, and that Skalnik's reputation as a snitch made it all but impossible that Jim had confided in him. "Without Skalnik's testimony the state would not have had sufficient evidence to convict Mr. Dailey," they wrote.

Brody and Hazen pointed to other evidence that Jim did not receive a fair trial. They leveled charges of misconduct at the prosecution for presenting snitch testimony that it "knew was incredible." The lawyers also provided the sworn statement Jack gave in 1993 in which he conceded that he had made up Jim's role in the killing. And they cited Leitner's about-face. "Leitner now admits that his testimony regarding Mr. Dailey's 'confession' was fabricated and false," they wrote. The totality of the evidence, they concluded, amounted to more than just reasonable doubt. "Mr. Dailey is innocent of the crime for which he was convicted and sentenced to death," they wrote.

Nearly a year passed before Judge Thomas Penick, who still presided over the case, handed down a decision. On September 22, 2000, he agreed that Jim's conviction deserved a second look, ruling that an evidentiary hearing should be held to determine whether he was entitled to a new trial. It was the best possible outcome, in an area of the law where victories are few and far between. "On a scale of one to ten, it's about a fifteen," Jim wrote in an exuberant letter to Marieke. "Judges just never, ever grant a hearing on all the important issues. It almost seems as if this judge is having second thoughts about my conviction." But his joy was short-lived. When Governor Bush appointed a new director to the CCRC's Tampa office, a career prosecutor named Bill Jennings, he promptly fired half its staff, including Brody and Hazen.

Bush's decision to install Jennings at the Tampa office left the impression that he did not want the CCRC's lawyers defending its clients too zealously. Where capital defenders like Brody and Hazen saw a swamped system straining to meet their clients' basic legal needs, the governor saw defendants who had already been convicted of heinous crimes needlessly dragging out appeals that demanded resolution. He vowed to speed up capital appeals, calling for legislation to sharply limit the ability of death-row prisoners to challenge their convictions and sentences. His top policy adviser on capital punishment, Bradford Thomas, told a reporter that the goal was to emulate a death-penalty state that was carrying out executions at the breakneck pace of nearly one per week. "What I hope is that we become like Texas," Thomas said. "Put them on a gurney and let's rock and roll."

Jim's case was reassigned to Eric Pinkard, one of the attorneys whom Jennings had decided to keep on. Pinkard had been practicing law for fifteen years, working as both a prosecutor and a private defense attorney before joining the agency. But early on, Jim began to feel uneasy. He was used to the ferocious attention that Brody and Hazen gave his case. He rarely heard from Pinkard.

"I'm very tired of trying to climb what seems like insurmountable mountains of legal roadblocks," Jim wrote in the fall of 2001 to Marieke, who had recently married her longtime boyfriend and taken his last name, Laauwen. He lamented that he seemed to be running in place; fourteen years after his conviction, the only thing that had changed was the reflection he saw in the mirror. "Kiddo, I'm getting old," he wrote. To drive home his point, he enclosed a photo of himself in which he wore his usual wide grin, his smile brightening his otherwise worn, lined face. His hair was almost entirely gray, and he looked at the camera from behind thick-framed, prison-issued glasses. Around his neck hung a gift from Mary Kay and Dick: a silver medallion of Saint Jude, the patron saint of lost causes.

Both Mary Kay and Dick had been faithful visitors as long as Jim had been in prison. During Jim's first few years on death row, the Florida Department of Corrections required married women visiting male inmates to be accompanied by their husbands; only female blood relatives were allowed to visit on their own. So Mary Kay and Dick always made the trip together. Dick would have come even had he not been needed to serve the peculiar role of chaperone; he and Jim had been friends since their early twenties, when they were stationed together in Tucson, and their unusual shared history—with Dick having adopted Jim's children, and both men having married Mary Kay at different points in their lives—had drawn them closer.

The drive to Starke was two and a half hours from their home in Tampa, and Mary Kay knew each shift in the landscape by heart. Her chest tightened every time the pine forest finally gave way, and the hulking white monolith of Florida State Prison came into view. If she was supposed to put it out of her mind that this was the same place where the state planned to one day carry out Jim's execution, she could not. She often felt short of breath as she and Dick waited in line and submitted to the pat downs that were required to gain entry, and once inside she felt as if she had stepped through the looking glass. One day while standing in line at the commissary, she saw the infamous serial killer Ted Bundy. He stood so close to her that she could have tapped him on the shoulder, just another prisoner ordering butter pecan ice cream.

When she visited Jim, they sat in a bare cinder-block room at steel picnic tables bolted to the ground. Only death-row prisoners who had clean disciplinary records were afforded these face-to-face meetings, which allowed them to spend a few hours out of their cells. Jim was always jubilant when he caught sight of Mary Kay and Dick, and her first glimpse of his broad smile would flood her with relief. She was grateful that they could disrupt his loneliness, but seeing his joy only sharpened the awfulness of his situation. She updated him on their grandchildren, and Dick held forth about his beloved University of Florida Gators; Jim told them of the absurdities of prison life. In the strangest of places, the three of them made easy conversation, a family unto themselves.

Mary Kay and Dick's visits stopped in the mid-1990s, when Dick's health began to deteriorate. He was diagnosed with progressive rheumatoid arthritis, a painful and debilitating disease in which the immune system turns on the body and attacks itself, eroding joints and damaging organs. Dick had a particularly aggressive case. He underwent years of medical interventions—skin grafts, an emergency colostomy, heart surgery—but he continued to decline. "Mary Kay wrote that Dick isn't doing well and is in constant pain," Jim wrote to Marieke in the summer of 2000.

"To see him suffering this way cuts me to the quick." By the following summer, Dick was in a wheelchair and relied on an oxygen machine to breathe. To come see his friend took everything he had, but Dick made the trip three times.

Then, in the fall of 2001, Dick died at the age of fifty-eight. "I sat here in my cell with tears streaming down my cheeks and having to hold back huge sobs," Jim wrote to Marieke afterward. "I've never felt so alone in my whole life. Dick was my very good and solid friend for over 35 years and I loved him." The grief he felt only deepened, he explained, knowing that he could not be there for Mary Kay to lean on. "I feel so damn bad for Mary Kay and I wish I could take her pain away," he told Marieke. He did the only thing he could think to do: He wrote to Mary Kay. He wrote to her again and again, from the confines of his six-by-nine-foot cell, to reassure her life was worth living.

18

SMALL FICTIONS

On March 1, 2002, Skalnik walked out of prison, having served his decade-long sentence for the sexual assault of Misty Anderson. He had nothing more to his name than $50 and a one-way Greyhound ticket, courtesy of the Texas Department of Criminal Justice.

Misty had fought to make sure that he served every day of those ten years. She was a junior at a private Baptist university southwest of Fort Worth when she was first notified, in 1996, that Skalnik was eligible for parole. By then, he had served nearly half his sentence. Distraught, Misty wrote to the parole board, urging it to deny him early release. She explained that she still suffered from intrusive thoughts and flashbacks of Skalnik's abuse, and was sometimes jolted awake by a recurring nightmare in which he showed up on her doorstep. At twenty-one, she did not yet feel safe enough around men to go on a date. She implored the parole board to get Skalnik a psychiatric assessment and counseling, cautioning that he would pose a danger to society until his mental health problems were meaningfully addressed. Prisoner "00647713 has avoided these evaluations in the past," she wrote, referring to Skalnik by his inmate number, "and I believe it is because he knows he is a sick man."

The board declined to grant Skalnik parole. Each year that

his case came up for review, Misty appealed to board members. "Would you be willing to invite Paul Skalnik into your community to live near your family?" she wrote in 1998. They denied him parole again.

Angling for a way out, Skalnik filed a lawsuit against the Texas Department of Criminal Justice in which he portrayed himself as a persecuted whistleblower whom corrections officials had dispatched to a remote Panhandle prison in retaliation for speaking out about prisoners' civil rights. Despite Misty's entreaties that he receive a proper psychiatric evaluation and mental health treatment, there is no evidence that he did, and as his time in prison wore on, his grandiosity was matched only by his baroque imagination. He claimed to be at work on a tell-all book, for which he had secured a New York publisher and a sizable advance, that would expose the corruption and rot inside the Texas prison system. "I wish I could have received the advance that Hillary Clinton was afforded," he wrote to one of his ex-wives about the interest he said his book proposal was generating in Manhattan, "but it's substantially more than the initial offer!"

Rather than register as a sex offender upon his release in 2002, as he was required to do by law, Skalnik simply disappeared. Then, later that spring, the fifty-two-year-old surfaced just outside Boston, in the guise of an attorney named Avery Harrison. Living at an extended-stay hotel that sat in the shadow of a highway interchange, he fleshed out his new persona, which he accessorized with business cards that listed a tony address in Boston's financial district and an imaginary law partner he christened Lloyd Wright. His clients, who initially overlooked his ill-fitting suits and frayed shirt collars, soon came to realize that he was not performing the legal work they had paid him thousands of dollars to do. Two of them went to police, and on May 18, 2003, a little more than a year after his release from prison, he was arrested and charged with larceny and the unauthorized practice of law.

Skalnik's arrest, which brought his short run as Avery Harrison to an end, was recorded in the Interstate Identification Index, an FBI database that is accessible to law enforcement agencies around the country. This seemed to be a rare stroke of good fortune for Jim. Skalnik was central to the claims that Jim's new CCRC attorney, Eric Pinkard, hoped to present at his evidentiary hearing, and the discovery of Skalnik's whereabouts ensured that Pinkard could subpoena him to testify.

When they had represented Jim, Brody and Hazen had envisioned spending up to two weeks calling witnesses, effectively retrying Jim's case. They understood that the evidentiary hearing was a singular opportunity, and they believed the defense should try every possible avenue.

Pinkard took a narrower approach. He sought to have Jim's conviction overturned by demonstrating four main points: that the fundamental facts of the prosecution's case rested on the perjured testimony of multiple witnesses; that the state had withheld evidence of a deal it struck with Skalnik; that Jim's defense attorneys had not provided him with effective representation, depriving him of a fair trial; and that newly discovered evidence pointed to Jim's innocence. But Pinkard had a high bar to clear: In this kind of evidentiary hearing, the burden of proof rests on the defense.

Calling Skalnik to the stand was risky. Skalnik would effectively be a hostile witness, and what he had demonstrated, time and time again, was that he would not hesitate to stonewall, dodge, and lie when he was under oath. To effectively expose his fraudulence and his coziness with the state attorney's office would require extensive research and preparation. Pinkard would have to carefully thread the needle, showing that Skalnik was both a fabulist whose testimony could not be trusted *and* someone who had fleetingly told the truth when he turned on prosecutors in 1988. The problems he posed as a witness might only be outweighed if Pinkard undertook a sweeping examination, methodically walking Skalnik through every criminal case in which he had testified for the prosecution and each plea deal the state had offered him.

Skalnik was in the witness box for less than an hour. As Pinkard led him through the kinds of routine questions he had fielded many times before, Skalnik refused to give the lawyer an inch. When Skalnik was asked about the basic details of his criminal record, he feigned amnesia. "I don't even remember today," he said. When Pinkard inquired whether he had testified for prosecutors in other cases, Skalnik squinted, considering the question for a moment. Finally, he said, "I think I have."

When Skalnik repeatedly denied ever vying for, or receiving, a deal—"I never discussed a deal with the state, ever, or with any police officer," he said—Pinkard tried another tack. He turned to Skalnik's 1988 claim that prosecutors had coached him on how to testify and then concealed from juries the rewards that prosecutors gave him in return. But when Pinkard asked him about the legal filing bearing his signature that laid out these allegations, Skalnik testified that he had never actually read it; his public defender, who he claimed harbored a grudge against the state attorney's office, had tricked him into signing it.

"You signed it, but did not read it?" Pinkard asked, skeptical.

"That's correct."

"It was notarized, but you did not read it?"

"That's correct."

"That motion declares specific allegations against the State Attorney's Office and specific state attorneys that knew your testimony in various cases in Pinellas County were lies," Pinkard said. "Isn't that what the motion says?"

"That my testimony was a lie?" Skalnik said, with some annoyance. "I never lied."

Pinkard, who found himself badly outmatched, did not challenge Skalnik forcefully enough to alter the narrative. As a result, Skalnik's insistence that he had always testified truthfully, and that prosecutors had never given him a deal in exchange for his cooperation, became part of the official court record. This record would become a reference point not only for Judge Jack Espinosa Jr., who was overseeing the hearing, but for all subsequent appellate courts that had to evaluate whether Jim received a fair trial.

When Pinkard called the case's lead prosecutor to the stand, he only compounded the problem. Beverly Andrews, who was sworn in by her married name, Beverly Andringa, told the court that she had found Skalnik credible. "I did not put on testimony that I didn't believe," she said. "I believed his testimony to be true and I put him on the stand. I never offered him any deals that weren't disclosed to the defense or in open court."

Jack Pearcy was similarly unhelpful. Pinkard introduced the sworn statement in which Jack admitted he had lied to investigators, falsely claiming Jim took part in the killing. But when Jack was called to the stand, he remained silent on the matter. Staring ahead, he never glanced at Jim, who sat a few paces away at the defense table. "I currently have an appeal pending right now," Jack muttered, before invoking his Fifth Amendment right to remain silent.

Pinkard did raise some of the key facts the jury never heard. He called Dwain Shaw to the stand to state that Jim was not in the car when Jack and Shelly dropped him off at the pay phone, and he offered the Southwestern Bell telephone bill as corroborating evidence. The woman Dwain phoned, Betty Mingus, also took the stand to corroborate his account. Pinkard then interrogated Jim's lead trial attorney, Henry Andringa, about tactical decisions he made during the trial, including not making use of the telephone bill. "Can you relay any strategic reason why you wouldn't have used that to impeach Gayle Bailey?" Pinkard asked.

"Not as I sit here today, no, sir," Andringa replied.

But Pinkard himself did not call to the stand any of the men who had been held in the jail at the same time as Jim—witnesses who could have spoken about Halliday coming to the jail to look for a snitch and Skalnik's reputation. Pinkard, too, failed to bring forth all the evidence at his disposal.

Jim, who had gradually warmed to Pinkard, trusted his attorney's assurances that a pared-down strategy was the best way forward. He did not protest when Pinkard told the judge that they were abandoning half of the legal claims Brody and Hazen had raised in their motion. "I just have to wait now for the judge to make his ruling," Jim wrote to Marieke on March 9, 2004. "That, my sweet friend, is going to be the longest wait of my life. It could take him a year or more to write his ruling. I just pray that he is smart and fair enough to see what the state did to me and that he has the courage to overturn my conviction. It's just a wait-and-see-what-happens thing now. I've done all I can do."

There were no surprises, however, when Judge Espinosa handed down his ruling in the summer of 2005, denying the defense's request for a new trial. He did as every judge before him had done: He took Paul Skalnik at his word. "Mr. Skalnik testified that his testimony at Mr. Dailey's trial was truthful," Espinosa wrote. "Beverly Andringa testified that she would not have called Mr. Skalnik to the stand if she felt his testimony was not truthful." Furthermore, he wrote, "it is clear that no evidence of preferential treatment in exchange for Mr. Skalnik's testimony existed." Espinosa's ruling was not unusual. Appellate judges—many of whom, like Espinosa, are former prosecutors—often defer to the trial judge as a matter of course and are reluctant to second-guess a jury verdict, even when appeals bring to light the very evidence that jurors never heard. Once a witness like Skalnik takes the stand and gives his testimony, it is almost impossible to unring the bell.

MARY KAY DOLLAR, JIM DAILEY, AND THEIR DAUGHTER, STACEY, AT UNION CORRECTIONAL INSTITUTION IN RAIFORD, FLORIDA, IN 2007

. . .

Jim would wait two years for the Florida Supreme Court to consider his appeal. By the time oral arguments were held in the white-domed courthouse in Tallahassee on February 2, 2007, Pinkard had left the CCRC and Jim's case had been assigned to yet another attorney at the agency, a longtime government lawyer named David Gemmer. Jim was not in court that day to see his lawyer argue on his behalf, but from the moment Gemmer stepped up to the lectern, he appeared flustered and unfamiliar with the evidence.

"This is a forest," the stout, bespectacled attorney began, glancing toward the ceiling as he searched, in vain, for the right words. "There's a lot of trees and it just occurred to me sitting here that I need to talk about the forest, so to speak."

Chief Justice R. Fred Lewis looked down from the raised oak bench where he sat with the other justices, and shot Gemmer a disapproving look. "We have a very limited amount of time," he said. "I wish you would give us some kind of a focus here."

As was customary, the state and the defense were allotted twenty minutes each to present their case, but in practice each side would effectively have just one or two minutes to get across their argument before the justices jumped in with their own questions. To successfully advocate before the court required intense preparation and diligence; attorneys needed to know the evidence inside and out, to be able to distill the intricate narratives of their cases into a few clear, powerful points. But as Gemmer spoke, he stumbled through basic facts. Barbara Pariente, considered by many one of the court's more liberal justices, threw him a lifeline, reminding him of testimony that suggested Jim had never left the house with Jack and Shelly. "Shaw *did* say that he saw the co-defendant alone with the victim," she offered. Gemmer did not follow her lead.

Pariente quickly grew exasperated, pressing him to explain why he could not take them through the evidence that helped his client. "There's all this other evidence now that really points to a different conclusion," she said. "If you can't give us a word picture of that, how do you expect us to be able to carry law on this?"

Gemmer shook his head sheepishly. "I'm at the end of the line of a number of attorneys," he said. "I apologize for not having all the facts at my fingertips. I read everything and"—at this, he threw up his hands and invoked his age, as if that were explanation enough—"I'm 56."

The justices continued to pepper him with questions, but before oral arguments came to a close, Chief Justice Lewis addressed the quality of Gemmer's lawyering. "Is there a problem at CCRC that we need to discuss?" he asked sharply.

"No, Your Honor," Gemmer stammered. "I just—I read it all, and I can't memorize it all." He assured the chief justice that he had spent months preparing.

The Florida Supreme Court issued its opinion on May 31, 2007, denying Jim a new trial. Echoing many of Espinosa's findings, the court cited the original testimony of the three jailhouse witnesses as proof that the state's case was well founded. The court explicitly threw its weight behind Skalnik, finding the testimony he gave at the evidentiary hearing—in which he denied ever alleging in court filings that he colluded with prosecutors—to be credible. "Skalnik disavowed the accusations," the justices ruled, and "unequivocally stated that they were false." The court accepted the government's assurances that prosecutors had not engaged in wrongdoing. "The prosecutor in Dailey's case also testified that she believed Skalnik's testimony to be truthful at the time of trial," the justices wrote.

With the Florida Supreme Court's ruling, Jim's state appeals came to an end. For the better part of the next six years, he would pursue his appeals in the federal courts—again, with no success. In 2013, the U.S. Supreme Court declined to hear his case. His last resort would be Florida's clemency process. Clemency is supposed to be a "fail-safe," in the words of William Rehnquist, the court's former chief justice: a final bulwark against miscarriages of justice. But for Jim, the odds were long. No Florida governor had spared a condemned prisoner from execution since 1983.

19

FAIL-SAFE

Late in the morning of September 10, 2015, Jim was led into a cramped room at Union Correctional Institution in Raiford, just a mile down the road from Florida State Prison. Here, two commissioners with the Florida Commission on Offender Review would hear his final plea for mercy as he sought to have his sentence commuted to life. Jim had been relocated to Union Correctional years earlier, when Florida transferred most condemned men there to accommodate the growing death-row population. But the change of venue did little to alter his daily existence: With the exception of the two hours each week he was allowed in the rec yard, he still spent twenty-four hours a day in his windowless, concrete cell.

Although the prospect of a sentence reduction was remote, Jim was no ordinary death-row prisoner. There were his twelve years of military service, including three tours in Vietnam. There was his scant criminal record prior to Shelly's murder. And there was his exemplary conduct in prison. He had been written up just four times in nearly three decades, for minor infractions—a monumental achievement in a place where every aspect of living was governed by arbitrary rules, and correctional officers exercised their power by citing prisoners for the tiniest lapses. Jim's last write-up had occurred sixteen years earlier, when he was cited for giving his then-investigator a stamped letter to mail.

By those measures, Jim was a good candidate. But many clemency boards expect the men and women who come before them to show remorse for their crimes. Prisoners who refuse to admit guilt are rarely considered viable candidates for mercy. One option is to reverse course and admit to crimes they have spent years denying. This, Jim was unwilling to do. Facing the officers, he began.

"I've been on death row for 28 years now, and I've never given up hope," he said, his hands cuffed in front of him. "I'm a good Christian, I read, and I love my family very much. I'm not going to tell you about my innocence or guilt because that's not what you're here for, but I am innocent."

Tena Pate, the chair of the Florida Commission on Offender Review, seemed perplexed. "You don't deny being there that night, correct?"

"No, I was *not* there that night."

"You were not there?" she asked.

"No, I was not," he said. "I was home in bed asleep." Having just promised not to relitigate his case, Jim could not resist. He explained that he had seen no hint of trouble between Jack Pearcy and Shelly when they left the house that night. "I'm extremely sorry for what happened to her, but I didn't see it coming," he said. "Nobody saw it coming. Gayle didn't see it coming, [Dwain] didn't see it coming. I don't know what happened or what caused it." Had he been with them that night, he said, he would never have allowed Jack to hurt her. "It wears on my soul that I couldn't do anything to stop it," but, he emphasized, "I was not there."

"I want to make sure that you understand how important this conversation is today," cautioned Pate.

"Yes, ma'am."

"And you deny being there at the time this happened?"

"Yes, ma'am."

Their conversation lasted more than an hour. When the commissioners asked him why he'd left Florida so soon after the murder, Jim referred to something Jack had said years earlier, in his sworn statement absolving Jim. On the early morning of May 6, 1985, Jack came home alone, and took Jim to a nearby causeway to get high. There, Jack told him to leave town, couching the request as one of domestic necessity. "Gayle, his girlfriend who was pregnant, wanted me to leave because she wanted to turn my bedroom into a nursery," Jim said he was told. "And I told him that was fine with me, I was ready to go to Tucson anyway. I had some good friends out in Tucson. I had no idea that a murder had even been committed, and Jack never said anything about it to me. And the next morning we woke up and he said, 'Let's go to Miami.'" Jim said he had taken off not long after that, eventually making his way to California.

It was only later, he said, that he learned what had happened to Shelly. "When Jack got caught, he got me involved," Jim told the commissioners. "I was in California with two friends of mine, and we'd opened a cabinet shop called United Craftsmen, and we were doing fine. And one day they just came and arrested me, and I didn't know what was going on. And this lawyer came to see me, and he had a copy of a statement Jack had made. And I read it, and I just couldn't believe it." Jim added, "I was out there working under my own name, under my own Social Security number."

The other commissioner, a former prosecutor named Richard Davison, was skeptical. "Out of the blue," Davison said, "he pins a murder on you that you had absolutely nothing to do with?"

"Yes, sir. That's exactly what happened."

"You have to understand the difficult position that we are put in whenever an inmate comes in and denies the offense that he or she is convicted of," Pate reminded Jim.

"All the evidence—the jury, the court case, everything from the judicial standpoint—said that you cut, choked, and drowned her," Davison said.

"But all that evidence has been disputed," Jim stammered.

"No," Davison said. "It's been determined beyond a reasonable doubt—beyond, and to the exclusion of, every reasonable doubt—that you are the person that did that."

Jim pushed back, but Davison, by then, had grown visibly frustrated, finding Jim's guileless explanations, and his insistence that he knew nothing about the murder, to be disingenuous. Steering him back to the early morning hours of May 6, Davison pressed him to say more about what happened when he and Jack went to the causeway.

"Jack came in and woke me up," Jim said. "And I grabbed a six-pack out of the fridge, and we left. We went to Belleair Causeway."

"It's just unfortunate that the same night she was murdered and found in the water," Pate interjected, "that you also opted to go to the lagoon."

"But that's what happened."

"Well, it's—" she began, doubtful.

"How was I supposed to know?" Jim said, cutting her off, his voice suddenly too loud for the small room. "If I had known something, don't you think I would have hidden or something? I didn't care that my pants were wet, I didn't care."

"All right, this concludes the interview at 12:48 p.m.," Pate said tersely. "Thank you."

20

E. PAUL SMITH, ESQ.

Six weeks after Jim's clemency interview, two law enforcement officers pulled up to a double-wide trailer on the edge of Lake Murvaul, in northeast Texas. It was a secluded spot, hemmed in by pine thickets and old-growth forest. The U.S. marshal Shirley Saathoff, a tall, plainspoken woman who was based in Tyler, more than an hour to the west, remained silent as they stepped out of the patrol car. She had worked some of the region's biggest cases, from the Oklahoma City bombing to the Texas Seven prison break, but she knew to let the local investigator, James Ferris, take the lead. Ferris, who worked for the Panola County Sheriff's Office, grew up in nearby Henderson and spoke with the long, slurred vowels of a Piney Woods native. "Ms. Nickell," he said to the woman standing outside the double-wide, squinting at the two officers. "We're conducting a fugitive investigation into a person you know as Paul Smith. We understand he's a friend of yours and we'd like to talk to you."

Ferris had begun investigating E. Paul Smith three months earlier when a young woman had contacted law enforcement, concerned that her mother's larger-than-life new boyfriend, known to them as an undercover federal agent, was not who he claimed to be. She'd discovered that E. Paul Smith was listed on the National Sex Offender Registry as one of many aliases of Paul Skalnik. She said Skalnik owned a Ruger 9 mm semiautomatic pistol—which, as a felon, he was prohibited from carrying. Ferris started digging and discovered that Skalnik had never reported for probation upon his release from prison in Massachusetts in 2006 and had multiple warrants out for his arrest. No sooner had Ferris started looking for him, however, than Skalnik disappeared. The investigator reached out to Saathoff, who routinely conducted multistate investigations to locate fugitives, and asked for her help.

To the locals who knew him as E. Paul Smith, Skalnik was a retired lawyer from Houston who had amassed vast wealth, stashed away in offshore bank accounts. He wore a large, gold class ring from the University of Texas, inscribed with "JD" for juris doctorate, the degree conferred by law schools, and often consulted a legal dictionary he kept at his fingertips, embossed with the words "E. PAUL SMITH, ESQ., ATTORNEY AT LAW." He was also slowly dying from late-stage brain cancer, and though he was undergoing experimental treatment at the VA hospital in Shreveport that was keeping him alive, the prognosis was terminal. He suffered from a host of other ailments, some of which were a legacy of his time as a prisoner of war in Vietnam—when, as a Marine Corps fighter pilot, he had been shot down and taken captive.

Ferris and Saathoff could find no evidence that Skalnik had ever practiced law, or received treatment at the VA hospital in Shreveport, or served in the military, beyond an unfinished stint in officer candidates school. All they could establish was that he had shaved his head to make himself look as if he were undergoing cancer treatment. He had kept busy working a number of scams: writing up wills, assisting people with minor legal matters, and cutting them in on what he assured them were lucrative investment opportunities. One of his clients, a cancer patient in Florien, Louisiana, told Ferris that she had given Skalnik $15,000 that she was later unable to recoup when she needed to pay her medical bills. Ferris also interviewed Judy Smith, his estranged wife, whose modest, tidy home in Carthage, the county seat, had been Skalnik's base of operations before he disappeared one day with her car. Ferris discovered that Skalnik had never really married her; the marriage license he'd had her sign after they exchanged vows on a riverboat casino in Shreveport was phony, and their union was not recorded in the parish's records. Judy told Ferris that "Paul put just enough truth into a lie to make you believe it."

Ferris and Saathoff's investigation had proceeded in fits and starts, constantly sidetracked by more pressing matters, and three months in they were no closer to locating Skalnik than they had been when he first disappeared. Skalnik had left no digital trail—no bank account activity, credit card charges, or cell phone records—and the investigators had little to go on. Frustrated with their lack of progress, they set aside a Friday in late October for an uninterrupted day of work on the case, and it was that afternoon that they arrived at the double-wide on Lake Murvaul where Shawn and Tammy Nickell lived. The investigators knew that he'd stayed with the couple after he'd left Judy Smith, and it was Tammy, a sturdy woman in her late forties with a mane of curly blond hair, who was standing outside when Ferris and Saathoff stepped out of the patrol car. After introducing himself, Ferris glanced up at the sky, which was heavy with rain clouds. "Can we come inside?"

Tammy told them to wait while she put her dogs up, and then she disappeared into the house for a long time. When she returned, she looked uneasy, but she told the officers to come in, motioning for them to take a seat while explaining that her husband was at work. "If you would just start at the beginning," Ferris said over the murmur of the TV, which was turned down low. "When did you first become acquainted with Paul Smith?"

Tammy explained that he had been a regular at the auto shop where her husband worked, and that his generosity had set him apart from other customers. "Shawn would say, 'Mr. Paul was in here today and he bought hamburgers for everyone,'" she said. "Paul didn't go up there often but when he was there, he just stayed and talked, and that's how Shawn got to know him." Tammy told the investigators that he had once been a high-flying attorney, and that when he learned that she and her husband did not have a will, he drafted them one for free. Soon they were meeting him for nice dinners out in Shreveport and Marshall, for which he footed the bill.

"Did Paul ever ask y'all to do him any favors like deposit a check?" Ferris asked. "Or transfer money or receive packages for him?"

"No, never," Tammy said.

Ferris explained that they needed any information she might have so they could locate Paul Smith. "He might be in Fort Lauderdale," Tammy offered. "He has a yacht there. And a Bentley in storage." He had let his law license expire because he had brain cancer, she explained. "There's no telling where he is," she said. "He has a pilot's license and bank accounts overseas, I think in the Bahamas."

"When did you all see him last?"

"A month, two months, maybe?" she said, shifting in her seat. "I'm not real good on dates."

"Did he say anything about when he'll be back?"

"No," she said, shaking her head.

Tammy seemed nervous, looking away from the investigators as she spoke, and Ferris asked why she seemed so on edge. "Because you haven't really told me why you are looking for him," she said.

Ferris leaned forward in his seat and proceeded to explain that her friend was not the dashing figure he portrayed himself to be. "He has a long criminal history that includes a lot of fraud, defrauding people of money," Saathoff added. "So a lot of the things he told you about his background were not true."

Tammy was quiet. "You think you know somebody," she finally said.

She looked as though she were about to cry. Ferris and Saathoff guessed that Skalnik, having claimed to be on death's door, had promised her part of his fortune. This was one of his signature manipulations: dangling the possibility of a vast inheritance in front of people, sometimes even drawing up a phony will, to get them to do his bidding. But Tammy said nothing more on the subject, and the investigators headed for the door. Another dead end.

Ferris and Saathoff had been back at the sheriff's office for an hour when Tammy came rushing in with her husband and asked to see the investigators. She spoke quickly, as if she couldn't get the words out fast enough. They needed to go to her house right away, she said; Paul Smith was holed up in her back bedroom. He had been at her house the whole time, but she had been too scared to say anything. "He has a gun," she warned.

Ferris, Saathoff, and more than half a dozen additional officers soon converged on the Nickells' property, forming a perimeter around the double-wide. A deputy sheriff commanded Skalnik to come out with his hands up, but there was no movement inside. Law enforcement was not in any rush; even though Skalnik had a gun, the area was contained, and there was no one else in the house. They would wait. Half an hour passed with the officers frozen in position, and still he did not emerge. The sky grew darker and it began to drizzle. A few minutes later, Skalnik slid his 9 mm under a mattress and walked out the front door, holding his hands in the air.

Once he was in custody, Skalnik slipped back into his old habits: He asked to speak with Ferris and told the investigator that he wanted to cut a deal. Ferris marveled at Skalnik's audaciousness; he spoke with the easy confidence of someone who had worked this angle before. He told Ferris to make sure that he would only be charged at the state level; "no federal charges," he instructed. In return, he said, he promised "to be useful" inside the Panola County Jail. Ferris—who had just looked through Skalnik's confiscated wallet, which included a pilot's license, Marine Corps and Veterans Affairs cards, bar association cards from Texas and Virginia, a Homeland Security special agent ID, and an American Express black card, all in E. Paul Smith's name—had to stifle a laugh. In what world did this guy think anyone would use him as an informant?

Skalnik was charged in federal court on two felony charges: failure to register as a sex offender and unlawful possession of a firearm by a felon. In 2016, he was sentenced to fifty months in federal prison. He was dispatched to the Federal Correctional Institution in Seagoville, south of Dallas, the collection of low-slung brick buildings where I met him in 2018. Here, he set up shop as a jailhouse lawyer. He quickly developed a reputation as an effective advocate, and in exchange for his services he had prisoners' families deposit money in his commissary account. In the margins of his King James Bible, he scribbled notes on case law and legal jargon, and he practiced his lawyerly writing ("It is essential in an equitable criminal justice system that an opinion is rendered based on the facts of law and a sense of fairness"). As his underground law practice grew more lucrative, he hired another inmate to serve as his typist, and he gorged on commissary candy bars, dictating motions with a mouth full of chocolate.

21

THE CALL

The Florida Commission on Offender Review declined to recommend Jim's case for a clemency hearing, ending any possibility for mercy. The only question that remained was how soon he would be chosen, from among the eligible prisoners on death row who had exhausted their appeals. All that stood in the way of his execution was the governor's signature on his death warrant.

Though there was no obvious legal path forward, his case remained with the CCRC. In 2017, it was assigned to a young lawyer named Chelsea Shirley. Only twenty-seven, she was younger than the case itself, and she was deeply troubled to see the paucity of evidence against Jim. Just three years out of law school, she was not yet worn down by the courts' failure to meaningfully review her client's claims or dissuaded by the near impossibility of overturning a death sentence. Rather than assume that nothing could be done to help Jim, she began brainstorming with her colleagues: What investigative avenues, if any, had not been explored? Who might be willing to say more about what happened on the night that Shelly had been killed?

It was this last question that brought her, on the morning of April 20, 2017, to Sumter Correctional Institution, an hour's drive north of Tampa, to see Jack Pearcy.

She had studied the various accounts Jack had given about the night of the crime, and it seemed to her that Jack had suggested—but never explicitly said—that he committed the killing by himself. Shirley did not even know if he would agree to meet with her, but she went with the hope that he might be ready, thirty-two years after the murder, to speak candidly.

When she worked as a public defender in Tallahassee after law school, she had learned to never underestimate who might agree to talk if she simply showed up in person. Those who were incarcerated often welcomed the diversion—Florida prisoners, on average, receive only two visits, total, from family and friends—and people were often willing to open up to Shirley. Her long blond hair and placid demeanor disarmed them, and her ability to listen without judgment made people who had been let down by the system feel safe enough to share what they knew. She did not advertise her faith, but it was her social-justice-oriented Catholicism that had led her to represent death-row prisoners, and it helped hold at bay the existential gloom that often accompanies such work. Recognizing the dignity and worth of every human being was a principle her churchgoing family had raised her with when she was growing up in southwestern Florida, and it was one that she carried with her into jails and prisons.

Waiting for corrections officials to check her identification, Shirley spotted Jack right away. At sixty-one, he was one of the prison's old men, and he had the hard-bitten look of someone who had spent more than half his life behind bars. But he was still barrel-chested and muscular, with penetrating blue eyes, and he carried himself with the confidence of his youth. Though he didn't know the purpose of the visit, he wasn't surprised by it, and he agreed to meet with Shirley and her colleague Lisa Bort. In a conference room with a large window facing into the prison, Jack took a seat across from the two lawyers.

Shirley began by explaining that Jim was now eligible for a death warrant. Jack did not register any emotion as she relayed this news, but he listened intently. "We're preparing to file a motion, but there probably will not be more chances—if any chance—to get back into court," she told him. "Before we filed the motion, we wanted to talk to you."

"All right," Jack said.

Shirley reviewed the previous accounts Jack had given of the hours surrounding the murder, moving chronologically through his statements to law enforcement. He nodded along, confirming what she ran by him: that he, Shelly, and Dwain Shaw had left the house that night without Jim. That he and Shelly had dropped Dwain off at a pay phone. That he had returned home in the early morning hours by himself. Eventually, Shirley arrived at the most damaging admission: his sworn statement from 1993 in which he admitted that the story he had told law enforcement about Jim being the killer was not only false but "a self-serving statement to exonerate myself." Again, Jack nodded.

When she finished, he picked up a document that she had placed on the table between them; it was an affidavit she had prepared that summarized his previous statements, but it concluded with a declaration that went one step further. "James Dailey was not present when Shelly Boggio was killed," it read. "I alone am responsible for Shelly Boggio's death."

Jack read the affidavit line by line, and when he finally spoke, he struck his usual nonchalant tone. "If you can give me a pen, I'll sign it." He did not offer up any other information or elaborate on what he had done to Shelly. But he said that he would be willing to testify to the accuracy of the affidavit; he just wanted to tell his mother first, he said, to prepare her. It was an astounding admission, and it was new evidence, enough, Shirley hoped, to win her client a new trial. As she and Bort left the prison and walked to her car, Shirley clutched the affidavit tightly, afraid that the two pieces of paper on which Jim's life now depended might slip through her grasp.

. . .

Jack had requested that she not file the affidavit with the court until he had a chance to tell his mother that he planned to testify on Jim's behalf. As the days and then weeks ticked by, Shirley kept her word. She understood that he might change his mind, but she felt cautiously optimistic that he would make good on his promise; he had seemed resigned and even a little relieved as they spoke, as if he had been expecting such a visit for a long time.

By then, Jack had been lucky twice. He had not only dodged the death penalty; he had been sentenced before the state eliminated the possibility of parole for capital crimes. During his conversation with Shirley, Jack had raised the question of whether his affidavit might impact his chances of parole, suggesting that he did not fully grasp how long the odds were that he would ever be released. His mother, also, clung to the idea that he might one day be freed. She urged the Commission on Offender Review in 2016 to recommend him to a highly selective program that prepares lifers to reenter the world after decades of incarceration. "While I recognize his mistakes of the past, I also recognize that his attitude and demeanor have changed for the positive," she wrote to the commission. "My husband and I have witnessed a 'softening' of Jack through the years."

The commission, however, had never held out false hope to either of them. When he first came up for parole, the commission cited the extraordinarily violent nature of Shelly's murder, Jack's previous escape attempt from the Pinellas County Jail, and his extensive disciplinary history, pushing his release date off to 2076. That date was extended by an additional year after synthetic marijuana was found in his locker. Barring some unforeseen circumstance, Jack would die in prison. Whether or not Jack had come to terms with this hard reality, when Shirley spoke to him again that spring, he seemed at peace with his decision to sign the affidavit. He told her that he was ready to move forward.

Before Shirley filed the affidavit with the court, she sought out the men who had been locked up with Jim before his trial but had not been called to testify at the 2003 evidentiary hearing. That May, she found James Wright living at his brother's house in St. Petersburg, and as soon as he understood what she had come to talk to him about, he straightened up in his wheelchair. Shirley feared that his memory might be fading—he was frail and in poor health, relying on a tracheostomy tube to breathe—but he needed no reminder of who Jim was, even though it had been thirty years since they were in jail together. Though the tracheostomy tube made it hard for Wright to speak more than a few words at a time, he recounted, bit by bit, what he remembered. He walked her through everything—from the newspaper articles about Shelly's killing that a detective gave him while probing for information to Jim's insistence, throughout their time locked up together, that he did not commit the murder.

Michael Sorrentino was similarly unreserved when Shirley and two colleagues came to see him in Miami. He talked to them for hours over Cuban coffee as he related an experience nearly identical to Wright's. "The detective asked me if anything in the newspaper articles 'looked familiar,' " Sorrentino told her, explaining that he thought the investigator—whose name he could not remember—wanted him to lie. Shirley was taken aback by how readily both he and Wright agreed to come to court if they were needed in the future, despite the effort it would involve. She was appalled that no judge or juror had ever heard their testimony. Not wanting to let any more time slip by, she filed a motion with the circuit court in Clearwater in which she asserted that Pearcy had admitted to being solely responsible for the murder. She also produced affidavits from Wright and Sorrentino which established that law enforcement actively sought out men in the jail to testify against Jim—a fact that cast into doubt the reliability of the three snitches, James Leitner, Pablo DeJesus, and Paul Skalnik, who did come forward.

After she filed the motion, she continued knocking on doors. One day in July she caught up with another neglected witness, Travis Smith, at home. Smith welcomed her into his living room, but he seemed confused; he said he had spoken to lawyers who represented Jim before, as far back as the 1980s and then again in the 1990s, but nothing had ever come of it. He echoed what his former fellow inmates Wright and Sorrentino had told her, but added more. He said he had a clear memory of hearing Leitner and DeJesus ironing out the details of a story they had made up about Jim confessing to them. As for Skalnik, he said Jim would never have confided in the man. "He was known as a liar and a pedophile," Smith said. "No one in the jail would talk to Skalnik because he was an ex-police officer and a rat."

Shirley cast an even wider net, working her way down a list of men who had been jailed with Jim. Some had died and others were impossible to find, but she located one man, Juan Banda, in prison in Dixie County, a three-hour drive north of Tampa. She had no luck when she went to visit him that summer; Banda refused to answer her questions, and he was skeptical when she told him that Jack—whom Banda had served time with in state prison—had signed an affidavit accepting responsibility for the killing. He told her he wanted proof that she was being straight with him, and only then would he consider talking to her. Shirley sent him a copy of Jack's affidavit once she returned to the office, and when she went back to visit him a few weeks later, his tone had changed. He handed her a written statement he had prepared for her, and as she read it, she realized why he had been reluctant to say anything when she first came to visit: He did not want to snitch on another prisoner. Jack's affidavit had given him permission to say what he knew.

"On two separate occasions," Banda had written, "Jack Pearcy confided in me that James Dailey was innocent." He explained that the first such conversation occurred when they were incarcerated at the same prison in north-central Florida in the mid-1990s. "I started bitching about doing time when Jack says, 'You think we got it bad?'" Banda wrote. "Jack tells me that James is innocent of the crime he is on death row for." The second such conversation took place a little more than a decade later, around 2007, when the two men crossed paths at a different penitentiary. Banda was working in the prison library when Jack walked in. "Jack and I got to talking and the conversation got around to James," Banda wrote. "Jack told me James was still on death row. I asked, 'How is that possible when you told me that James was innocent?' Jack once again states that James is innocent of the crime."

The circuit court judge Frank Quesada, who was assigned the case, agreed to allow the men to testify. Over the objections of the state attorney's office, he set an evidentiary hearing. All five witnesses would be subpoenaed to take the stand on January 3, 2018.

When Shirley arrived at the courthouse in Clearwater that January morning, she was accompanied by Jim's legal team: two colleagues from the CCRC, Maria DeLiberato and Julissa Fontán, and an out-of-state attorney, Laura Fernandez, who had joined the case only a week earlier. Fernandez possessed a unique expertise: an encyclopedic knowledge of Skalnik's history as a jailhouse witness.

Though Fernandez lived in Connecticut, where she was a clinical lecturer and research scholar at Yale Law School, she was well acquainted with Pinellas County. She had grown up in Tampa, and earlier in her career she worked on the post-conviction appeals of Richard Cooper, who had been sentenced to death in 1984 with the help of Skalnik's testimony. (Cooper was the youngest of the High Point murders defendants, whose youth Skalnik used against him, claiming the teenager bragged he would never be sent to the electric chair because of his "little baby face.") Fernandez had been part of a pro bono legal team that persuaded a federal appeals court in 2011 to vacate Cooper's death sentence. The court found that Cooper's trial lawyers failed to present mitigating evidence of severe abuse he suffered throughout his childhood, when his father repeatedly knocked him unconscious. In 2014, he was resentenced to life in prison.

While representing Cooper, Fernandez had looked closely at Skalnik's history as a snitch. Unlike the public defenders and court-appointed attorneys who had examined Skalnik's record before, Fernandez worked at a large, private law firm that could devote the kind of time and resources lawyers need to effectively challenge capital convictions. She was also singularly dogged, spending years piecing together a detailed paper trail of Skalnik's dealings with the state. Building on litigation that her firm, Holland & Knight, had undertaken in the Cooper case over access to public records—and studying the appeals of other defendants convicted on Skalnik's word—she filled in the remaining gaps with more research and record requests, eventually amassing enough documents to fill an entire conference room. She soon saw a damning pattern: Taken together, the documents showed that the state attorney's office had given Skalnik break after break, allowing him to repeatedly dodge any kind of serious punishment or accountability. Whether prosecutors ever made explicit promises to him or not, he would have known that he could expect leniency as long as he testified favorably for the state.

Shirley had been stunned, during their first phone call, by how much Fernandez managed to unearth. Most shocking was what no previous lawyer of Jim's had known or been able to prove: that prosecutors had dismissed twelve-year-old Karen Parker's molestation charge, and that this was part of a previously undisclosed, and extraordinarily lenient, plea arrangement brokered when he was acting as a jailhouse witness. Shirley wanted to present this evidence during the hearing, but Quesada made clear ahead of time that he would not allow it in. He faulted Jim's previous lawyers for failing to do their due diligence, finding that the evidence had come too late.

Perhaps, Shirley hoped, there was still a way to crack open the door, to make sure that Skalnik's role in Jim's conviction was not completely excluded. She saw an opening when, just three weeks before the hearing, the state attorney's office announced that it planned to call John Halliday as a witness. Fernandez had deposed the detective years earlier for Cooper's appeal, giving her a head start on the rest of Jim's legal team; she also knew Halliday's history with Skalnik inside and out. Shirley asked if she'd be willing to come to Clearwater at the start of January to handle Halliday's cross-examination. Shirley knew it was a big ask—Christmas was approaching, and Fernandez would have little time to get up to speed on the case—but Fernandez didn't hesitate. She started reading.

As Fernandez sat at the defense table that winter morning, she was still getting her bearings, after the frenzied days of preparation leading up to the hearing. But from her very first pass over Jim's trial transcript and police reports, she was struck by the illogic of the state's theory of the crime. As a kid, Fernandez had been a voracious reader of Agatha Christie novels—until she read *Murder on the Orient Express,* whose plot she found both overly complicated and implausible. Reading the record in Jim's case, she felt the same jolt of frustration. To her mind, thirty-one knife wounds indicated that the murder was an act of rage, as if the killer had erupted in furious anger; it did not suggest two perpetrators working in concert. The prosecution's case seemed even more far-fetched after she went to Florida and met Jim, whose equanimity and low-key, midwestern warmth struck her immediately. The cognitive dissonance she felt—how could *this* man have committed *that* crime?—only deepened once she watched Jack, with his flat affect and hard stare, take the stand that afternoon.

First, though, came the three witnesses who described Halliday's visit to the jail. Wright looked fragile and his tracheotomy made him unable to speak above a whisper, but both he and Sorrentino were steadfast in their assertion that the detective who grilled them—whose name they could not recall—had shown them newspaper articles about the murder. Smith was the most outspoken, asserting that in the 1980s prosecutors and investigators had routinely visited the jail looking for witnesses to help their cases. "A lot of state attorneys used to come over there," he told the judge. Leitner and DeJesus, he said, were among the men he saw taking advantage of this arrangement by inventing a story about Jim confessing to them. "That was a plot that they had to try to get their sentence reduced," he said. "And the state attorney reduced their sentence as a result of them, you know, fabricating their story."

Smith's testimony visibly rankled Jim Hellickson, a silver-haired prosecutor who had worked for the state attorney's office since 1976. As he leaned forward in his chair, poised to object, Smith turned toward Hellickson. "I was there, and I knew them. That was a common—not being disrespectful, sir, but that was just a common practice from the state attorneys."

Jim sat at the defense table, listening closely, quietly heartened by the direction the hearing was taking. The morning's testimony concluded with Banda recounting how Jack had on two different occasions, many years apart, told him that Jim did not commit the murder. "He told me Mr. Dailey was innocent of the crime that he was sentenced to death row for," Banda said.

When Jack took the stand, he looked uneasy. Seated in the front row of the courtroom was his mother, her gaze fixed on him. Shirley knew that Jack was under enormous pressure; two investigators with the state attorney's office had visited him weeks before the hearing, and though she was not privy to the message they delivered, she suspected that it echoed prosecutors' arguments to the judge that day: Jack should be warned that any admissions he made in court could be used against him at future parole hearings. Suggesting that his testimony would hurt his odds of winning parole was a cynical tactic, Shirley thought, since prosecutors would never back his release, but she worried that Jack would fall for it.

"Would you please state your name for the record?" she began.

"Jack Edward Pearcy," he said in his low monotone.

"And, Mr. Pearcy, how old are you?"

"Sixty-two."

"Do you know Mr. Dailey, James Dailey?"

"Yes, ma'am."

"Would you please identify him and point him out for the court?"

Jim was seated at the defense table in plain view, in the distinctive bright orange uniform that is only worn by the state's death-row inmates, but Jack paused. The two men had not glimpsed each other since Jim's last evidentiary hearing, almost fifteen years earlier. "I'm not sure I recognize this dude in orange," Jack finally said. "Looks different from the last time I seen him."

"Did you sign an affidavit in this case, Mr. Pearcy?" Shirley asked.

"I did."

"Is that your signature there on the bottom of page two?"

"It is."

"Did you sign that affidavit under penalty of perjury?"

"I reckon, if that's the law," he said.

"At this time, Your Honor, the defense would move defense exhibit number five into evidence," Shirley said, holding up the affidavit.

Glenn Martin, a veteran prosecutor who was assisting the state attorney's office that day, objected, arguing that the claims in the affidavit had not yet been corroborated by Jack's testimony. "The only way that this goes forward any further is if Jack Pearcy testifies today, 'I am solely responsible for the death of Shelly Boggio,'" Martin said. "We need to hear it from Mr. Pearcy's lips."

"Sustained," Quesada agreed.

Shirley was not sure how far Jack would go with this line of questioning. She had visited him in prison several times in the months leading up to the hearing, and he had always been cooperative, but he had told her that his family was worried about him testifying. "So you agree that you signed an affidavit in this case?" she asked him.

"I did," he said.

"And are the statements in the affidavit true?"

"No," he said.

Shirley stood very still, her heart thumping. "Which statements in the affidavit are not true?" she asked.

"I'm not sure," Jack said. "There's quite a few lines on there."

"Okay," Shirley said. "We're going to go through your affidavit line by line."

As she read the affidavit back to him, he confirmed the first sentence—"My name is Jack Pearcy"—and the second: "I was tried and sentenced to life imprisonment with the possibility of parole for the murder of Shelly Boggio." But when she asked him about each statement pertaining to the hours surrounding the murder, he invoked his constitutional right against self-incrimination. "I take the Fifth," he said.

Puzzled, Quesada turned in his seat toward the witness box. "Mr. Pearcy, I don't understand your position, as far as the Fifth Amendment goes," he said. "We're talking about a crime that you have been convicted of, and certainly I don't believe the state could try you twice for the same crime."

But Jack did not budge. "I'm still invoking my Fifth Amendment right," he said.

Shirley tried a different tack. "Mr. Pearcy, has your mother advised you not to testify?" she asked.

"I spoke with all my family, and they told me I needed to do what I thought was right, but that I needed to not make a rash decision since my parole just got denied for seven years." His family had advised him, he said, to "think about what I was doing."

Jim watched, stone-faced. "No further questions," Shirley said.

Before the hearing came to a close, the state called its only witness—John Halliday—to the stand. Halliday, who had retired from law enforcement more than a decade earlier, was no longer the imposing, muscle-bound interrogator he had once been, but his memory was sharp and his testimony definitive. As prosecutors led him through a series of questions, he stated clearly that he had not provided relevant newspaper articles or done anything else improper when he questioned men in the jail about Jim's case.

When it was time to cross-examine him, Fernandez stepped up to the lectern. She knew that Jack's decision to plead the Fifth had been enormously damaging, and that she had to make the most of Halliday's time on the stand. She began by asking whether his visit to the jail had not, in effect, signaled to the men there that he was looking for a snitch. "I don't know whether that was a well-known fact," he shot back. "How am I supposed to know that?"

Halliday had given the prosecutors straightforward answers, but with Fernandez he struggled to recall basic facts about the investigation. He claimed to remember little about the jailhouse witnesses who testified against Jim; he said he recalled "the name" Paul Skalnik, but not much else.

"You worked with Skalnik on several cases?" Fernandez pressed.

"I interviewed Paul Skalnik concerning other cases, yes."

"And he was a witness in other cases?"

"Yes. He was an ex–police officer."

But beyond that, Halliday was vague. "You'll have to show me a police report, deposition, trial testimony to refresh my memory," he said, later adding by way of explanation, "I've been involved in a lot of cases in the last 32 years."

That March, when Quesada handed down his ruling, Shirley and Fernandez both rushed to read it, searching for reasons to be optimistic, but found none. The evidence presented by the defense was "untimely," the judge wrote, again faulting Jim's previous lawyers for not bringing forward Smith, Sorrentino, and Wright earlier in the appeals process. Their testimony, the judge added, "otherwise does not give rise to any reasonable probability that the defendant would be acquitted on retrial." He also dismissed Banda's testimony as hearsay. The irony wasn't lost on the lawyers: Banda—unlike Skalnik during his days as a jailhouse witness—had no incentive to testify. The defense had no power to offer him a reduced sentence; if anything, Banda, who was still incarcerated, had taken a huge risk speaking out against another inmate. Quesada rejected the defense's bid for a new trial.

The logical next step for Fernandez would have been to put the case behind her and return to her research at the law school, where she focused on prosecutorial ethics and accountability. She had already spent most of her career in the trenches of capital post-conviction defense, and by 2014, when she took the position at her alma mater, she was eager for the relative calm of academic life. The relentless hours and emotional intensity of capital cases had consumed her. In her new role, she hoped to continue the work she cared about so deeply, but at a measured distance.

But after meeting Jim and seeing what had happened in Quesada's courtroom, she could not fathom walking away. She and Shirley began discussing the next step in the case: appealing Quesada's decision to the Florida Supreme Court. The two lawyers—along with another Yale Law–trained attorney, Cyd Oppenheimer—spent the spring writing a ninety-two-page analysis of the case which they hoped would ensure that the court's justices could not look away. The Innocence Project of Florida lent its credibility to the effort by signing on as co-counsel, a signal to the high court that Jim's claims should be taken seriously. The defense submitted its brief in the summer of 2018 and waited.

More than a year passed with no word from the court. Fernandez was confident that their brief laid out a convincing case that Jim deserved a new trial, but she knew better than to hope. Jim had what she called a "Murphy's Law case"—everything that could have gone wrong did.

On September 24, 2019, Shirley awoke feeling unwell, but she could not afford to miss a day of work, and she dragged herself into her office at the CCRC, where her files on the Dailey case sat in orderly rows of binders. By lunchtime, she could no longer ignore that she was sick; she could barely keep her eyes open. She went home to lie down and stopped checking her phone.

Fernandez had just gotten home from work when she discovered that she had a voicemail, and she pressed her phone to her ear as she hurried around her house, tidying up for the babysitter who would be arriving soon. "Hi, Ms. Fernandez," the message began. A woman was speaking, her tone friendly and informal, with a particular intonation that made each sentence sound like a question. "I'm calling from the legal office of Governor Ron DeSantis," she continued. "I see in some recent filings that you were involved in the representation of Mr. James Dailey." Fernandez, ever the idealist, momentarily entertained a bit of magical thinking. Perhaps someone at the Office of General Counsel had read the defense's pleadings and, seeing the obvious injustice in her client's case, wanted to discuss restarting the clemency process.

As she listened to the rest of the message, time slowed down. The late afternoon sun seemed to dim as it slanted across the floor; her children's voices receded. The woman on the recording was still speaking in her chirpy, matter-of-fact way. "I'm calling to give you notification," the woman continued, "that the governor has signed his death warrant and set his execution for Thursday, November 7."

PART IV

22

ELEVENTH HOUR

One week after Jim's death warrant was signed, I went in search of Paul Skalnik. I hadn't heard from him since he'd cut off communication with me six months earlier, but as I drove north out of Austin, I hoped he might agree to talk. Just past Waco, I turned onto Texas Highway 31, a two-lane road flanked by cotton fields ready for harvest, and followed it until I reached the town of Corsicana. Skalnik was no longer in prison, having served out his sentence, but I had some idea where he was; he appeared on the state's sex offender registry, his listed address a Corsicana nursing home. He had never backed away from his claim that Jim confessed to him, but if he were ever going to, it would have to be now: Jim's execution date was little more than a month away.

I found Skalnik splayed across a bed in a drab, cluttered room with the blinds drawn and a television on low. He seemed stunned to see me standing in his doorway—"How on earth did you find me?" he asked—and the sheer surprise of it seemed to disarm him for a moment. After a beat, he motioned toward the empty wheelchair next to his bed and told me to take a seat. He was mostly naked and barely concealed under a tangle of sheets, but he did not cover up when I sat down next to him. Instead, he just stared back at me as I asked how he had been faring. "Do you know that you're

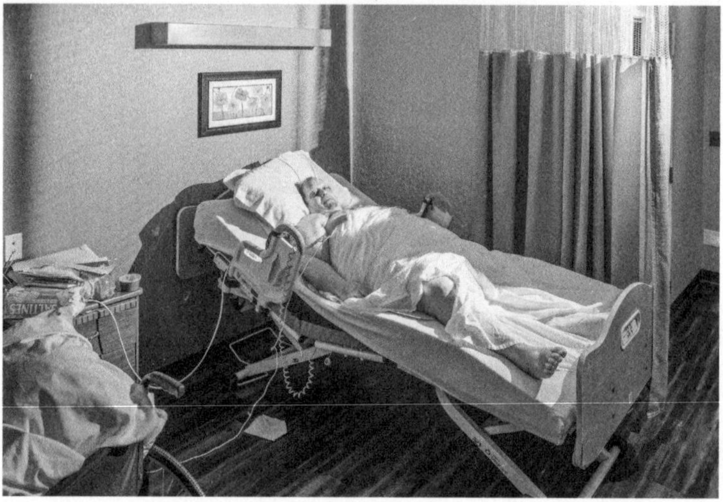

PAUL SKALNIK IN A NURSING HOME IN CORSICANA, TEXAS, IN OCTOBER 2019

the only visitor I've had?" he said, his eyes watering. "I appreciate you very much."

We talked for a while, carrying on a pleasant enough conversation. I listened as he rattled off a litany of infirmities he said he suffered from and gripes about his care. Even flat on his back, he cut a shockingly large figure, his protuberant belly undiminished, and he explained that it took a team of nurses to turn him so that he would not develop bedsores. Exactly what illness had left him so incapacitated, he did not say. But every so often, his body would suddenly go rigid. Teeth clenched, eyes squeezed shut, hands balled into fists, he would fall silent, gripped by what appeared to be exquisite pain. After one such episode, he told me that he did not think he had much longer to live.

"Do you remember a man named James Dailey?" I finally asked.

Skalnik shook his head.

"From the Pinellas County Jail?" I said.

After thinking for a while, Skalnik nodded. "He's on death row. He drowned a girl."

"His execution date has been set for November 7," I said.

Skalnik took in this news with no discernible sign of concern, or even interest. "It's October 1 today," I added.

"Huh," Skalnik offered. His manifest indifference should not have surprised me, but it did.

"I want to ask you some questions about the Dailey case," I said.

"I'll do my best," Skalnik said wearily, closing his eyes. "I had a stroke on June 14, and ever since then, my memory has been real"—he searched for the right word—"flaky."

"Do you remember testifying at his trial?"

"No," he said, shaking his head. "Did I?"

"You did."

"I really don't remember."

"What do you remember?"

"Not much," he said flatly.

I told him that the evidence in the case seemed to point to Jim's co-defendant, and suggested that Jim had been at home at the time of the murder.

"Oh, he was there," Skalnik said, suddenly engaged. "He told me. He said he could see her face underwater."

"I thought you said your memory wasn't great right now."

Annoyed, he gave me a sharp glance.

"He's going to be executed in less than five weeks," I said. "If there's any chance that your testimony against him was false—"

"No," Skalnik said firmly.

"Did investigators ever share details of the case with you?" I asked.

"No," he said. "Halliday is a straight shooter."

"Did he ever make you any promises?"

"No, he couldn't do anything for me."

I reminded him that Halliday had done a lot for him long before he testified against Jim, and that the detective had written to the parole board on his behalf.

"Did he?" Skalnik said, as if this were the first he was hearing about it.

Skalnik's relationship with the detective, I suspected, was key to understanding the role he had played in Jim's case. So I asked him about something he had claimed when he briefly turned against the state attorney's office in the late 1980s: Halliday, he said, once took him out of the jail for a conjugal visit with his then-fiancée. There is reason to believe this actually happened. Logs indicate that the detective checked Skalnik out of the jail for two and a half hours on May 15, 1984—a month after Skalnik's testimony helped secure a death sentence for Richard Cooper, the youngest of the High Point murders defendants. When Halliday was later questioned under oath about facilitating a meeting with Skalnik's fiancée, the detective gave a tepid denial. ("I don't remember taking him out of the jail to meet her," Halliday said in a 2000 deposition. "If it happened, it happened, but I don't specifically have a memory of it.")

When I asked him about this particular story, Skalnik affirmed that Halliday and another detective had once taken him out of the jail and driven him to see his fiancée. "They put me in civilian clothes and took the cuffs off of me," he told me. He denied, though, that the purpose of the visit was sex; he and his fiancée had merely eaten lunch, with detectives keeping a close watch over them. "I wasn't allowed to put my hands on her," he said. Then he seemed to insinuate the opposite. "She was a good cook," he told me with a wink.

That brief sojourn into the free world had been carefully coordinated to ensure his safety, Skalnik said, explaining that his movements around the jail always had to be mapped out so he was not put in harm's way. "It would be a major production, like Jack the Ripper was coming," he said. "It got to the point where they would have to secure the entire facility, every inch of it, before I could be moved."

"Because everyone knew you were an informant?"

"Oh, absolutely," he said. "The whole place knew."

I pressed him to explain how it was possible that Jim had told him anything self-incriminating if everyone in the jail knew that he was feeding information to detectives.

"He drowned a girl," Skalnik said. "He said it to my face."

Skalnik made no effort to explain how both things could be true at once. But my revulsion at that moment was not reserved for Skalnik, who had known he would be rewarded, all those years ago, for telling just the right story; it was for the entire apparatus that enabled and encouraged him. For the detectives who incentivized him. For the prosecutors who represented him as a truth teller. For the trial judge who allowed jurors to hear Skalnik's testimony. For the appellate judges who rubber-stamped it all, paving the way for the governor to one day sign a death warrant.

It soon became clear that the last person who could provide a deeper understanding of Skalnik was Skalnik himself. He sidestepped my questions, portraying himself as the unfairly maligned hero of a story that featured a supporting cast of scheming and vindictive women. Of both charges of child molestation, he insisted that he had been wrongly accused, a victim of girls who lied to the authorities. His ex-wives? Greedy opportunists who were only after his money. The people who accused him of conning them? "You try to do people a favor," he said, "and they turn on you."

When I asked him about a woman named Donna Mackey, he at first feigned ignorance.

"Donna?" he said innocently.

"Donna, the woman you were engaged to earlier this year," I said.

"Oh—Donna," he said, gazing up at the ceiling. Then his eyes darted back to me. "Have you been talking to Donna?"

Early that spring, I had received a call from Donna, who explained that she was Skalnik's fiancée. (When Skalnik had bragged to her that a reporter came to interview him in prison, she'd scribbled down my name.) She had not heard from Skalnik in more than a week, which concerned her because they normally spoke every day, and she wondered if I'd heard from him. I hadn't—by then, he had already shut me out—but Donna was warm and friendly, and we kept talking. She told me they'd met through her son, whom Skalnik had taken under his wing when he and the young man were briefly incarcerated together. And she repeated what Skalnik had told her: He was a retired Houston attorney with properties around the globe whose ex-wife had falsely accused him of molesting her daughter.

Donna and I stayed in touch after she and Skalnik reconnected, and in the coming months we spoke regularly. At first, I was guarded: Was Donna in cahoots with Skalnik, and trying to gather information about my reporting? But the more we talked, the more I grew to trust her, and to feel for her. Donna told me that she had weathered a series of losses before Skalnik came into her life. Her husband had died from a heart attack in 2012, and not long afterward she was laid off from her pharmacy job and became her ailing mother's live-in caretaker. Then her son was arrested for a financial crime he committed while in the grip of drug dependency. "I was just treading water," she told me. Skalnik began writing to her—first, assuring her that he was looking after her son, and then lamenting, in his old-fashioned, looping script, how his life of adventure had been unfairly cut short by his arrest.

Donna had never traveled widely; when her son was little, she told me, they'd sit in her mother's blue Ford LTD outside the hospital in the East Texas town of Longview, ice cream cones in hand, and watch ambulances roar past—the closest thing to adventure she could give her little boy. She was captivated by Skalnik's travel stories, and read them aloud to her mother before her mother died in 2017. He wrote of the yacht he dry-docked every winter; his favorite haunts in Europe; the vacation home he owned on the coast of Belize. Before long, he was professing his love for her and telling her that he wanted to show her the world. "I took a long time before I gave in and told him I loved him," Donna told me. "And when I finally did, he didn't think I was sincere, and he started to cry." It was then that he started asking her about the property that her mother had left her.

Late that spring, Donna called me, sounding both excited and apprehensive. Skalnik was going to be released from prison in early June, she had just learned. He would be moving in with her until his health improved, and then they planned to travel the world. Skalnik couldn't wait, she added, to finally meet her five-year-old granddaughter.

Until that moment, I'd agonized over how much to tell her. I'd taken my cues from her about how much she wanted to know, truthfully answering any question she raised. She had not asked much, but I sensed that she had kept in touch because, consciously or not, she harbored doubts about her future husband. She had told me about her granddaughter before, mentioning that the little girl sometimes spent the night. "Donna," I said. "How soon can I come see you?"

Days later, I went to meet her at her home in a rural community outside Longview. As we sat on her back porch, overlooking the pastureland that Skalnik had expressed such interest in, I told her everything. She listened with a sort of defeated acceptance—not entirely surprised, I thought, but still shaken. On some level, she had always known he was too good to be true. Quietly, she studied everything I'd brought with me: arrest warrants, police reports, mug shots. After I explained that I had spoken to several women whom he had molested when they were girls, she sat back in her chair, staring out at the property where she'd imagined building a life with him.

When our time together was over, she stood up and asked me to wait there. When she returned, she was holding a stack of love letters, more than fifty in all, that Skalnik had written to her over their three-year relationship. They professed his undying devotion and provided glimpses of their imagined future together; in one, he provided her with the combinations to the safes on his yacht in Costa Rica. "Please take these," she said, handing them to me. "I don't ever want to look at them again."

As I sat at Skalnik's bedside, he expressed bewilderment over Donna, who had broken off their engagement. I couldn't tell whether he had put two and two together, but if he had, he did not let on. "Donna was supposed to pick me up on June 14," he said, recalling the day he was released from prison. "I told everybody she was coming. They unshackled me and said, 'You're a free man today.' But she didn't come." His voice caught and a little sob escaped him. "I had a stroke either that day or the day after, because I was so depressed. I never figured she wouldn't show."

As Skalnik talked, I eyed his tattoos. His right shoulder was emblazoned with two crossed swords and the letters "U.S.M.C."—a nod to the Marine Corps—and his left shoulder bore the words "1970: From Texas to Vietnam." Skalnik told me that he had been a decorated fighter pilot before his life went sideways. "I was probably the best pilot the Marine Corps ever had," he added. Tracing a jagged scar across his knee, he recounted how he had been wounded in combat; shot down over the jungles of Laos during the height of the Vietnam War, he was taken captive and held prisoner before he managed to escape, he said—a feat that earned him a Purple Heart.

Skalnik had traded on this story throughout his time in Texas, frequenting American Legion Halls where he befriended veterans;

portraying himself as a war hero to the women he pursued; and keeping a shadow box that held medals, campaign ribbons, and pilot wings. But his military records show that he never served overseas; briefly a reservist, he remained stateside throughout the war. (The redacted file offers no explanation for his abrupt discharge from the reserves in 1971.) The scar on his knee was sustained not when he was shot out of the skies over Laos but in a car accident in Austin—or at least that was what he told me during our first interview, though he had apparently forgotten. The contrast between him and Jim could not have been any starker. Jim, who had suffered the real costs of Vietnam, rarely spoke of his service, and certainly never to aggrandize himself.

Before our time together was over, I circled back to the subject of Jim's impending execution, but Skalnik showed little interest in discussing it further. It was not until I mentioned another man he had testified against, Freddie Gaines, that he grew animated. Gaines was the twenty-four-year-old who stabbed his girlfriend's ex-lover in a bar brawl. "Short little Black guy," Skalnik said, with a half smile, remembering the perennially upbeat young man. "He was three cells down from me."

Skalnik's divergent reactions to each man were telling, I thought. Gaines was clearly someone he knew. But Jim, I suspected, was a stranger.

I had asked about Gaines because he appeared to be the last man—aside from Jim—who was still serving a prison sentence enabled by Skalnik's testimony. In the nearly forty years since Skalnik began peddling information in Pinellas County, the other defendants he testified against had served their time, seen their convictions or sentences reversed, or died in prison. Of the four men he had testified against who were sentenced to death, two—Richard Cooper and Kenneth Gardner—were no longer on death row, having been resentenced on appeal to life in prison. A third, J. D. Walton, succeeded in getting Skalnik's testimony against him thrown out and was later resentenced to death on the strength of other evidence.

Freddie Gaines, however, was trapped in a life sentence secured with Skalnik's testimony. Without that testimony, Gaines could have gotten as little as fifteen years for manslaughter. But Skalnik's account had Gaines bragging of carrying out a calculated, premeditated killing—allowing prosecutors to seek, and win, a first-degree murder conviction. Thanks to Skalnik, and a state attorney's office eager to use the kinds of stories he hawked, Gaines would likely die in prison.

Though Skalnik had been blasé throughout our conversation about the suffering he had caused, he seemed taken aback when I told him that Gaines was still in prison. The young man he remembered, I explained, was now sixty.

Skalnik looked away and was quiet. "He doesn't need a life sentence," he finally said. "I'd give him ten years and let him go home."

When I reminded Skalnik of the role he played at Gaines's trial, he appeared shocked. "This was your testimony, that he had planned this," I reminded him. "Does that ring true to you? Do you think he told you that?"

"No!" Skalnik cried. "No." He shook his head resolutely.

But when I later returned to this apparent recantation, his tone shifted. "I won't retract what I said," he told me, his voice rising. "Whatever I testified to was fact."

Then I understood. Skalnik was never going to admit that he lied on the stand because there was nothing in it for him. In Florida, there is no statute of limitations on perjury in capital felony cases; a jailhouse witness who later changes his story can face the threat of criminal prosecution. Once a verdict has been rendered, there is more incentive to perpetuate a lie than admit error; it's a system designed for finality, not necessarily for correction.

"So all these people over the years told you their deepest, darkest secrets," I said.

"That's true."

"How did you get people to tell you everything?"

"I wish I could tell you."

"Well, try to help me understand."

"I listen and I probe a little. And then we're off to the races. Guys at the jail would say, 'You got to really watch what you say around him because he can get anything.' The ones that talked to me thought I was the most trustworthy person in the world."

"Did you ever feel bad about that?"

"Remorse?" he said.

I nodded.

"I don't feel bad about Dailey," he said. "I'm sorry, I just don't. I really wouldn't want him walking the streets."

When the afternoon light behind the blinds began to fade, I closed my notebook and thanked Skalnik for talking to me, but it was clear that he was not ready for the conversation to end. He tried to draw me back in with stories of stashing his money in Abu Dhabi and taking luxury shopping trips to New York City, where he said he liked to stay at the Plaza hotel. ("Ivana Trump really messed that place up," he said, referring to the renovation she undertook after her then-husband bought the property in 1988. "Stupid woman.") He said he had frequented the finest stores on Fifth Avenue: Tiffany, Cartier, Bergdorf Goodman. "You can't make this shit up," he said. "How many people, if you walked out in this hallway right now and said 'Bergdorf Goodman,' would know what it is?"

I told Skalnik I needed to get on the road before dark. When I rose, a look of panic crossed his face. He reached for my hand, squeezing it. "When I'm ready to die," he said, gripping my hand with surprising strength, "will you come sit with me?"

23

ZOMBIE CASE

Jim had always tried to imagine the moment when his luck would run out. Still, he was floored when, late in the afternoon on September 25, 2019, a knot of prison officials stopped outside his cell and a sober-faced captain stepped forward to announce that his death warrant had been signed. Jim, who had turned seventy-three that summer, complied with the officers' orders, standing still as his hands were chained to his waist and his ankles were shackled together. But he told them that there had to have been a mistake: His case was still under review by the Florida Supreme Court. His legal team had appealed Judge Quesada's decision to deny him a new trial, and the court had not yet issued a ruling. As he was led out of his cell, he stammered, "I still have things in the courts," but no one seemed to hear him or to be concerned about what he was saying.

Jim was taken to a holding cell, where he was strip-searched and instructed to put on a fresh uniform. Then he was told to wait. He closed his eyes and thought of Mary Kay. He wanted to spare her the pain of what was to come.

A Department of Corrections van transported him a little more than a mile down State Road 16, to Florida State Prison—the penitentiary where he was first held when he came to Starke in 1987. He

JIM DAILEY, EARLY IN HIS DECADES-LONG CONFINEMENT ON DEATH ROW, AT HIS 1993 RESENTENCING HEARING

was to spend his final days there in an isolation cell inside Q Wing, a restricted area within the prison known as the death house.

The lieutenant who oversaw the death house, an incongruously friendly and good-natured man in his sixties named Dennis Cauwenberghs, led Jim down into the bowels of Q Wing. Jim was to remain there, in isolation, for the next forty-three days, until his execution on November 7. He shuffled into the cell, which measured twelve by seven feet. The walls, painted the color of fresh butter, gleamed under the fluorescent lights. The execution chamber was just down the hall, thirty feet away.

Cauwenberghs locked the cell door, reached through the bars to remove Jim's shackles, and pulled up a chair. Speaking to Jim through the bars, the lieutenant explained that they needed to discuss final arrangements. Thumbing through a small stack of papers, he identified the most urgent matters at hand. First, Cauwenberghs explained, there was the question of what Jim wanted for his last meal. Then there was the matter of the disposition of his body and who would handle his funeral arrangements. If Jim wanted anyone to have his meager belongings, he needed to figure that out too. Cauwenberghs did not hurry him. "I know this is an awful lot to take in right now," he said. The lieutenant advised Jim to spend some time thinking over what he wanted to do.

That night, the death house was quiet. A correctional officer stationed at the end of the hallway was the only other human presence. Jim calculated how many days he had left. Five in September. Thirty-one in October. Seven in November.

Mary Kay was in Kansas City visiting her sister when she got the call. "I'm so sorry to have to give you this news," her daughter-in-law began. A flurry of calls followed, and soon Mary Kay, desperate to see Jim, was on the phone with the warden's office. She was told she could schedule a time to come to Florida State Prison, but only a non-contact visit would be allowed; the small gestures of physical affection she and Jim had shared on prior visits—holding hands, a loose hug—were now off limits. Mary Kay strained to keep her tone civil. "So when someone is told they have a death warrant," she said, "no one can touch them?"

Early that October, she went to see Jim. Mary Kay felt only raw terror as she was led into the visitation room in the death house, but to reassure Jim, she forced a smile. He was so close to death, and yet there he was, full of life, overjoyed to see her. She took a seat and placed the palm of her right hand on the glass partition that separated them. Jim pressed his palm against his side of the glass, lining up his fingers with hers. Wordlessly, they stared at each other.

Thirty-four years had come and gone since Shelly's murder. One by one, across the intervening years, the people who knew her best had each passed away. Her father, Frank, and her big sister, Sherry, both died of cancer. Shelly's twin, Stacy, who spent years tormented by the question of whether she could have protected her sister if she had stayed with her that night, died of an overdose in 2006, when she was thirty-five. None of them lived to see Jim given an execution date.

Prosecutors don't always level with victims' families, before making the calculation to seek the death penalty, about what actually lies ahead: appeals that can drag on seemingly without end. Defendants who face execution are afforded more opportunities than other prisoners to challenge their convictions, but those appeals are complex; capital cases are often tainted with problems like prosecutorial misconduct, ineffective legal representation, and racial bias, which appellate courts, at least in theory, are supposed to thoroughly examine. As a result, death sentences may not be carried out for decades, if at all. Florida's death row includes scores of prisoners who were convicted in the 1980s, and some as far back as the 1970s; the state's longest-serving condemned men committed their crimes when Gerald Ford was president.

The ostensible reason the state attorney's office had sought a death sentence for Jim had been to secure justice for Shelly, and to exact a punishment that would, in some small way, help assuage the pain suffered by her family. Instead, the Boggios had been subjected to a nightmarish, decades-long legal saga. Rather than get any semblance of closure, they had suffered the repeated trauma that came with each court date and legal filing: a protracted ordeal that had, thanks to the state's stubborn reliance on Skalnik and the weakness of the evidence, stretched on for more than twice the length of Shelly's own life.

"End Moves Closer for Teen's Killer," read the front page of the *Tampa Bay Times* on September 27, above a decades-old, hollow-eyed photo of Jim. The accompanying article described Shelly's murder—a crime that, despite its abject horror, had long faded from public consciousness—and recapped the archaic, Reagan-era investigation. "There was no forensic evidence, even by 1980s standards," the *Times* story explained. "The case relied on jailhouse informants." A quotation from one of Jim's prosecutors, Beverly Andringa, who had by then retired from the state attorney's office, inadvertently demonstrated how tenuous the evidence against Jim still was, just forty-one days before his execution date. "It was a circumstantial case; it's not like there was an upstanding citizen eyewitness," she told the *Times*. "So speculation is all we have as to what happened."

Jim's conviction was deeply rooted in the tough-on-crime 1980s, but by the time he was slated for execution, the death penalty in America was in steep decline. Since his trial, a convergence of forces had moved the country further and further away from capital punishment. Violent crime rates plunged in the 1990s and early '00s, and gradually the public's zeal for draconian punishments softened. Death-row exonerations—brought about by newly available DNA testing—began to erode confidence in the death penalty. New sentencing laws gave juries the option of choosing life without parole over death. Supreme Court rulings narrowed who was eligible for execution. Nowhere was the shift away from new death sentences starker than in Florida. In 1987, it sent forty-four people to death row, including Jim. Thirty years later, in 2017, that number was just three.

Yet death rows across the country were straining under a backlog of prisoners condemned to die decades earlier. They had what Stephen Bright, one of the nation's preeminent capital defense attorneys, calls "zombie cases": relics of a time when prosecutors pursued the death penalty with fervor. Perversely, as the country turned away from capital punishment, it was these cases—cases like Jim's—that were chosen for execution.

What remained unclear was why, of the 340 prisoners on Florida's death row, the governor had settled on Jim. There was no discernible pattern to whom DeSantis sent to the death chamber. In the eight months since he had taken office, he had dispatched two men, both serial killers whose cases had nothing in common with Jim's. DeSantis did not explain his decision, nor did he have to. Unlike many other death-penalty states, where the responsibility of setting executions falls to the courts, in Florida, the governor has absolute discretion over which death-row prisoners live or die. How a governor culls the list of eligible candidates is cloaked in secrecy, as is the timing of death warrants, which are handed down without warning. "For all we know," one capital defender told me of the selection process, "the governor throws a dart at a list of names."

On October 3, a week after Jim's warrant was signed, Florida's highest criminal court rejected his appeal, clearing the way for his execution to proceed. Once again focusing on procedural rules rather than the merits of the defense's arguments, a court had found that much of the new evidence had come to light too late. This included recently discovered Indian Rocks Beach police reports, which showed that Dwain Shaw told investigating officers, in 1985, that Jim was not with Jack and Shelly when they gave him a ride to the phone booth. "Dailey neglects to explain why this information could not have been discovered earlier," the ruling stated—in essence faulting his lawyers for not uncovering facts that the state had spent years obfuscating.

At a news conference, DeSantis insisted it was time to move forward. The governor conveyed his belief that the courts had done their work, and that the lengthy appeals process had been more than sufficient. He did not appear troubled by the issues the defense had raised; a graduate of Harvard Law School and a former military prosecutor, DeSantis expressed his confidence in the system and the multiple stages of review that are built into capital convictions, which are meant to provide assurance that the most severe penalty is imposed only after exhaustive scrutiny. The only injustice in the case, he told reporters, was that both defendants were not facing execution. "This was one of the most gruesome crimes in the history of Pinellas County," DeSantis said. "This has been litigated over and over and over, and so at some point you need to do justice."

As news of Jim's execution date circulated on social media, Marieke caught sight of his photo in her Facebook feed, and froze. She knew there were only two reasons he would be the topic of discussion in her Florida death-penalty group: Either he was dead, or he was slated to die. She stared at her phone screen, afraid to read the solitary sentence that ran below his picture, but then she made herself. "Dailey will be the oldest death row inmate executed in Florida," it said. He was still alive, but not for long.

After years of intense friendship, she and Jim had fallen out of touch. Their letters had slowed in the years that followed the birth of her children; Marieke's life had felt fuller and harder, and sometimes Jim, who had no good news to share about the state of his appeals, could not bring himself to write. Gradually, their correspondence had dwindled down to a few letters and cards a year. Then a letter went missing or unanswered, and they lost the thread. By the time the death warrant came down, five years had passed without a word between them.

As Marieke stared at Jim's photo, she felt the urgent need to make contact. The guilt she felt over not writing to him had become so crippling that it had prevented her from reaching out, but now, in an instant, it lifted.

She walked the streets of Groningen, the cheerful university city where she lived with her husband and children, in a daze. She wanted to find a card with a meaningful message that she could send to Jim, but she soon realized this was an impossible task. "Apparently no one makes cards you can give to people who just heard they will be murdered by the state," she joked darkly to a friend. It was not until she stepped into a store that featured some work by local artists that she found a card emblazoned with a single word that captured everything she was feeling—one, she hoped, that might even make Jim laugh. In large capital letters, the front of the card read, simply, "FUCK."

As the machinery of death kicked into gear, Chelsea Shirley and the rest of Jim's legal team embarked on a frantic quest to uncover any new evidence or missed leads that might persuade a judge to halt the execution. The investigator Colin Kelly woke every morning at 4:00 and drove to the Capital Collateral Regional Counsel's office in Temple Terrace, northeast of Tampa. Combing through the thousands of pages that made up the case file, he looked for any forgotten details or overlooked witness that hadn't yet been chased down. An amiable twenty-nine-year-old with a master's in social work, Kelly would head out at 9:00 a.m., armed with names and addresses, for a day of door knocking. When it grew dark, he would return home and work the phones, cold-calling people into the night.

Representing a client whom the state planned to kill, who would die unless the legal team found a way to stop it, was an assignment that drove Kelly and his colleagues to their limits. Kelly subsisted on black coffee and energy drinks, finding that the pressure of working under a death warrant robbed him of his appetite. Shirley lay awake most nights, puzzling through the labyrinth of arcane procedural rules that governed their eleventh-hour litigation. Nothing in law school had prepared her for what it felt like to try to save another human being, or for how painfully inadequate her efforts felt when measured against the enormity of the task at hand. What awaited them if they failed went unspoken. The specter of having to witness their own client's execution so disturbed

Laura Fernandez that one night after flying to Florida, she awoke barefoot in the lobby of her hotel, having sleepwalked there in a nightmare-induced fog.

Even as the long nights bled into days, there were always new leads to chase. One oppressively muggy afternoon, as Shirley and Kelly were driving around Pinellas County making unannounced visits, they pulled up outside a Spanish-colonial-style home on a quiet, well-manicured cul-de-sac in Seminole. They had little confidence that the lawyer who lived there, James Slater, would speak to them, but they knocked on the door. Slater was the original prosecutor assigned to Shelly's case in the spring of 1985. Though he left the state attorney's office before the case went to trial, he was the lead prosecutor during the critical period of the investigation when Jack was arrested and brought to Florida. Slater had questioned Jack under oath, when Jack was vying for a deal, and worked closely with investigators when Jack became distraught during a polygraph and admitted to having "cut" Shelly.

Slater had eased into retirement after spending three decades in private practice, and he greeted the two strangers warmly, talking to them in the easy, unhurried way of someone who no longer tracks his billable hours. Shirley explained that they worked at the CCRC and had come to speak to him about a murder at Indian Rocks Beach that he had once been assigned to prosecute. Slater did not seem to know about Jim's death warrant, but he immediately recognized the case; he remembered that he had been called out to the scene, as prosecutors often are when a serious crime has taken place, to get a firsthand look at the evidence. A girl had been found nude in the water, he recalled. He stood in his doorway as they talked, the ice-cold air-conditioning drifting outside. After they chatted for a while, he invited them in.

Shirley and Kelly were used to being stonewalled by anyone affiliated with the state attorney's office, but the former prosecutor ushered them into his living room and handed them bottled waters, gesturing for them to take a seat. They gathered from Slater's willingness to speak to them, and his lack of awareness about the warrant, that he was not in close contact with prosecutors. At first, as they sat and talked, it was not clear that he could be of any help. The lawyer could only summon scattered impressions of the case; he did not remember Shelly's name or anything more than the broad contours of the investigation. Then, casually, he mentioned something they had never heard before.

Slater said that "law enforcement"—he couldn't recall exactly who—told him that Jack had tried to have sex with the girl but couldn't perform.

Shirley and Kelly, who sat opposite him, listened in shocked silence. They had spent years poring over the case file but had never heard or seen this story before.

Slater continued, recounting what he said he'd been told: Jack perceived something that the girl said as teasing. Enraged, he stabbed her.

Suddenly all the disparate facts and details of the crime scene fell into place. Shirley and Kelly had reviewed the evidence again and again, and come up with theories about what might have triggered Jack, but nothing felt satisfactory. The state had never successfully answered the question of motive—it remained an enduring mystery at the center of the case—but Slater's story aligned with what they knew about Jack's temperament, as well as the evidence itself. It helped explain why no semen or forensic evidence of sexual assault had ever been found. In that moment, everything clicked, and it felt as if they finally understood what had really happened that night.

Slater's account, which he committed to a sworn affidavit, gave Jim's lawyers a way back into court. On October 8, with thirty days until the execution, they filed a motion asking the circuit court to vacate

Jim's conviction. The state had violated its legal and ethical duties, they argued, by not disclosing Jack's admissions to investigators—statements that created reasonable doubt about Jim's culpability. Those statements provided "a clear and direct motive that was Pearcy's, and Pearcy's alone." The allegations were serious enough that the latest judge who had been assigned to the case, the circuit court judge Pat Siracusa, set a hearing for October 14.

But what had appeared to be a last-minute lifeline for the defense quickly began to fray. When Shirley reached out to Slater to let him know that he would be subpoenaed to testify, he no longer sounded like the unguarded retiree she had first encountered; his voice was tense, and he picked his words carefully. The ex-prosecutor had been contacted by the state attorney's office, and that exchange appeared to have rattled him. It would emerge at the hearing that not just one prosecutor but at least three were on the call Slater received—though exactly what they told the lawyer remains unclear. Shirley felt sure that it had not been a pleasant conversation; Slater's recollections threatened to blow up the state's case.

Slater assured her that he would come to court to testify, but he said he felt pulled in two different directions and was no longer comfortable speaking to her alone. Moving forward, he said, he would only discuss the case in the presence of the state's attorneys.

Outside the courtroom on the afternoon of the hearing, Slater dabbed sweat from his forehead before he went inside to take the stand. He looked ill at ease as Kara Ottervanger, a CCRC attorney who worked with Shirley, led him through a series of questions. Initially, Slater confirmed what was in the affidavit. "I am positive that those statements were made to me," he said. He also recalled his impression, when he signed it, of the importance of what law enforcement had told him. "I had a general overall feeling that that's what this entire case was about," he said. But he explained that as the hearing approached, he had started second-guessing himself. He could not recall who had made those statements to him, "which makes me question whether it had anything to do with this case," he said. Maybe, he suggested, he had "gotten confused with another case."

Prosecutors seized upon Slater's uncertainty. His hazy memories were far too vague to have any bearing on the case, they told the judge.

In an exasperated but firm voice, Shirley addressed the court, laying the blame for Slater's equivocation on the state attorney's office. "He signed an affidavit under penalty of perjury—as an attorney, knowing exactly what that meant," she said. "It wasn't until after he got a phone call from Glenn Martin, Jim Hellickson, and Marie King that he started wavering," she said, referring to both current and former assistant state attorneys. She scoffed at the notion that Slater might have been thinking of a different fatal knifing beside an inland waterway, in Indian Rocks Beach: "In what other case in Pinellas County was a fourteen-year-old girl stabbed in this exact location, by the exact motive of this defendant, in 1985?"

The judge did not see things the same way. Two days later, Siracusa ruled not only that the defense was too late in bringing Slater forward as a witness but that his uncertain recall of facts showed him to be "wholly without credibility."

With three weeks left until Jim's execution, the ruling left his lawyers with few options beyond continuing to chase down potential witnesses. Yet Slater's story underscored just how little they knew about the original police investigation. As far back as 1999, when Harry Brody and Jeff Hazen were on the case, Jim's lawyers suspected that law enforcement had not turned over all their work, and had shared only what supported their two-man theory of the crime. By the end of the Slater hearing, the defense was more certain than ever. And more afraid that the answers they needed might always remain beyond their reach.

. . .

As each day in October slipped by, Fernandez felt the knot in her stomach tighten. *They are going to kill him,* she thought, astonished by the crushing indifference of the courts and the obliviousness of the world around her. Her mentor, George Kendall—a revered figure in the field of capital defense who had won landmark victories overturning death sentences across the South—received a distraught call from her one morning as she drove to Florida State Prison to see Jim. What could she possibly say to her client, she wanted to know, with his execution date fast approaching? "You'll be surprised by his strength," Kendall told her. "He's had time to think about this in ways that you and I haven't, and can't."

If Jim ever gave in to fear or despair, he did so privately. When Mary Kay and their daughter, Stacey, came to visit, or when his attorneys made the drive to Starke, Jim kept the mood upbeat, as if he could offset the pain of the people around him. Though the State of Florida planned to execute him, he refused to give it the satisfaction of stealing the last weeks of his life. He kept his mind focused, studying the legal briefs his attorneys brought him and frequently meeting with a lay Catholic prison chaplain who had become a trusted confidant. Every other day, he pushed through his exercise routine—500 jumping jacks, 300 push-ups, 250 sit-ups, 250 squats, and 200 curls—using a makeshift dumbbell he fashioned by filling a pillowcase with his legal paperwork.

Then, on October 23, with fifteen days to spare until his execution, he was pulled out of a visit with Mary Kay for an emergency legal call from the CCRC. The lawyer on the other end of the line, Ottervanger, was speaking quickly. She had another attorney on the call, the federal defender Brenna Egan, who jubilantly told him the news: A federal judge had granted him a limited stay of execution. The U.S. district judge William Jung was giving Jim's newly appointed federal defenders—who would raise final constitutional challenges while racing against the execution timeline—seven extra weeks to familiarize themselves with the case's long and byzantine record. Jung's decision was only a delay, not a reprieve, but it bought Jim and his lawyers a little more time. The stay would be in effect through December 30, at which point the governor would be free to set a new execution date. Jim would remain on death watch.

Jim's response was subdued. He would later apologize to his attorneys for not meeting their joy with his own, but he explained that he had already reconciled himself to the idea that his life would be ending on November 7. A limited stay of execution meant mentally preparing himself—again—for a date that was now just a bit further in the future. He later told Marieke that he was embarrassed by how he had reacted. "But I had resigned myself," he wrote. "I was so tired of it."

She wrote back, "It's hard to prepare to die, and to live at the same time."

24

CATCH THE DEVIL

That fall, for the first time since the 1980s, Jim's case started to attract attention. The *Tampa Bay Times* ran a front-page article in October on the flimsiness of the state's evidence, and the Florida Conference of Catholic Bishops sent a letter to Governor DeSantis that read, "While we urge you to stop every execution and end the use of the death penalty in Florida, this case of a veteran with evidence of innocence is especially alarming." Four death-row exonerees—all innocent of the crimes for which they were once condemned to death and sent to Florida's death row—traveled to the governor's office in Tallahassee to press their case that Jim's life should be spared.

I had spent the better part of that year digging into Jim's case and piecing together the crucial role that Skalnik played in helping prosecutors win a conviction and death sentence. On December 4, ProPublica and *The New York Times Magazine* jointly published my investigation, "False Witness," which traced Skalnik's path of destruction through the criminal justice system, and how he had helped to seal Jim's fate. Afterward, Harry L. Shorstein, Jacksonville's former top prosecutor, wrote in an editorial for the *Miami Herald*, "I urge Gov. Ron DeSantis to grant executive clemency to James Dailey and not to execute a man who was convicted and sentenced to death on the basis of unreliable jailhouse informant testimony." Smaller newspapers' editorial boards also exhorted the governor to act. "It seems clear that the state never had enough real evidence to convict Dailey," *The Daytona Beach News-Journal* wrote, "so it turned to lies—lies that have come undone." The novelist Carl Hiaasen wrote in the *Miami Herald* that "sending a man to his grave on the worthless word of Paul Skalnik wouldn't be justice. It would be a shameful travesty."

While reporting the story, I had reached out to the two attorneys who prosecuted Jim in 1987 to see if they would speak to me. Beverly Andringa did not grant me an interview, writing in an email that she had "very little memory" of the more-than-thirty-year-old case but asserting that she "never willfully and intentionally provided false evidence or testimony to a court or jury on any case." Robert Heyman did agree to speak to me, and in the course of a wide-ranging conversation he forcefully pushed back on the idea that Skalnik was unreliable. Law enforcement had vetted Skalnik, he reminded me, and other prosecutors had previously called Skalnik to the stand. "If we did not believe that his testimony was truthful, we wouldn't have had him testify," Heyman told me.

In a subsequent interview with a local TV news reporter, Heyman went a step further. "As the old saying goes, 'You've got to make a deal with a sinner to catch the devil,'" he said.

Detective Halliday declined to talk to me, referring me to the state attorney's office. By then, the office was led by Bernie McCabe, an uncompromising figure who had worked there for nearly half a century. James Russell—the former state attorney who had built the office's reputation on aggressive prosecutions—had handpicked McCabe as his successor. When I reached out for comment, McCabe did not respond. After I sent a detailed list of my findings, stretching back to the plea deal that had allowed Skalnik to avoid punishment for molesting Karen Parker, his office issued an unequivocal statement: "The state attorney's office never provided any leniency to Paul Skalnik in exchange for his testimony."

It went on to say that all details Skalnik supplied had been verified. "The state attorney's office," the statement concluded, "has never received any information to indicate that testimony from Paul Skalnik was incorrect."

On December 10, the federal judge who had granted Jim the limited stay of execution rejected a request from his attorneys for a longer stay that would allow them the time they needed to meaningfully pursue his innocence claims. "The Court has personally read every single page of this lengthy record," Judge William Jung wrote. "A thorough review shows the state's trial case against Dailey was not strong, but it was sufficient."

Time was running out, and with the stay of execution about to expire, Jim's attorneys had few good options. One of the only avenues left was a path they had traveled before: asking Jack to tell the truth about who had killed Shelly, and to say so in open court. It was a long shot, but Josh Dubin, the newest member of the defense team, believed it was worth trying. Dubin ran his own trial strategy firm in New York City and did pro bono work for the wrongly convicted in his native Florida. He had managed world champion boxers earlier in his career, an experience that gave him a knack for connecting with streetwise clients, and he told the team he thought he should go see Jack.

When Dubin arrived at Sumter Correctional Institution on a mild afternoon one week before Christmas, he was wearing jeans and a black T-shirt that showcased his tattoos—a gesture meant to establish common ground with Jack, who he knew was also heavily inked. He could see Jack eyeing him from across the concrete courtyard through a chain-link fence, and he met the sixty-four-year-old's gaze as they waited. Jack, gray-haired and weathered but still muscle-bound, was smaller than Dubin had anticipated. The lawyer was curious to see what kind of man Jack had become. His disciplinary record reflected a gradual but unmistakable change: For the first eighteen years he was behind bars, he had racked up a long list of violations, most involving drugs and alcohol, and had been sent to solitary confinement for months at a stretch. But since his last violation—when he was found, in 2015, to have stimulants in his possession—he had stayed out of trouble. That shift made the lawyer wonder if Jack might be more open to talking to him.

A corrections officer led the two men into a small visitation room. Dubin gestured toward the nicer, high-backed chair behind the desk, offering it to Jack, and settled into the smaller chair opposite him. The prison had given Dubin a beeper-like device upon his arrival—a panic button he could activate, if he felt threatened at any time by Jack, who was not handcuffed—and Dubin made a point of nonchalantly setting it aside. "I don't think I'll be needing this," he said, sliding it down the desk away from him.

Jack stared back at him and said nothing.

The corrections officer stepped outside, leaving them alone.

"Look, man, do you know why I'm here?" Dubin asked.

"I think I have an idea," Jack muttered.

"My client's stay is up in less than two weeks," Dubin said, "and then they're going to kill him."

That elicited no reaction, so Dubin forged on, explaining that while he was new to the case, he had more than a passing understanding of the evidence. "I've read every letter of every sentence of every line of the transcripts in your trial and his trial," he told Jack. "I've read every piece of discovery. I've done my own investigative work. I have a pretty good idea of what happened."

As Dubin continued, making the argument that Jim had not taken part in the murder, Jack did not challenge him. He just listened, unfazed, as the lawyer picked apart the state's narrative. Dubin laid out the sequence of events on the night of the killing, which the defense team had plotted out on a timeline. He moved through each hour of that evening and early morning, using the pay phone records to pinpoint the time at which Dwain Shaw watched Jack drive off into the night with Shelly. Dubin was suddenly aware that he was doing all the talking, and he did not know how his words were landing, but Jack never looked away.

"You know that Jim had nothing to do with this," Dubin said. "You know it, and I know it. So really, you're in a rare position right now."

"How do you say?" Jack asked.

"You've taken a life, and it's up to you whether or not you want to be involved in taking another life," Dubin said. He let Jack contemplate that for a minute. "I'm asking you to do one easy thing, and that's just to tell the truth."

Jack looked out the small window on the door, beyond which the corrections officer stood. He stared into the distance without saying a word.

The two men sat in silence. Dubin, who did not want to show his nervousness, rested the palms of his hands on the desk in front of him so that he would not fidget. He began counting to himself, reaching ninety-seven before he stopped.

Finally, Jack said, "You got something for me to sign?"

Dubin had come with a prepared statement that made a simple admission of guilt, and he slipped the single sheet of paper across the desk. If Jack signed the declaration, it would likely trigger another hearing at which he would be called to testify. Jack read it over, studying it for several minutes. The statement, though brief, was more definitive than the affidavit he had signed in 2017. "James Dailey had nothing to do with the murder of Shelly Boggio," it read. "I committed the crime alone. James Dailey was back at the house when I drove Shelly Boggio to the place where I ultimately killed her."

Jack picked up the pen the lawyer had placed on the desk. Before signing his name to the bottom, he looked up at Dubin. "I don't want my mother there this time," he said.

. . .

At midnight on December 30, the stay of execution expired. With that protection gone, Governor DeSantis now had the legal authority to set a new date for carrying out Jim's death sentence. But Jack's signed statement had already changed the trajectory of the case. Jim's attorneys had filed a copy of it with the court three days earlier, putting the circuit court judge Pat Siracusa on notice that there was new evidence to consider. The *Tampa Bay Times* trumpeted, "Other Man Claims Killing."

Upon reviewing the new evidence, Siracusa scheduled an evidentiary hearing. Jack would be called to the stand and asked, under oath, about his declaration. The hearing was to be held on March 5, 2020. DeSantis indicated that he would hold off on setting a new execution date until the courts resolved the matter. In the meantime, Jim was to remain on death watch.

That March morning, Judge Siracusa's cavernous courtroom hummed with activity. Prosecutors conferred in low voices; reporters bent over screens and tapped notes; spectators filtered in to claim their seats. Although TV cameras flanked one side of the courtroom, the lawyers and the judge went about their business, pretending to be oblivious to the presence of the media. Mary Kay sat one row behind Jim and the attorneys at the defense table, looking expectantly forward, clasping the hand of their daughter, Stacey. Also seated in the gallery was an observant, dark-haired man named Clemente Aguirre-Jarquin, who had spent a decade on Florida's death row before being exonerated in 2018. He had come to show his solidarity for the man who had become his friend behind bars.

Toward the back of the courtroom were two young women who looked uncannily like Shelly. They had the same sea-green eyes, the same high forehead, the same sandy-colored hair brightened by the Florida sun. Born three and six years after the murder, respectively, they were her half sisters, Brittany and Kalli: Frank Boggio's youngest daughters. They had never known Shelly, but they had grown up in the shadow of her killing, and after their father's death they carried on the campaign he had left unfinished. Both sisters had already gone on the local news to say that their family wanted to see Jim executed.

But the person who commanded the attention of Jim's attorneys was a white-haired woman with slightly stooped shoulders who sat silently observing from the back row. Jack's mother, Sally Simon, had come to hear what her son had to say. She lived in nearby Lakeland, and learned of his signed confession not from him but from the newspaper.

In the weeks following that shocking discovery, she had made sure Jack understood what he risked losing if he stuck with his admission that he had killed Shelly. Over the course of twelve phone calls, she told him she was devastated that he had signed the declaration, reminding him that she had stood by him since his arrest, and had proclaimed his innocence for thirty-five years. Like all such phone conversations, theirs were recorded by the Department of Corrections. "You're my son and I have been here for you 100 percent," she said. "I don't want you to sign your life away." She recalled how upset their family had been about his 2017 affidavit taking responsibility for the killing, and especially how much Jack's admission had shaken his son, Justin.

Again and again, Simon had circled back to the subject of his son, who had always exerted a particular hold on Jack. Years earlier, when Jack had fled Florida after Shelly's murder, it was Justin—then just a little boy—whom Jack had snuck back into Olathe to see, in a gamble that ended in his arrest. Their bond had endured; Justin, now forty and living in the same small city as his grandmother, remained close to his father. Simon explained that Justin did not know about the latest signed confession, but that he was bound to learn about it if Jack testified. "I'm sure when things do happen, it will be front-page news," she warned. "I don't know how he will escape it." That, she said, would be the breaking point: "Justin will probably never come visit you again, Jack. It's that serious."

At the time of the hearing, Jim and his legal team were aware only that Jack was under tremendous pressure. That pressure had become obvious ten days before the hearing, on February 24, when Jack announced that he would not be testifying. Jack's about-face prompted the defense to request recordings of recent communications between him and his mother—recordings that Jim's lawyers did not receive until the eve of the hearing. They forged ahead with their plan to put Jack on the stand, hoping that if he were made to face Jim in person, at this most desperate juncture in the case, he might be moved to back up his sworn declaration. The statement was worthless unless he was willing to corroborate it in open court, under oath.

"All right, let's bring him in," Judge Siracusa said.

As Jack was led into the courtroom, he strode past the TV cameras and took a seat in the witness box. Quickly, he glanced over at Jim, then looked away.

"Good morning, sir," Siracusa said. "Welcome back to Pinellas County."

Before swearing him in, the judge turned to address the witness, acknowledging both Jack's reluctance to testify and the court's limited power to compel him to do so. "I'm asking you as a gentleman," Siracusa said. "You're not on drugs now. You've had a lot of time to reflect: three and a half decades. If you are a good person at heart, that's who I want to appeal to today." Siracusa explained that he had asked Jack's mother to step out of the courtroom, and that he could have her stay outside while he testified, if that's what Jack wanted. "It will be my goal to make this as easy for you to do as possible because we've all been waiting a long time to hear from you."

"I didn't kill Shelly," Jack said. "I really don't plan on testifying any further."

Siracusa persisted. "We've gone to a lot of trouble to arrange this," the judge said. "You've made many sworn statements over the years, many that contradict each other. Today, I need to know the final truth. Today is when I want you to testify to what really happened."

"Well, testifying is not going to change my situation whatsoever."

"The Boggio family is here today, and I'm sure they would like to hear you testify."

"I can't help bring Shelly back or the pain her family has already suffered. I don't want to testify any further."

"I'm not accepting that as your final answer, okay?" Siracusa said.

The judge briefly excused his witness and solicited advice from the attorneys about how to persuade Jack to testify. When the discussion failed to produce a viable solution, Siracusa ordered him to return to the stand.

"Do you swear or affirm to tell the truth, the whole truth, and nothing but the truth?" Siracusa asked.

Jack held his right hand up and muttered, "I do."

"It's my hope that you're going to answer the questions of the attorneys," the judge said. "Do you have any questions for me before we start?"

"No questions, but I'm not going to testify."

"Well, we'll see what happens." The judge gestured at Dubin to step forward.

"Good morning, Mr. Pearcy," began Dubin, who today wore a gray suit and the more formal demeanor of the court. "You and I met for the first time on December 18th, 2019, at the Sumter Correctional Center, correct?"

Jack stared straight ahead and said nothing.

"Mr. Pearcy, I'd ask that you answer the question," Siracusa said sharply.

Jack remained mute.

Dubin persisted, continuing to pose questions. Each was met with silence.

The lawyer drummed his fingers on the lectern; he glanced up at the ceiling. Finally, Dubin conceded, "He's obviously an adverse witness, Your Honor."

Visibly frustrated, the judge turned toward Jack. "I have to tell you I'm pretty disappointed here," he said. He went on to explain that Jack would not be afforded any more chances to clear up the confusion he had caused with his contradictory accounts of the murder. "You've given basically two different stories," the judge said. "Why can't we just get another two hours of your time and hear your testimony? And we'll all be done with this and we can go our separate ways? Can we do that?"

"No, sir," Jack said, his voice barely audible.

"Nothing I can do or say to change your mind?"

"No, sir."

Siracusa shook his head. "All right," he finally said. "Mr. Pearcy can go."

Jack kept his gaze fixed on the floor as two bailiffs led him out of the courtroom. Jim stared after him.

25

LOCKDOWN

None of us who sat shoulder to shoulder in Judge Siracusa's courtroom understood that life as we knew it was about to end. Headlines warned of a deadly respiratory virus that was rapidly spreading across the globe, yet for most of us COVID-19 still remained something of a willful abstraction—a distant threat. Six days after the hearing, on March 11, 2020, the World Health Organization shattered any illusions by announcing that COVID-19 was officially a pandemic, making clear that nowhere would be spared. Two days later, President Donald Trump declared a national emergency.

Jim was already back at Florida State Prison, on death watch. The irony was not lost on him: where better to preserve his life, as a lethal virus spread uncontrolled, than in near-total isolation, cut off from society? The prison suspended all nonessential visits, barring everyone except attorneys who needed to meet with their clients. There would be no more time with Mary Kay, whose physical presence, even through a glass partition, had kept his hope alive. No more discursive conversations with Brother Dale Recinella, the death-row chaplain whose companionship comforted him. Jim watched on the small TV just outside his cell as the rest of humanity retreated into its own kind of solitary confinement. The news showed him a world he barely recognized: empty streets and highways, vacant office buildings, darkened storefronts, closed schools and deserted playgrounds, churches and sports arenas that had descended into ghostly silence.

From the isolation of my own home in Austin, I kept reporting in the stolen moments I found between helping my children navigate online school and the strange new rituals of pandemic life. Sitting down at my laptop one night after dinner, the house quiet for the first time all day, I pulled up something I had been eager to read: the transcript of a hearing held in Jim's case that February, weeks before the evidentiary hearing at which Jack refused to testify. I hadn't been in Florida at the time of the February hearing, but afterward I learned that the state attorney's office had mentioned my reporting on Skalnik in its comments to the court, calling my account of Karen Parker's case misleading. One prosecutor had apparently gone so far as to attack Karen's own truthfulness. Now, with the transcript in front of me, I could finally see for myself exactly what had been said.

The hearing focused on an issue that Jim's lawyers wanted to explore at the upcoming evidentiary hearing: whether prosecutors knew that Skalnik had been charged with lewd-and-lascivious conduct on a child when they called him to testify at Jim's trial. Skalnik had not disclosed the charge when he took the stand. Handwritten notes from the trial, which Robert Heyman had recently acknowledged were his, had brought the issue to the forefront; by Skalnik's name, the words "sex assault" had been crossed out. Jim's lawyers argued that the state had allowed Skalnik to give misleading testimony, leaving the jury without crucial information to assess his reliability. But reading the transcript, I could see that the state attorney's office had gone to great lengths to shift Judge Siracusa's attention away from the prosecutors' handling of Skalnik and toward the character of his twelve-year-old accuser.

"I wanted to address the 1982 lewd and lascivious [case]," said the assistant state attorney Sara Macks:

> These most recent Skalnik pieces from *The New York Times,* along with statements that have been made in court today, do not paint an accurate picture of the problems that were in that case. There were a lot of problems with the trial witness herself. Unfortunately, lewd and lascivious charges are always difficult to prove. They are difficult to take to trial. It is often a he-said-she-said type of case, and there were some credibility issues with the witness herself, unfortunately. In the end we investigated the case, and we determined that we couldn't bring it to prosecution. In fact, we investigated the case, and unfortunately some of the facts that we found out about the case was that this young girl had multiple issues. You know, she had—eventually, she ran away from home not too long after reporting this to law enforcement. But there had been multiple issues with her and her family in the past, some concerns about her sexual activity in general. And then more particularly Paul Skalnik was someone who was known to the family. He had found out about some of her sexual activity and went to her parents. Not long after he went to her parents, these allegations were made. As always, that's a concerning fact for prosecution. So this isn't a very simple case of somebody gets a deal and then, based on testimony, we drop the charges.

I read the passage again and again. *There were a lot of problems with the trial witness herself.*

A cold transcript never captures the nuances of the spoken word, but even on the page, with the words stripped of all tone and inflection, I could feel, in Judge Siracusa's response to the prosecutor, his unease. It was not the 1980s, but 2020, when the #MeToo movement had already reshaped public conversations about power and consent. Macks was suggesting that a twelve-year-old who had reported a sexual assault to law enforcement was both promiscuous and untrustworthy—all in service of shoring up the credibility of the state's witness. Yet rather than probe what Macks was saying, the judge quickly reframed the prosecutor's comments, making them sound more palatable than they were. "Just to be clear—and, in an abundance of caution, so your statements aren't misunderstood—the rape shield laws in Florida didn't come into effect until the mid-nineties," he said, referring to legal safeguards that protect sexual assault victims from having their sexual history used against them in court. "Are you suggesting that is one of the possible problems that you had, with the prior activity that the victim had in her past?"

"Correct," Macks said. "There was some concern about that becoming an element of the trial."

Macks did not move on; she continued to press the point that it was Skalnik's accuser, not Skalnik himself, who was unreliable. "We also never got any corroboration," she told the judge. "You can't always get corroboration in these lewd-and-lascivious cases, and that was another factor. There was never any corroboration that we were able to obtain. Mr. Skalnik always denied it from the beginning. He was insistent that it never happened." Of course, the investigative reports in the case tell a different story, because they include eyewitness accounts of the assault from Karen's neighbor and the neighbor's boyfriend.

LISA ROGERS IN 1977, WHEN SHE WAS FOURTEEN YEARS OLD

As I read Macks's words, I felt sick. Weeks earlier, I had received a wrenching phone call from Lisa Rogers, now in her fifties and running an animal rescue for injured horses. There was a part of her story that she hadn't shared with me, she said—from back when she was a teenager in Friendswood, Texas, watching helplessly as Skalnik charmed her mother, Penny, and upended their lives. Lisa confirmed what I had long suspected: Skalnik, she said, had molested her too.

I thought of Lisa as I stared at the transcript, and how she had endured decades of shame and silence. I thought of Karen Parker, who had been brave enough to take a polygraph exam and say that she wanted to move forward with a criminal prosecution, only to be abandoned by a prosecutor's office that was still second-guessing her. I thought of Misty Anderson, who had lived in private terror before confiding in an adult that Skalnik was sexually abusing her—a fate she might have been spared had Skalnik been held to account for what he did to Karen. I thought of all the other girls he had hurt; I was sure there were more. And then I thought of the lawyers at the state attorney's office, so determined to preserve a conviction that they were willing to defend the indefensible.

In those first terrifying weeks of the pandemic, as nursing homes locked down and barred outside visitors, my mind often turned to Skalnik, now trapped in a place that made him particularly vulnerable to the virus. Late one evening, when my children were asleep and my laptop was open before me, I pulled up Texas's sex offender registry, the database that had led me to the nursing home in Corsicana. Where detailed information had once appeared next to his name, now there were only two words: "status change."

When I contacted the nursing home the next morning, I was told that Skalnik was no longer there, but no other information was forthcoming. My repeated calls to his federal parole officer went unreturned. Eventually, I reached a health aide who had cared for Skalnik, who informed me that he had been very ill and transferred to a local hospital weeks earlier. When I contacted the hospital, I was informed that the institution was not currently caring for any patients by that name. *Not currently.* I turned that phrase over in my mind. Only then did it occur to me that Skalnik might be dead.

Skalnik had professed to be on death's door for so long that I had assumed, even in the diminished state I had seen him in, that he was exaggerating his condition, if not outright faking. This assumption had only been reinforced when I spoke with a former cellmate of his, who contacted me after the publication of my story to tell me about the different schemes Skalnik had run when they were in federal prison together just two years earlier, including feigning an illness to get transferred to a Dallas hospital. He was sure Skalnik was not actually bedridden, as I had described him in the article. "If you presented him with a moneymaking opportunity, he'd get up and walk out the door," the former cellmate said.

But now doubt crept in, and I continued making calls. There could not have been a worse time to try to shake loose information. Government offices had sent most of their employees home, and anyone I was able to reach was overwhelmed. I called the Navarro County Sheriff's Office, the Corsicana Police Department, and the county's four justices of the peace, but made little headway. Finally, a friendly voice answered the phone at one of the local funeral homes. "Paul Skalnik?" she said. "Yes, ma'am, we have him. Are you family?"

Skalnik had died on March 10, the woman at the funeral home told me. She did not know the cause of death, and despite the many calls and record requests I would make in the months to come, I was never able to find out what, exactly, had killed him. COVID was likely *not* to blame; Navarro County would not record its first coronavirus death until April. Later, I would marvel at Skalnik's timing; he died just one day before the virus was declared a pandemic. The man who had spent a lifetime evading consequences had skipped out on the collective hardship and heartbreak that was to follow.

I told the woman on the other end of the line that Skalnik had few living family members, and the relatives he did have were estranged from him. Assuming no one came forward, I asked, what would become of his remains? She explained that the county would pay for cremation services, and the funeral home would keep them indefinitely. He wouldn't even have the modest dignity of a pauper's grave, I realized. It was a humble end for a man with delusions of grandeur: a box of ashes on a shelf, unclaimed.

My relationship with Skalnik had begun with a con. When I first met him, in federal prison, he sized me up instantly. He saw my hunger for a story no other journalist had—not just any story, but a story that mattered, a story with real life-and-death consequences. So, he gave me exactly what I wanted: He promised he would reveal everything, and in the end, of course, he delivered nothing. My reporting became an attempt to remedy that—to uncover and reconstruct what really happened. But I never forgot how strong that pull was to believe him. We hear what we want to hear.

Skalnik had cast such a long shadow over the lives of the people I had met in my reporting that as I reached out to share the news of his passing, I encountered uniform disbelief. Many suggested that his death must be another elaborate deception. Even after I obtained a death verification letter from the Texas Department of State Health Services, suspicion lingered that he had somehow, as a final act, managed to dupe everyone.

Perhaps it was easier to imagine him as a criminal mastermind who had faked his own death than to confront the truth: What made him so dangerous was not his intelligence or cunning, but rather how readily the institutions that were supposed to uphold the law and protect the most vulnerable had amplified his lies. These institutions indulged his pathologies, granting him power and influence he could never have achieved on his own, effectively giving him license to commit greater crimes. Without them, Skalnik would have been nothing more than a small-time con man.

EPILOGUE

For the first half of 2020, Jim remained marooned on death watch. Like nearly everything else during the pandemic lockdowns, the criminal justice system ground to a halt. Courthouses were shuttered, jury trials suspended. Florida ceased carrying out executions, and as the COVID-19 crisis deepened, the death penalty receded as a priority for Governor DeSantis. On the last day of June, Jim was shackled, driven a little more than a mile down State Road 16, and returned to Union Correctional Institution, to death row. He had endured 279 days on death watch.

Jim felt certain that he had only dodged the executioner temporarily. A different specter loomed now that he was no longer in isolation: Prisons had become viral hot spots. In late August, COVID reached death row, and many of the men were running fevers; in September, two inmates at the prison died from the virus. With death row's close quarters and poor ventilation, Jim figured it was only a matter of time before the virus found its way to him—though he had still not gotten sick by the time he received the vaccine in the spring of 2021. The absurdity of receiving a lifesaving treatment from the same system that was methodically planning his death was not lost on Jim. Yet with executions in Florida at a standstill, he found himself carrying on in a strange limbo. The pandemic had accomplished what decades of appeals could not: suspending his execution indefinitely.

Mary Kay and Stacey came to see Jim as soon as visits resumed that summer, and their reunions, in which their voices overlapped in their eagerness to share their news, sustained him. The hardest moments came afterward, knowing they were heading home without him, and he had to return to his cell alone. Yet Marieke was struck by his refusal to succumb to hopelessness. She introduced him to a Dutch expression—*met de moed der wanhoop*, or "with the courage of despair"—for which there is no exact English translation. "It acknowledges that you are trying to do something despite knowing it probably won't work, but that you have to do it anyway," she wrote to him. "It is often accompanied by a 'What can you do?' kind of shoulder shrug. It acknowledges that you can be simultaneously scared, and even know you might fail—but that you are still going to try, and to continue to hope. It acknowledges the resilience you only find when tested."

In the late summer of 2022, as talk of DeSantis's presidential ambitions grew, two Florida-based political websites published articles that took aim at the governor for not carrying out more executions. "DeSantis, who presents himself as a 'law-and-order' leader, lags far behind his most recent Republican predecessors," observed *The Capitolist*. "His inaction could leave him open to criticism for being soft on violent criminals." *Florida Politics* ran a similar story under the headline "Not So Deadly DeSantis," which referenced Jim's case. The article explained that the Florida Supreme Court had denied Jim's latest appeal in the fall of 2021, adding, "DeSantis, though, hasn't signed a subsequent death warrant."

As the *Florida Politics* report had made clear, Jim was in a precarious position; without any claims left in court, there was nothing to shield him should DeSantis choose to resume executions.

Though Jim's attorneys had petitioned the U.S. Supreme Court, its justices declined to intervene. At any moment, the governor could set another execution date, and the news would arrive suddenly, without warning. Then, on January 23, 2023, four months before launching his presidential bid, DeSantis signed a death warrant, but the warrant was for another prisoner: Donald David Dillbeck. After more than three years of uncertainty, executions were resuming—but not with Jim.

DeSantis signed three more death warrants that spring, none of which bore Jim's name. Just as the process by which the governor had originally selected Jim for execution had been inscrutable, so too were the reasons why DeSantis now decided to pass him over, leaving Jim unsure of when he might fall into the governor's sights again. "Of course I'm thankful I'm still around," he wrote to Marieke. By then, he had watched eighty-five death-row inmates—some of whom he had grown to count as friends—go to their deaths. "But I'm so very tired of being locked up. I'm tired of the same prison routine, I'm tired of the same faces all the time, I'm tired of the courts not giving me a chance to go home, I'm tired of the added warrant pressure. In fact, I'm just plain fucking tired."

DeSantis launched his presidential campaign that May, and as he crisscrossed early primary states, he signed two more death warrants: again, for other men. A law-and-order agenda anchored his political platform, and in early polling DeSantis emerged as the most formidable challenger to Donald Trump. But as a candidate, he never lived up to his early promise, and his momentum was short-lived. Unable to match Trump's dominance in a crowded field, DeSantis dropped out of the race on January 21, 2024. There was guarded hope among the lawyers who represented Florida's condemned that, at least for a time, death row would not serve as a stage for the governor's national political ambitions. For the remainder of that year, DeSantis signed just one death warrant.

. . .

That fall, the National Registry of Exonerations published a little-noticed report on the prevalence of jailhouse witnesses in wrongful convictions. Overall, the report found, their testimony had been a factor in 7 percent of cases listed on the registry. But in death cases specifically, the picture was starkly different. Of the 142 people on the registry who had been freed from death row, a full 25 percent had been condemned with the help of a jailhouse witness. The report's authors emphasized that capital cases are uniquely high stakes; they bring unparalleled public attention, intense pressure to win a conviction, and life-or-death consequences. "Those high stakes," the authors wrote, "encourage prosecutors to cut deals or do other favors for prisoners in return for testimony, which can lead to perjury."

Twenty years earlier, in 2004, a seminal study conducted by Northwestern Law School's Center on Wrongful Convictions came to a similar conclusion, finding that testimony from jailhouse witnesses and other criminal informants was the leading cause of wrongful convictions in capital cases. Nevertheless, its authors wrote, "the reality is that neither legislatures nor courts are about to ban snitch testimony in the prevailing tough-on-crime political climate." Their prediction proved accurate in the years that followed. More recently, as criminal justice reform has gained momentum, the idea of subjecting such testimony to greater scrutiny has begun to gain traction. Since 2017, at least a dozen states have enacted legislation that tries to curb or regulate the use of jailhouse witnesses, such as mandating pretrial "reliability hearings" to vet testimony before it can reach jurors and establishing tracking systems that show whether a jailhouse witness has testified in other cases.

Still, in a vast majority of states, no reforms have been passed at all. Perjury charges for jailhouse witnesses are rare, even when their testimony is later proved to have been demonstrably false.

So, too, are any meaningful consequences for prosecutors who fail to disclose agreements made with a jailhouse witness at the time of trial, or who mislead juries into thinking that the witness will not receive rewards after testifying, or who conceal facts about the witness's criminal history that might undermine his credibility. No legislation has yet addressed the outsized but largely invisible role that jailhouse witnesses play in plea deals, in which prosecutors may use the mere specter of their future testimony to intimidate defendants into not taking their cases to trial. And more radical ideas—like an outright ban on jailhouse witnesses in capital cases—have stalled, allowing prosecutors to continue using snitch testimony to secure the harshest, most irrevocable punishment.

Trump's return to power ended the relative calm on Florida's death row. After taking office on January 20, 2025, the new president urged prosecutors to more aggressively seek the death penalty, and DeSantis began signing death warrants with renewed intensity. By the end of the year, Florida had executed nineteen men, far outpacing every other state that carried out executions. DeSantis also signed legislation broadening the list of crimes punishable by death and expanded the way executions can be carried out, paving the way for alternative methods such as hanging, nitrogen gas, or firing squad. The sharp rise in executions, wrote the *South Florida Sun Sentinel*'s editorial board that summer, "gives rise to wonder: Why the sudden rush? Is it another sign that he's planning another run for president in 2028? Would he campaign as the governor who tried to empty his state's death row?"

Jim came to dread the afternoons, when the warrants were typically delivered to death row. Prison officials would appear unexpectedly, their approach heralded by the jingle of the restraint chains they carried. As the delegation advanced down the row, the prisoners would listen; from their cells, they could only see their

MARY KAY DOLLAR AND JIM DAILEY AT UNION CORRECTIONAL INSTITUTION IN RAIFORD, FLORIDA, ON APRIL 8, 2023

neighbors, so they tracked the procession by sound, straining to hear who would be taken to death watch. Not a word was spoken until the officials reached the right cell, and one would ask, "Name and ID number?" Then there would be the groan of a cell door opening, the clatter of leg irons, feet shuffling as another man was led away. "Every afternoon," Jim told Laura Fernandez when she paid him a visit, "I wonder if they are going to come and get me."

Jim is, as of this writing, still on death row, but he has never given up on the possibility of a happy ending. In his visits with Mary Kay, conversations with his lawyers, and letters to friends, he always strikes an upbeat note, telling them that he still harbors hope that he will one day return home. But coming so close to execution has stripped him of any pretenses. He understands that the future he longs to share with Mary Kay, in which they would live together and care for each other as they grow old, might lie beyond his reach. Where he had once prefaced his thoughts about the future with "When I come home," now he sometimes says, simply, "If I come home."

When he first arrived at death row and heard some of the prisoners speak about how long they had been there, ten years had seemed unfathomable. Now he is closing in on forty. Jim knows there are other men like him on death row whose cases are also clouded with questions, who are trapped in a judicial limbo that will neither free nor kill them. Many of them are, like him, senior citizens. Though he had at first jokingly called himself "Old Man" in his correspondence with Marieke, now he really is one. June 11, 2026, marked his eightieth birthday.

After nearly four decades of imprisonment, his body is surrendering to time. His heart, once strong, now flutters. Cataracts cloud his vision. He has lost many of his teeth—nineteen in all—and the partial dentures he has been issued sit uncomfortably in his mouth, making the simple act of eating a daily struggle. Gout has settled into his joints, sometimes flaring with such intensity that he is almost blinded by the pain. Though his mind is still sharp, he can feel that he is no longer as strong or resilient as he once was. Having watched prisoners older than him grow frail or succumb to the end stages of terminal illnesses, he knows the cold reality that awaits him, even if he is never called up for execution. A natural death behind bars means dying alone.

His escape is his daily practice of painting—mostly landscapes, which he renders with modest art supplies from the commissary, images of a natural world he no longer inhabits. They pulse with life: a sugar maple that stands orange crimson against a row of evergreens; a stream shrouded by ferns; a rose-streaked sky ablaze at sunset; a solemn, snow-draped peak cloaked in shadows; a wave cresting in moonlight, the moment before it breaks; a farm half buried in snow; a single white water lily reflected in dark emerald water; a cobalt-blue swimming hole in Kansas that he frequented as a child. He works from photographs and old memories, bending over his canvases until his back aches.

Should Jim receive another execution date, and should the courts not step in to stop it, he will be the oldest person ever put to death in Florida. If that day comes, he will be told to walk from a holding cell to the execution chamber, where he will lie down on the gurney. Leather restraining straps will be fastened across his body, and an IV line will be inserted into his arm. Finally, the signal will be given to begin the flow of lethal drugs: a sedative, followed by a paralytic, and then potassium acetate to stop his heart. At that moment, the State of Florida will be asking its citizens to trust that Jim killed Shelly that night beside the dark water, and that he received a fair trial, and that justice has finally been served. It will be asking them, as it has time and time again, to believe the word of Paul Skalnik.

ACKNOWLEDGMENTS

Karen Parker told me a story that I never forgot. After running away from home and dropping out of high school, she earned her GED and became a corrections officer, steadily climbing the ranks at a maximum-security penitentiary outside of Pensacola until she reached the role of captain. Every so often, when she was catching up on paperwork, she would log into the inmate database and type in her best approximation of the name whose spelling she didn't quite know: *Scalnick, Scalnik, Skalnick, Skalnik.* She searched year after year, until she retired from the Florida Department of Corrections in 2013, but her searches never turned up anything. What happened to Skalnik, and how he was able to avoid prison time, are laid out in this book, but to her it remained a mystery until we first spoke.

I'm grateful to Karen and everyone else who took the time to talk to me. While elements of Skalnik's past are still unknown, I hope this book offers some clarity to the people whose lives he altered. I'm particularly thankful to Karen, Misty Anderson, and Lisa Rogers for entrusting me with their stories; to Suzanne Bourdeau and Donna Mackey, who sleuthed with me into Skalnik's past; and to Mary Kay Dollar and Marieke Laauwen, who helped me better understand Jim Dailey. For the many people who unearthed old letters, photos, and journals and revisited painful memories, I am deeply appreciative.

This book exists only because Laura Fernandez began digging into Skalnik's role as a jailhouse witness more than a decade ago, while she was trying to keep a Florida prisoner named Richard Cooper from being executed. Without her, Skalnik's story would have remained buried. I'm profoundly thankful to her for her meticulous investigative work and the foundation it provided—and for the countless hours she spent helping me understand the complex, often comically byzantine, record. It was Rachel Aviv who connected me with Laura, setting me on this path. I will forever be grateful.

Hilary Redmon, my editor, was a brilliant, hands-on partner throughout this project. Time and again, her instinct for what this book could be—and how to get it there—was uncannily correct. I'm grateful that she pushed me to make this manuscript the very best it could be, and for often seeing it with more clarity than I did. Working with her has been one of the great privileges of my career.

Kate Rodemann, my longtime friend and former magazine editor, read multiple drafts and counseled me at every stage of this project. Book writing can be a lonely endeavor, but Kate provided equal parts moral support, cheerleading, and tough love. From small tweaks in language to big ideas that animate the manuscript, her guidance is evident throughout. She always made this book feel possible.

David Patterson, my agent, spent many years pretending to believe me when I assured him that I would never write a book, even as he was quietly laying the groundwork for when I was finally ready. I'm enormously grateful for his guidance. Thanks as well to Chandler Wickers, who provided critical support, and to Jane Finigan, who looked out for my interests in the UK and beyond.

This book evolved from an article co-published by ProPublica and *The New York Times Magazine*. It would be hard to overstate the brilliance of my editors, Tracy Weber and Ilena Silverman, who took my mountain of reporting and sharpened it into a clear and powerful narrative. I carried the lessons I learned from their editing with me into the book, which is better in every way because of them. Steve Engelberg at ProPublica and Jake Silverstein at the *Times Magazine* supported this book from the beginning and gave me precious time to write it. Jake, whom I've been lucky enough to work with for much of my career, suggested early on that I frame my article on Skalnik around the case of Jim Dailey.

Thanks to the original *New York Times Magazine* fact-checkers who worked on this piece, Cynthia Cotts, Rob Liguori, and Steven Stern, whose rigor ensured that the story withstood scrutiny. Thanks to Arya Sundaram, for early book research, and Steve Merlan, who helped me obtain Skalnik's FBI file. Thanks to photographer Eli Durst, who traveled with me to Florida's death row and later persuaded Skalnik to be photographed in a Texas nursing home. Special thanks to Cyd Oppenheimer for her spreadsheets and keen insight, and, perhaps most crucially, for pointing me toward the indispensable Kenny Rodgers.

This book would not have been possible without the Watchdog Writers Group, a fellowship that backs investigative reporters while they work on ambitious, long-term projects, and that provided crucial financial and emotional support during the writing of this book. I will forever be grateful to Chris Leonard, its director; I hope I can pay forward even a fraction of the generosity he showed me. It was thanks to WWG that I had the good fortune of working with Steve Garrison, a dogged investigative reporter who did essential research early on in the book-writing process. I'm also grateful to those who were in the fellowship with me, particularly Michael Grunwald, Mya Frazier, and Shoshana Walter.

I would like to thank Jordan Pavlin for her wholehearted belief in this book. I feel incredibly lucky to have such a supportive publisher. Thanks to everyone at Knopf who worked tirelessly behind the scenes to champion this book: Gabrielle Brooks, Claire Leonard, Emily Murphy, Nora Reichard, Kelly Shi, Betty Lew, Tyler Comrie, Kayla Miller-Sissoko, and Erinn Hartman. I am deeply grateful for their dedication and for the faith they placed in this project. Special thanks to Sierra Fang-Horvath for patiently and expertly guiding me through the editorial process. I'm also thankful to Mala Sanghera-Warren at Octopus Books, my UK publisher, whose feedback on my first draft was invaluable. I'll always be grateful to Andy Ward, at Random House, for his wise words when I asked him how to reimagine a magazine story as a book: "Forget the magazine story exists."

Nicole Cásarez, Elon Green, and Sarah Weinman read the manuscript when it was still finding its shape and gave indispensable feedback. I'm grateful to each of them for their insight, generosity, and steady friendship over these last few years. Thanks to the other exceptional journalists who provided essential guidance while I was writing: Ken Armstrong, Nate Blakeslee, Keri Blakinger, Maurice Chammah, Kate Winkler Dawson, Jessica Goudeau, Michael Hall, Pat Meisol, Janet Reitman, Dan Sullivan, and, in particular, Ethan Brown. I'll always be indebted to Skip Hollandsworth, Evan Smith, and Mimi Swartz for teaching me how to tell a story.

Gilbert King, whose menschiness is unmatched, has championed this book since the very beginning. Megan Abbott, Rachel Aviv, Bryan Burrough, Stephen Harrigan, Patrick Radden Keefe, Bob Kolker, and Lawrence Wright were kind enough to take time away from their own writing to read this book and offer their early support. I will forever be grateful. Thanks to Casey Cep and Kathryn Schulz for a particularly helpful conversation during the book-writing process, and to David Grann for another. I deeply appreciate the kindness of these extraordinary writers.

Thank you to Paul Tough and Paula Shapiro, who gave me a place to work on this book during the pandemic and in the summers that followed. Your encouragement and generosity made this project possible. I'm also grateful to David Brearley and Molly O'Halloran for opening their doors to me. Thanks as well to the village that ensured my children were thriving while I was writing this book—in particular, Jenny Ford, Lisa Henken and Randy Ramirez, Angie Marshall, Stephennie Mulder, and Robyn Strelitz. I'm lucky to count them as friends, and luckier still that they have been such steadfast co-parents. Special thanks to Daniela Di-Capua.

My thanks also go to the multitalented Lauren Smith Ford, who swooped in at the last minute when I needed her help most, and to the freakishly talented Peter Yang, who made me feel comfortable in front of the camera. Additional thanks to the many other friends whose enthusiasm for this project buoyed me at different points along the way, including Sarah Andre, Andrew Case, Tucker Carrington, Kim Green, Hal Humphries, Jason Neulander, and Tisa Watson.

I'm grateful to Sarah Jane Lapp for always offering me encouragement and understanding. To Margaret Brown for the way her work challenged me to rethink how these stories can be told. To Jenny Lloyd for reminding me that I needed to step away from my desk and go outside. To Karen Olsson for making me want to be a better writer. To Katy Vine for our precious morning phone calls, which always leave me feeling better than when we began. To Glenn Brown and John Spong for much-needed mirth. And to Sarah Hepola for running this marathon alongside me. We did it.

I would not have been able to write this book without the steadfast support of my family. My mother, Margery Colloff, has championed my writing since I was eight years old, when she photocopied and bound a "book" I'd written about a Scottish terrier. Her encouragement has meant everything to me. The steady, calming presence of my brother, David, helped me on my most anxious days.

Chad Nichols, my husband, never asked when this book would be done. Instead, he made sure I always had the time and space to write. I can't imagine a greater act of patience, or of love. No words can express how thankful I am to him and our two amazing children, Jake and Lucy, who made me laugh even when I was writing about difficult things. I'm grateful for every moment we have together.

NOTES ON SOURCES

To reconstruct Paul Skalnik's forty-three-year odyssey through the criminal justice system, I drew on voluminous court records dating back to the 1970s, in both Florida and Texas, from nearly forty different criminal cases, including trial transcripts, pretrial interviews, and depositions. I also relied on thousands of pages of police reports, arrest records, jail logs, probation and parole records, and correspondence I uncovered by filing more than a hundred public records requests. This research built on the extraordinary groundwork laid by the attorney Laura Fernandez, whose years of meticulous investigation into Skalnik's history produced a vast archive of documents and an exhaustive timeline of his cases and movements through Florida's courts and jails. When I first saw the timeline, it was close to one hundred pages long; with the addition of new material, including findings from my reporting that traced Skalnik's earliest cooperation with prosecutors to Texas in the 1970s, it reached 257 pages. That provided the architecture for my understanding of Skalnik's long career as a jailhouse witness.

When key figures in this story declined to be interviewed, I relied on affidavits and sworn testimony they had given over the years, as well as prior statements, investigative reports, or notes of theirs that I was able to locate. The book also draws on interviews I conducted with upwards of eighty people who crossed paths with Skalnik, some of whom are not named. They include men who served time with him, victims of his crimes, defendants he testified against, ex-wives and former fiancées, and members of his family.

I reached out to the state attorney's office in Clearwater, Florida, for comment on material included in the book that had not appeared in my earlier magazine reporting but received no response. Beverly Andringa (who was known as Beverly Andrews at the time that she prosecuted Jim Dailey) reiterated that she never willfully or intentionally presented false testimony. Robert Heyman, who prosecuted the case with her, emphasized that, apart from Skalnik's testimony, the state's case rested on other evidence—including Jack Pearcy's statements placing Jim at the crime scene and witness testimony about Jim's wet pants—which were central to the prosecution's theory of events. The lead investigator in the case, John Halliday, did not respond to requests for comment, nor did Henry Andringa, who represented Dailey at trial.

I'm grateful to the *St. Petersburg Times* reporters who covered the Pinellas County courts in the 1980s; their day-to-day accounts of the proceedings preserved details that would otherwise have been lost. Their contemporaneous reporting—particularly that of Pat Meisol—was essential to rebuilding the events of that period.

This book was deeply informed by the scholarship of the Harvard Law School professor Alexandra Natapoff. Her book *Snitching: Criminal Informants and the Erosion of American Justice* (New York University Press, 2009) is essential reading.

A brief note on language: I decided to use the term "jailhouse witness" throughout the book instead of the more common "jailhouse informant." To me, "informant" suggests a reliable source with direct knowledge of the evidence; the term implicitly lends credibility to the person's testimony. Some legal scholars and attorneys use the term "incentivized informant" or "incentivized witness" to highlight that much of this testimony is offered in exchange for benefits or leniency. While more precise, those phrases can be unwieldy, so for readability I stuck with "jailhouse witness."

This book would not have been possible without Florida's expansive public information laws, which are meant to ensure transparency and accountability. Those statutes, which guarantee public access to most government records, are now under threat as some lawmakers seek to weaken them.

CHAPTER 1: SKALNIK

Conversations I had with Lisa Rogers over the course of several years formed the foundation of this chapter. Without her, I would have had little understanding of this critical period in Skalnik's life. Lisa's brother, Lynn, was also kind enough to talk to me. Their mother, Penny, died in 2005.

Public records provided the scaffolding of this chapter. Skalnik's arrest records, jail records, and marriage records were crucial, as were offense reports and investigative notes that chronicled his criminal activity. In Texas, these records came from the Harris County Clerk's Office and the Harris County Sheriff's Office. (The Galveston County Sheriff's Office and the Friendswood Police Department did not retain records from this period.) In Florida, these records are held at the Orange County Clerk of Courts Office in Orlando. Marriage records came from the Clark County Clerk's Office in Nevada.

My descriptions of Skalnik—and how he spoke, moved, and acted—were informed not only by interviews but by my own observations of him when I spent time with him in 2018 and 2019. For background on Southwest Airlines, I consulted Joseph Guinto, "Hot Pants, Love Potions, and the Go-Go Genesis of Southwest Airlines," *Texas Monthly,* July 2021.

I'm indebted to Kenny Rodgers, who illuminated one of the biggest questions I had when I began working on this book: How and why did Skalnik first become a jailhouse witness? Rodgers went so far as to dig up his old journals, which laid out his work, day by day, during the late 1970s and proved to be invaluable. So, too, did details from his memoir, *Special Crimes: Memoirs of a D.A. Investigator* (Special Crimes Press, 2020). My conversations with Rodgers deepened my understanding both of this time in Houston and of how prosecutors work with these kinds of witnesses.

Rodgers's memories of Skalnik from their time together at the New Mexico Military Institute aligned with those of two other classmates I interviewed, John Glover and Tom Rogers (no relation to Penny). Additionally, Rodgers's impression of Skalnik's brief time in the Marines was consistent with dates in Skalnik's military records, which are housed at the National Archives' National Personnel Records Center in St. Louis.

CHAPTER 2: FOOL ME ONCE

This chapter drew from the work of the late Tom Curtis, whose groundbreaking reporting on the Houston Police Department in the 1970s, including the José Campos Torres case, was revelatory both in its time and today. His cover story for the September 1977 issue of *Texas Monthly*, "Support Your Local Police (or Else)," is the definitive contemporaneous account of the Torres case and the toxic culture that pervaded the police department at that time. His investigative feature "The Throwdown," *Texas Monthly*, August 1979, was also essential. Several pieces he wrote for *The Washington Post* were helpful, especially his June 12, 1977, story, "Police in Houston Pictured as Brutal and Unchecked."

An important companion piece to Curtis's work, which also informed this chapter, is Jim Atkinson's "The Ragged Edge," *Texas Monthly*, December 1982. My description of the bayou drew on my personal observations as well as Geoff Winningham's breathtaking book of photography, *Along Forgotten River: Photographs of Buffalo Bayou and the Houston Ship Channel, 1997–2001* (Texas State Historical Association, 2003).

Two excellent pieces of audio journalism were also key to my understanding of this period: Maggie Freleng, "Remembering Moody Park: The Death That Sparked a Houston Riot," *Latino USA*, October 21, 2016; and the first two episodes of the 2021 podcast *Chicano Squad*, by Cristela Alonzo and Eva Ruth Moravec.

I gleaned added details about the Torres case and the greater context of police brutality at that time from Dan Berger's *The Hidden 1970s: Histories of Radicalism* (Rutgers University Press, 2010) and Dwight Watson's *Race and the Houston Police Department, 1930–1990: A Change Did Come* (Texas A&M University Press, 2005). Additionally, I was lucky to find the Texas Archive of the Moving Image's repository of local TV news coverage. It includes raw footage of the Moody Park riot, which helped me visualize what happened that night.

My description of the Moody Park Three trial drew from the appellate record in *Thomas Hirschi v. The State of Texas*, Texas State Library and

Archives, Austin. That record includes most of the transcript of the 1979 trial. I also relied on Gary Taylor's coverage for the now-defunct *Houston Post.* Taylor was kind enough to unearth his original clips and share his memories.

The prosecutor Andy Tobias passed away in 2012. However, I was fortunate enough to speak with all of the Moody Park Three: Thomas Hirschi, Travis Morales, and Mara Youngdahl, whose memories were indispensable.

This chapter wove together Kenny Rodgers's memories with available public records on Skalnik at the Harris County District Attorney's Office and the Harris County Sheriff's Office, in Houston. I also found information on Skalnik in the case files of the co-defendants Robert Avila and Claude Lee Wilkerson. Aron Frank confirmed Rodgers's account of recovering the diamond ring Skalnik stole.

I also relied on Lisa Rogers's memories of her late mother Penny's absence during this time, which dovetailed with Kenny Rodgers's work records and recollections. The letter Penny wrote to the judge overseeing Skalnik's 1979 probation violation case resides at the Orange County Clerk of Courts Office in Orlando.

To better understand the specific context of domestic violence in the late 1970s, I relied on M. R. Klatt's "Rape in Marriage: The Law in Texas and the Need for Reform," *Baylor Law Review* 32 (Winter 1980). I also consulted contemporary sources, including Larissa MacFarquhar's "A House of Their Own," *New Yorker,* August 19, 2019, and Rachel Louise Snyder's *No Visible Bruises: What We Don't Know About Domestic Violence Can Kill Us* (Bloomsbury, 2020).

I learned from Lisa that Skalnik disappeared from Penny's life without a trace. I gleaned additional details from Penny's 1980 divorce papers at the Harris County Clerk's Office in Houston.

CHAPTER 3: SUNSHINE STATE

For the early history of Pinellas County, I consulted a range of local histories and scholarly accounts, including the Pinellas County Planning Department's superb 157-page report, *Pinellas County Historical Background,* 3rd ed. (2008); James Anthony Schnur, *Historic Pinellas County: A*

Centennial History (Community Heritage, 2012); Federal Writers' Project of the Works Progress Administration, *Florida: A Guide to the Southernmost State* (Oxford University Press, 1939); Gary R. Mormino's insightful *Land of Sunshine, State of Dreams: A Social History of Modern Florida* (University Press of Florida, 2008); and U.S. census data.

For the Church of Scientology's arrival in Pinellas County, I relied on the *St. Petersburg Times*'s 1979 series "When Scientology Came to Town." Later reporting by the paper (after it became the *Tampa Bay Times*) was also helpful, particularly the 2019 project "Clear Takeover" by Tracey McManus.

My description of Skalnik's early years in Pinellas County drew on conversations I had with his then-wife, Suzanne Bourdeau, who patiently answered my many questions and joined me in sleuthing for answers about the mysterious man with whom she had once shared a life. I corroborated key details with public records. Their wedding announcement ran in the *St. Petersburg Times* on April 20, 1980.

Information about Skalnik's previous wives was gleaned from public records, including county marriage records, and wedding announcements.

The newspaper article that caused Skalnik to skip town ran in the *St. Petersburg Times* on May 23, 1981, and was written by David Henry. Details about Skalnik's bail-bond revocation came from jail intake records and his own testimony in a deposition on November 11, 1981, in *The State of Florida v. Melvin F. Glazener.*

My assertion that newspapers were widely available in the Pinellas County Jail is based on interviews with men who were incarcerated there during the early and mid-1980s, including Tony Capers, Terry Van Royal, and Michael Sorrentino. My claim that Skalnik held himself out within the jail as a legal adviser to gather information is based in part on a special investigation report, dated August 10, 1981, that was generated by the State Attorney's Office for the Sixth Judicial Circuit. It documents that Skalnik told prosecutors that he worked in the law library and held himself out as knowledgeable about the law and that Peter Pfluger, in turn, brought legal documents to Skalnik, looking for legal help.

My exploration of Skalnik's August 1981 plea deal, and the subsequent work Skalnik did as a jailhouse witness over the nine months that followed, relied on numerous court documents in six criminal cases in Pinellas County. The defendants in those cases were Clarence Clark, Melvin Glazener, Edward Lee Green, Jerome Hall, Roger Peterson, and Peter Pfluger. These documents include special investigation reports produced by the state attorney's office, depositions, and trial testimony. I also relied on a letter that Skalnik wrote to Judge Thomas Penick Jr. on August 27, 1981. Many of the key figures from this period—including Judge Penick, the prosecutor Larry Bergman, and the then–defense attorney Susan Schaeffer—have passed away. However, I was fortunate to speak with James Eckert and Lee Fugate, the defense team for the late Melvin Glazener.

Details about Skalnik's work for the private investigator Johnny Touchton were drawn from a 2005 affidavit that Touchton gave during postconviction proceedings in the capital case of Richard Cooper. Touchton died in 2016. The scene I describe is based on the recollections of Karen Parker, who lived next door to the Touchtons in Seminole.

CHAPTER 4: CONFIDENCE MAN

This chapter drew from extended conversations with Karen Parker, who was gracious enough to revisit a very difficult time in her life with me. I also drew heavily from the redacted case file at the Pinellas County Sheriff's Office, which included interviews with Karen (whose name was blacked out), her neighbors, and Skalnik, as well as the polygraph report. I located Karen in 2019 after a lengthy search that began with context clues found in the redacted case file; until we spoke, she never knew what happened to Skalnik or why he was not prosecuted. Additionally, I relied on records pertaining to the case at the State Attorney's Office for the Sixth Judicial Circuit. I have referred to Karen by her married name.

To better understand how law enforcement handled sexual assault cases during this time, I turned to Joanne Archambault's work. Archambault—a former sergeant for the San Diego Police Department who supervised the Sex Crimes Unit—has created guidelines and best practices for sexual assault investigations and prosecutions. Her 2018 paper, "Interviews with Victims vs. Suspects: Start by Believing and the Question of Bias" (published by End Violence Against Women International), was particularly helpful. Additionally, I looked to Ken Armstrong and T. Christian Miller's *A False Report: A True Story of Rape in America* (Crown, 2018). Also instructive was the *St. Petersburg Times*'s coverage from the early 1980s of Pinellas County's nascent Victim Advocacy Program.

My account of Skalnik's life outside jail during this time was based on interviews with Suzanne Bourdeau and Karen Parker, as well as many public documents, which proved essential since many of Skalnik's victims from this time, including the Garners and the Seidenbergs, have passed away. These records included a 1982 probation violation report; investigative reports, witness statements, and notes from the Pinellas County Sheriff's Office in the three grand theft cases in which he was charged; a 1984 Florida Department of Law Enforcement report documenting a complaint lodged by one of Skalnik's girlfriends against the state attorney's office; a deposition Skalnik gave that same year in *The State of Florida v. Terry Van Royal;* and a 2005 affidavit given by Johnny Touchton during post-conviction proceedings in the capital case of Richard Cooper.

Maria Konnikova's *The Confidence Game: Why We Fall for It . . . Every Time* (Viking, 2016) was essential reading that helped me gain a deeper understanding of the psychology of the con.

CHAPTER 5: FALSE WITNESS

My portrait of James Russell, who retired in 1992 and died in 2006, was informed by interviews with local attorneys who practiced during his tenure and reporters who covered the courts at that time, most crucially the generous Pat Meisol. I also relied on the following articles in the *St. Petersburg Times:* Steven A. Marquez, "Swapping Sides," June 20, 1983; Lori Denise Booker, "Justice System's Problems Blamed on Lack of Money," February 17, 1985; Earl Rinehart, "State Attorney Roasted at Luncheon Fundraiser," August 30, 1988; William Yelverton, "Changing Times," March 15, 1992; Craig Basse and Curtis Krueger, "Former State Attorney Dies," January 3, 2006; and David Sommer, "State Attorney Spent Decades Taking On Corrupt Politicians," January 4, 2006.

Two excellent books helped me better understand the forces and reward structures that can drive prosecutors to adopt a win-at-all-costs approach: Emily Bazelon's *Charged: The New Movement to Transform*

American Prosecution and End Mass Incarceration (Random House, 2019) and Deborah Rhode's *Character: What It Means and Why It Matters* (Oxford University Press, 2019).

To quantify the rise in violent crime in the 1970s and 1980s, I drew on historical data from the U.S. Bureau of Justice Statistics and the Murder Accountability Project. To gain insight into the broader tough-on-crime era, I consulted Michelle Alexander's *The New Jim Crow: Mass Incarceration in the Age of Colorblindness* (New Press, 2011), James Forman Jr.'s *Locking Up Our Own: Crime and Punishment in Black America* (Farrar, Straus and Giroux, 2017), and John Pfaff's *Locked In: The True Causes of Mass Incarceration—and How to Achieve Real Reform* (Basic Books, 2017).

My account of the Miami drug wars drew from testimony given before the House Select Committee on Narcotics Abuse and Control in 1986, which can be found in "Narcotics Interdiction and Enforcement Efforts in South Florida: Hearing Before the Select Committee on Narcotics Abuse and Control, House of Representatives, Ninety-Ninth Congress, Second Session, May 16, 1986" (Congressional Sales Office, 1987). Three articles helped me paint a picture of this time: Gregory Jaynes, "Miami Crime Rises as Drugs Pour In," *New York Times,* August 12, 1981; James Kelly, "South Florida: Trouble in Paradise," *Time,* November 23, 1981; and Francisco Alvarado, "Miami's Deadliest Summer," *Miami New Times,* August 10, 2011.

The plea deal, in which the State Attorney's Office for the Sixth Judicial Circuit offered to dismiss the lewd-and-lascivious charge against Skalnik in exchange for his guilty plea in the grand theft cases, is formalized in a transcript of Skalnik's plea hearing, which took place on March 10, 1983. Eleven days later, the state attorney's office filed a notice with the court, stating that there was insufficient evidence to proceed with the lewd-and-lascivious case. The circuit court judge who accepted the plea deal was Susan Schaeffer, who, as a defense attorney representing Peter Pfluger two years earlier, had accused Skalnik of fabricating testimony against her client. Schaeffer died in 2016.

Two letters from the state attorney's office to the Florida Department of Corrections document prosecutors' efforts to keep Skalnik in the county jail. (One was written on March 12, 1984, and another is undated.) These letters are part of Skalnik's parole records at the Florida Commission on Offender Review. Internal documents from the Pinellas County Jail show that Skalnik was widely known, at the time, to be a snitch. These include notes and reports documenting Skalnik's cell assignments, beginning with a transfer on January 12, 1983, into administrative segregation; reclassification notes; and a memo sent to the jail's then-director, Charles Felton, dated October 24, 1983.

Suzanne Bourdeau and Karen Parker were, again, invaluable sources. Also helpful were letters that members of Suzanne's church wrote to the Parole and Probation Commission on Skalnik's behalf in 1984.

My account of the Gaines case is based on the transcript of *The State of Florida v. Freddie Charles Gaines;* two pretrial depositions that Skalnik gave in the case in 1983; an interview I conducted with Gaines in the Taylor Correctional Institution in Perry, Florida, in 2019; and subsequent correspondence I exchanged with Gaines, who is still incarcerated.

CHAPTER 6: THE CLOSER

For my account of Skalnik's early work as a witness in cases where the death penalty was sought, I relied on transcripts of *The State of Florida v. Richard Michael Cooper, The State of Florida v. Kenneth Michael Gardner,* and *The State of Florida v. Jason Dirk Walton.* I also interviewed Cooper and two of his post-conviction attorneys, Marty McClain, who passed away in 2022, and Laura Fernandez. As I explain at greater length in part 3, it was Fernandez's persistent investigation into Cooper's case, undertaken decades after his conviction, that first revealed the breadth of Skalnik's role as a jailhouse witness. Drawing on public records and case files, she uncovered evidence that Skalnik had provided information on nearly forty other men held in the Pinellas County Jail during the 1980s.

Key insight into this period came from Lynda Richardson's "With Growing Resolve, Pinellas Condemning Its Killers to Death," *St. Petersburg Times,* October 21, 1984.

My account of Skalnik's life during this time drew from his Florida Department of Corrections records, which include a letter written by the prosecutor Bruce Young to the agency on March 12, 1984; an undated letter from Young to the agency sent after Skalnik testified against Gardner and Cooper; an interoffice memo documenting a phone call placed by Detective John Halliday to a commissioner on the Florida Parole and Probation Commission on October 5, 1984; and a letter Halliday sent to the commission on November 14, 1984. These records include letters written by Skalnik, including one to Senator Lawton Chiles on June 9, 1984, and one to Young on August 21, 1984. Also included are classification and admissions summaries that contain prison officials' assessments of Skalnik, and a report penned by his parole officer, Becky Anderson, on August 1, 1986.

My descriptions of Skalnik's criminal behavior during this period draw from investigative reports, witness statements, and notes at the Pinellas County Sheriff's Office in the Viola Giovanniello case; investigative reports from the Clearwater Police Department in the Dolores Wengatz case; and investigative reports and notes at the Austin Police Department in the stolen Rolex case.

CHAPTER 7: JIM

This chapter drew on interviews with more than a dozen people who knew Jim Dailey at different phases of his life, from his childhood in Manhattan, Kansas, to his tours of Vietnam, to his return to civilian life. I am particularly indebted to Mary Kay Dollar, who spent innumerable hours with me, helping me to draw a more complex portrait of him than was presented at his trial, and to members of Jim's family—in particular, his daughter, Stacey, and his sister, Joan Channel.

The gaps were filled in by friends and former classmates in Manhattan, most notably Jan Ballard and Max Fritz. My portrait of Jim's early life was informed by testimony that his mother, Grace Davies, gave in 1987 during the sentencing phase of *The State of Florida v. James Milton Dailey,* as well as information gathered by his first team of post-conviction attorneys for their 1999 Motion to Vacate Judgments of Conviction and Sentence. I'm grateful to Judy Specht Rickerson for sharing the story of her near drowning with me.

My portrait of Jim's military service is based on his extensive military records, 252 pages in all, from the National Archives and Records

Administration. I also relied on Jim's statements in 2015 to the Florida Commission on Offender Review; an interview I conducted with him in 2019; and letters he sent me in 2020 responding to questions about his military service.

Deepening my understanding of this time were conversations I had with four men who served with Jim in the Air Force: Dave Jandecka, Thomas Lesko, Larry Rasmussen, and Wilbur Sarlls. Lesko, in particular, helped me understand the sense of vulnerability that came with being stationed at an air base in South Vietnam at the height of the war.

I also drew on a number of historical sources on the Vietnam War. They include George C. Herring, *America's Longest War: The United States and Vietnam, 1950–1975* (McGraw-Hill, 2002); Stanley Karnow, *Vietnam: A History* (Viking, 1991); and Robert Mann, *A Grand Delusion: America's Descent into Vietnam* (Basic Books, 2002). To better understand the Tet Offensive, I relied on Bernard C. Nalty, *Air War over South Vietnam, 1968–1975* (Air Force History and Museums Program, U.S. Air Force, 2000), and Ronald H. Spector, *After Tet: The Bloodiest Year in Vietnam* (Vintage, 1994). I also consulted "Operation Homecoming," *Air Force Magazine,* February 13, 2009; John Gross, "Tet Offensive: The Battles of Bien Hoa and Long Binh," History Net, December 3, 2007; and Rebecca Maksel, "The Battle of Bien Hoa Air Base," *Air & Space Magazine,* February 1, 2018.

To reconstruct Jim's descent after leaving the Air Force, I consulted a 1978 Tucson Police Department report that documented his assault of another man in a bar fight, as well as relevant court records about the case's disposition in Pima County, Arizona. I also drew from Jim's comments, in both his correspondence with me and his statements before commissioners with the Florida Commission on Offender Review in 2015, about his past drug abuse. Last, I consulted an interview that the Olathe police detective Mark Kessler conducted with Jack Pearcy on May 21, 1985.

CHAPTER 8: SHELLY

To reconstruct the discovery of Shelly Boggio's body and the early days of the investigation into her murder, I relied on the autopsy file at the Pinellas County Medical Examiner's Office and reports and investigative notes written by detectives at the Pinellas County Sheriff's Office and the now-defunct Indian Rocks Beach Police Department. Much of this material was generated by the lead detective, John Halliday, who declined to speak with me. His investigation is documented in hundreds of pages of records, including his reports, testimony in both *The State of Florida v. Jack Pearcy* and *The State of Florida v. James Dailey,* a lengthy deposition he gave in 1986 in the Pearcy case, and partial audio of interviews, among them his conversation with Gayle Bailey, who passed away in 2024. I gleaned additional details for this chapter from the trial testimony of Jay Hoff, the bridge tender, and Dr. Joan Wood, the chief medical examiner for the Sixth Judicial Circuit of Florida.

CHAPTER 9: JACK

My portrait of Pearcy emerged from public records documenting his extensive criminal history. In Colorado, these included a 1973 Colorado State Reformatory evaluation and El Paso County District Court records. In Kansas, these included offense reports from the Lenexa Police Department, Olathe Police Department, and Johnson County Sheriff's Office, as well as Johnson County District Court records. I also consulted three un-bylined articles in the *Colorado Springs Gazette-Telegraph:* "Extensive Probe Leads to Arrests by Local Police," June 3, 1973; "Theft Charge Brings Innocence Plea from Youth," July 7, 1973; "Jail Break Duo Facing Felony Rap," September 1, 1973.

Martha "Lori" Cupp died in 2011, but I was able to include her perspective thanks to her interview with Pinellas County investigators on May 23, 1985, and her testimony in the Pearcy trial. Informing my understanding of law enforcement's response to domestic violence in the 1980s were two in-depth examinations: the National Institute of Justice's 1995 research report "The Criminalization of Domestic Violence: Promises and Limits," and its 2000 research report "Extent, Nature, and Consequences of Intimate Partner Violence: Findings from the National Violence Against Women Survey."

My description of the Duncan Danforth murder-for-hire case is based on the trial transcripts of *The State of Missouri v. Michael Stith* and *The State of Missouri v. Loretta Ollison Danforth,* as well as related case files held by the Camden County, Missouri, Sheriff's Office and the Camden County, Missouri, Prosecuting Attorney's Office, and by the Missouri State Highway Patrol. Interviews with Michael Stith, who died in 2021, provided additional context and insight into the case. Pearcy's comments about knives are drawn from a statement he gave on September 9, 1980, at the Johnson County, Kansas, Sheriff's Office, and from his testimony in the Stith and Ollison trials.

Much of this chapter is based on a videotaped interview of Pearcy, conducted at the Olathe, Kansas, Police Department, on May 21, 1985. To provide context, I filled in gaps with information gleaned from investigative reports. I also interviewed Joe Pruett in 2023.

Pearcy sent a very brief written response after I shared the findings of my investigation; his note did not address the murders of Duncan Danforth or Shelly Boggio.

Biographical information on Halliday was drawn from his personnel file at the Pinellas County Sheriff's Office and his parents' obituaries. Terry Buchaus passed away in 2014, but details about his career and his certainty that the murder was perpetrated by two people came from a deposition he gave in the Pearcy case on June 11, 1986.

My understanding of how early decision-making in an investigation can shape, and sometimes distort, the inquiry that follows draws from a seminal article on the subject: Keith A. Findley and Michael S. Scott, "The Multiple Dimensions of Tunnel Vision in Criminal Cases," *Wisconsin Law Review* 2 (2006). I also consulted the Innocence Project's "Criminal Investigations, Cognitive Bias, and Wrongful Convictions," by Vanessa Meterko, Glinda Cooper, Rebecca Brown, Amshula Jayaram, and Chantá Parker, published online in 2019.

CHAPTER 10: DARK WATERS

This chapter was defined as much by what was missing from the record as by what was present. Unlike detectives in Kansas, the Florida investigators did not record the interrogation they conducted of Pearcy. They recorded only discrete portions of their interviews with Gayle Bailey and Dwain Shaw, making it impossible to know what was hashed out before the tape recorder was turned on, or what other information they might have provided that did not fit their vision of the case. I drew from audio of Shaw's interview that came to light in 2019 after it was located by attorneys with the Capital Habeas Unit of the Office of the Federal Public Defender, who were appointed to the Dailey case that year. My description of the questioning of Shaw's girlfriend, Betty Mingus, relies on investigative reports and the audio recording of her interview in Olathe, Kansas, on May 22, 1985.

My analysis of the two investigators' interrogation of Shaw was influenced by a detailed assessment that Alan Hirsch, a law professor at Williams College and an expert in criminal interrogations, conducted in 2019. Hirsch was retained by the Federal Public Defender's Office. As he notes, "Information is most reliable when elicited by open-ended questioning ('Tell us what happened') rather than leading or suggestive questioning. The latter may encourage certain responses and may also supply information to the person questioned that compromises the reliability of their responses."

There is a curious lack of information about Shelly Boggio in the voluminous case file that documents the investigation into her death: no interviews with her mother or father, no school records, no statements from friends. Her older sister, Sherry, and her twin sister, Stacy, were called to testify in both the Pearcy and the Dailey trials, but the scope of their remarks was limited to the night leading up to their sister's murder and the subsequent identification of her body. Sherry, Stacy, and both of their parents, Frank and Cheri, have since passed away.

To create a portrait of Shelly, I drew upon the details that are in the record. These include 1986 depositions in the Pearcy case with Gayle Bailey, Stacy Boggio, and Deborah North; Bailey's statements to police and trial testimony; Frank and Cheri Boggio's divorce records and obituaries; and the Sixth Judicial Circuit medical examiner's report on Shelly's murder. I also relied on the following articles in the *St. Petersburg Times:* "School Had an Abundance of Misfortune," March 6, 1985; Pat Meisol, "Sixteenth Street School: Inventiveness Turned It Around; More Is Needed in Wake of Arrests," March 11, 1985; Christina K. Cosdon and Elizabeth Mauer, "Nude Body Identified as Young, Troubled Girl," May 9, 1985. Additionally, I consulted two pieces that ran in *The Tampa Tribune:* Lesley Collins, "Exterior Blights School," November 1, 1987; and an unsigned editorial, "Barbed Wire Fence Around School Should Come Down," November 5, 1987.

The end of the chapter relied on the transcript of sworn testimony that Pearcy gave on June 19, 1985; an account in the investigative reports of the polygraph exam he was administered on June 20, 1985; and additional statements Pearcy made to law enforcement on May 21 and July 17, 1985. Details about the search for Jim and his apprehension come from Halliday's deposition on April 16, 1985, his investigative reports, and Jim's testimony before commissioners with the Florida Commission on Offender Review in 2015.

CHAPTER 11: SNITCH

My description of Henry Andringa's handling of the case is based on his testimony at Jim Dailey's first evidentiary hearing, on March 19, 2003, as well as Jim's testimony at the same proceeding. I also relied on facts compiled and presented by Jim's later attorneys Harry Brody and Jeff Hazen in their 1999 motion for post-conviction relief. Deborah North's quotations come from her 1986 deposition. The subsequent description of Pearcy's trial is drawn from the trial transcript. For additional details about the case's prosecutors, I relied on three articles in the *St. Petersburg Times:* Pat Meisol, "Judge Bows Out of Trial Because of Ties to Lawyer," August 13, 1986; Pat Meisol, "Trial's Players Attract Attention," June 8, 1987; David Barstow, "Jurors Rate a Back Seat," August 31, 1990.

My account of Bob Graham's use of the death penalty was informed by an interview I did with Stephen Bright, one of the nation's preeminent capital defense attorneys. Bright litigated death-penalty cases in Florida throughout this period and gave me an essential overview from the perspective of an attorney who was fighting for his clients' lives. Deepening my understanding was David Von Drehle's *Among the Lowest of the Dead,* one of the finest books ever written about capital punishment. Articles that proved helpful included Donna Blanton, "Death Warrant a Political Bonus for Governor," *Orlando Sentinel,* January 22, 1989; Michael Mello, "Outlaw Judiciary: On Lies, Secrets, and Silence: The Florida Supreme Court Deals with Death Row Claims of Actual Innocence," *City University of New York Law Review* 1 (Fall 1996); Michael Grunwald, "Running

Scared," *Washington Post,* May 4, 2003; William Saletan and Ben Jacobs, "The Worst of Bob Graham," *Slate,* September 2, 2003; and Diane Rado, "Chiles' Execution Record: 5 of 13," *St. Petersburg Times,* October 9, 2005.

My exploration of the popularity of capital punishment in Pinellas County and the "Death Belt" relied on a number of sources, including Robert Sherrill, "Death Row on Trial," *New York Times Magazine,* November 13, 1983; Charles J. Ogletree Jr., "Black Man's Burden: Race and the Death Penalty in America," *Oregon Law Review* 100 (2002); Robert J. Smith, "The Geography of the Death Penalty and Its Ramifications," *Boston University Law Review* 92 (2012); and four stories in the *St. Petersburg Times:* Lynda Richardson, "With Growing Resolve, Pinellas Condemning Its Killers to Death," October 21, 1984; Martin Dyckman, "Overruled," March 3, 1986; *Times* editorial board, "Those Hanging Judges," March 3, 1986; and Paul L. McGorrian, "Defense Attorneys Criticize Death Penalty Motions," June 19, 1988. James Russell's quotation about "burning people" comes from Lynda Richardson's "Florida Death Row Is Biggest in the Country," *St. Petersburg Times,* October 21, 1984.

Also helpful was an address delivered on January 26, 1985, by the then–U.S. Supreme Court justice John Paul Stevens at Florida State University's College of Law, and published in the *Florida State University Law Review*'s spring 1985 issue under the title "Legal Questions in Perspective."

Two articles proved essential for my understanding of the material in this chapter: Bennett L. Gershman, "The Prosecutor's Duty to Truth," *Georgetown Journal of Legal Ethics* 14 (2001); and Barbara O'Brien, "A Recipe for Bias: An Empirical Look at the Interplay Between Institutional Incentives and Bounded Rationality in Prosecutorial Decision Making," *Missouri Law Review* (Fall 2009).

My account of the jail sweep conducted by Detective Halliday is based on his handwritten notes from December 4, 1986, and his testimony over the years describing his visit that day to the jail. He first discussed the visit in a 1987 deposition in the Dailey case, and he offered a fuller account in his testimony at the 2018 evidentiary hearing. In a 2005 affidavit, the jail's former director Charles Felton described how detectives were given unrestricted access to inmates held there. Among those questioned that day at the jail was Michael Sorrentino, whom I interviewed. He and three other men—Edward Coleman Jr., Travis Smith, and James Wright—testified at the 2018 hearing about being approached in the jail by a detective seeking information in the Dailey case. Their accounts helped me reconstruct what took place inside the jail's interview room.

My account of Skalnik's activity during the first half of 1987 comes from jail logs; pretrial interviews in the cases of James Clifford, David McPartland, and Willie Zene Moore; and letters Skalnik wrote to Governor Bob Martinez, the circuit court judge James Case, Assistant State Attorney Richard Mensch, and members of the Florida Parole Commission. Jail records from March 1987 show that Skalnik was briefly transferred to the jail's medical wing following what officials described as a depressive episode, and that in May, Jim was moved from the lower G Wing of the jail to the upper G Wing, where Skalnik was held. Skalnik subsequently met with Halliday and the case's prosecutors and reported Jim's alleged confession, as documented in a synopsis of a May 7, 1987, interview.

CHAPTER 12: A SIMPLE LIE

This chapter drew from the transcript for *The State of Florida v. James Dailey* and the invaluable memories and insights of Mary Kay Dollar and her daughter, Stacey. One of the prosecutors, Robert Heyman, discussed the evidence with me, the role that Skalnik played at trial, and his certainty that Jim committed this crime and was deserving of the death penalty. Last, I drew on my interviews with Paul Skalnik: one in the fall of 2018, and two in the fall of 2019.

CHAPTER 13: CONVICTION

The chapter opens with a quotation from the 1991 majority U.S. Supreme Court decision in *Arizona v. Fulminante*, which speaks to the power of a confession. That power, I learned, endures even when the confession is what researchers call a "secondary confession"—a jailhouse witness's account of another person's admission of guilt. Studies by the research psychologists Stacy Wetmore, Jeffrey Neuschatz, and Scott D. Gronlund show that jurors are significantly more likely to convict a defendant after hearing *any* testimony that he confessed—including confessing to another prisoner. In their 2014 article, "On the Power of Secondary Confession Evidence," published in *Psychology, Crime & Law,* the researchers found that such confessions are more powerful than other forms of evidence, even eyewitness testimony. "Secondary confessions," they wrote, "are unduly persuasive."

Like the previous chapter, this chapter drew from the transcript from the Dailey trial and the invaluable memories and insights of Mary Kay Dollar and her daughter, Stacey. I also discussed the trial during my interviews with Paul Skalnik, and my correspondence with him, in 2018 and 2019.

My conclusion that Skalnik was released in exchange for his testimony in the Dailey trial is based on a Florida Parole and Probation Commission memo, dated September 25, 1987, found in his Department of Corrections records. Additional records confirming that he was freed include an order for release on personal recognizance dated August 12, 1987, and Pinellas County Jail logs.

CHAPTER 14: STARKE

There is little agreement among journalists over whether to say that Florida State Prison is located in Starke or Raiford. The facility sits just outside Raiford, in Bradford County, but Starke—the county seat and the larger nearby town—appears more often in news reports. The Associated Press, for example, consistently uses Starke in its dateline when reporting on executions at the prison. For consistency and clarity, I've followed that practice throughout.

On the area being distinctly southern, I relied on one of my favorite quotations on the subject, from *Florida: A Guide to the Southernmost State,* by the Federal Writers' Project of the Works Progress Administration (Oxford University Press, 1939): "Politically and socially, Florida has its own North and South, but its northern area is strictly southern and its southern area is definitely northern."

My account of daily life and the physical environment on Florida's death row comes from my firsthand observations when I visited Florida State Prison; my correspondence with Jim Dailey; and Michael Lambrix's vivid firsthand account of life on death row, particularly "My First Day at Death Row," *Doing Life on Death Row* (blog), April 2009. The State of Florida executed Lambrix in 2017.

For historical data on death row and the state's condemned prisoners, I drew on the Florida Department of Corrections' death-row web page and the Death Penalty Information Center's database. Also helpful was Amnesty International's 2018 report *The Death Penalty and Juveniles.*

Accounts of unrest inside Florida's death row came from four UPI stories published on October 16 and 17, 1980: "Prison Officials, Thursday, Ordered a Total Lockdown of the Florida State Prison," "Death-Row Inmates Start Prison Disturbance," "Recent Outbreaks of Violence at Florida State Prison," and "Ten Weapons Found at Prison Under Lockdown." The layout of the death house and other physical details were informed by Nick Broomfield's 1992 documentary, *Aileen Wuornos: The Selling of a Serial Killer.*

My reconstruction of John Spenkelink's execution drew from first-person journalistic accounts that ran on May 26, 1978: J. Paul Wyatt, "Victim's Eyes Held No Hope," UPI; Thomas B. Slaughter, "Eyewitness to an Execution," AP; Wayne Ezell, "Witnessing Final Moments of Condemned," *Tallahassee Democrat;* Willard P. Rose, "Death Penalty Reborn as Spenkelink Dies," *Miami Herald;* Wayne King, "Florida Executes Killer as Plea Fails; Electrocuted Is Spenkelink," *New York Times.* Also essential to my discussion of the Spenkelink case was David Von Drehle's *Among the Lowest of the Dead* (Times Books, 1995) and Peter Ross Range's "Will He Be the First?," *New York Times,* March 11, 1979.

My descriptions of early executions and the use of the electric chair are drawn largely from accounts from that time, including the following un-bylined newspaper reports: "Troops Guard Blacks in Prison for Murder," *Shreveport Journal,* February 9, 1924; "Fortune Ferguson Has Been Extended a New Lease on Life," *St. Petersburg Times,* September 21, 1924; "Negro Slayer Dies in Chair," *Orlando Sentinel,* October 8, 1924; "Governor Martin to Sign Negro's Death Warrant," *Orlando Sentinel,* January 1, 1926; and "Condemned Negro's Sanity Questioned as Plea Fails," *St. Petersburg Times,* March 2, 1927.

The discussion about declining public support and legal challenges ending the death penalty in 1972, and the efforts in the years that followed to restore it, was informed by Maurice Chammah's *Let the Lord Sort Them* (Crown, 2021); Martin Waldron, "Ruling Cheered on Florida Death Row," *New York Times,* June 30, 1972; Martin Dyckman, "Life Arrives on Death Row in an Embrace," *St. Petersburg Times,* June 30, 1972; Tim Thornton, "Florida's Legislative and Judicial Responses to *Furman v. Georgia:* An Analysis and Criticism," *Florida State University Law Review* (Winter 1974); and Phoebe C. Ellsworth and Samuel R. Gross, "Hardening of the Attitudes: Americans' Views on the Death Penalty," *Journal of Social Issues* 50, no. 2 (1994).

The remainder of the chapter is based on my correspondence with Jim Dailey, interviews with Marieke Laauwen (who went by her maiden name, Jansen, at this point in the narrative), and Jim's letters to Marieke, which she fortunately held on to and was generous enough to share with me.

Florida's execution of Leo Jones continues to spark debate about whether the state put to death an innocent man. For a detailed look at the case, see Steve Mills, "Questions of Innocence: Legal Roadblocks Thwart New Evidence on Appeal," *Chicago Tribune,* December 18, 2000.

CHAPTER 15: THE ART OF THE DEAL

For the account of Skalnik's broken engagement and flight from authorities, I'm indebted to Pat Meisol, who wrote the vivid piece "Con Man Cops Out," *St. Petersburg Times,* October 21, 1987. My account of Skalnik's time in Austin, Texas, is drawn from detailed case files maintained by the Travis County District Attorney's Office and the Austin Police Department. I also relied on documents, namely notes that prosecutors with the State Attorney's Office for Florida's Sixth Judicial Circuit kept in the Viola Giovanniello case, and a September 23, 1988, memorandum written by an investigator in the office, after a Texas Department of Public Safety detective called and provided additional information about Skalnik's criminal activity in Austin.

My account of how the state's prosecution of David James McPartland fell apart without Skalnik testifying for the state drew on the McPartland case file, court filings, and two newspaper articles: Pat Meisol, "True

Confessions or Truly Unbelievable," *St. Petersburg Times,* September 13, 1987; and Earl Rinehart, "Murder Charge Tossed Out," *Tampa Tribune,* July 15, 1988.

My description of the rupture between Skalnik and prosecutors, his allegations of misconduct, and the plea deal that followed relies on internal memoranda from the state attorney's office, as well as related legal filings and affidavits dating from the summer of 1988 through the spring of 1989, beginning with Skalnik's motion to dismiss for prosecutorial misconduct, filed August 5, 1988.

To recount Skalnik's brief time in the Texas prison system and the confusion over both the length of his punishment and which state had jurisdiction, I relied on correspondence between the Texas Department of Corrections (now the Texas Department of Criminal Justice), the Florida Department of Corrections, and the Texas Board of Pardons and Paroles, along with internal records from the Florida Parole Commission. The quotation from Skalnik that closes the Pinellas County portion of the chapter comes from a letter he wrote to an unnamed judge on August 8, 1988.

To tell the story of Skalnik's early years, I relied on interviews with three members of his family, all of whom asked to remain anonymous, and with Skalnik himself. Skalnik talked to me at length about his difficult relationship with his father. Three incidents he recounted involving Emile—Emile knocking a man unconscious, arriving drunk at a high school baseball game, and forcing Skalnik to practice baseball late at night—aligned with his family members' accounts of Emile's temper and alcoholism. I also consulted two high school classmates of Skalnik's, as well as his birth records, education records, military records, and high school yearbooks.

For my account of his life after high school, I consulted the University of Texas at Austin registrar records, Austin Police Department employment files, the report generated by the U.S. Department of Justice's 1973 civil rights investigation into his violent treatment of a man he arrested, and a remarkable thirty-eight-page résumé, which is in his case file at the Orange County Clerk of Courts Office in Orlando. Newspaper ads in the *Austin Statesman* archives alerted me to the fact that he worked as a life insurance agent. Additional details came from his criminal court records in Orlando.

I'm profoundly grateful to Misty Anderson for sharing her memories of one of the most challenging periods of her life. Misty is identified by her married name, and her mother, who declined to be interviewed, is identified by a pseudonym to protect her privacy. My interview with the attorney Margaret Hindman, who prosecuted the case against Skalnik for the Galveston County District Attorney's Office, was invaluable, as were the court records from these criminal proceedings.

CHAPTER 16: AN UNREAL DREAM

A great deal of this chapter is based on interviews I conducted with Harry Brody and Jeff Hazen; Hazen, in particular, spent extensive time talking to me.

News accounts that helped me describe the Capital Collateral Regional Counsel's Tampa office in the late 1990s included Jackie Hallifax, "One Death Row Appeals Office Is Struggling with Its Case Load," *Tallahassee Democrat,* October 1, 1997; Sydney P. Freedberg, "State's Death-Row Lawyers in Turmoil, Under Attack," *St. Petersburg Times,* January 2, 1999; and David Karp, "The Innocence Defense," *St. Petersburg Times,* February 9, 2003. Karp's deeply reported story informed my description of John Moser's leadership of the state agency.

Jack Pearcy's attempted escape and subsequent disciplinary violations are laid out in his Florida Department of Corrections disciplinary records and related criminal charges filed against him in 1988.

My examination of the first death warrants that Governor Jeb Bush signed and the renewed debate over the electric chair was informed by the following articles: Editorial, "Shocking Findings of Old Sparky Study," *Orlando Sentinel,* May 19, 1999; Diane Rado, "Gov. Bush Signs His First Death Warrants," *St. Petersburg Times,* June 10, 1999; and Editorial, "Heed Court Warning on Electric Chair," *South Florida Sun-Sentinel,* July 6, 1999.

My description of the execution of Jesse Tafero and its aftermath is drawn from Ellen McGarrahan, "Execution in Florida Goes Askew," *Miami Herald,* May 5, 1990; Mark Davis, "Killer Executed amid Sparks, Flames," *Tampa Tribune,* May 5, 1990; and Barry Bearak, "Dispute over Fiery Death Idles Florida Electric Chair," *Los Angeles Times,* July 23, 1990.

The execution of Allen Lee Davis and its immediate fallout are depicted in several firsthand accounts, most notably Lesley Clark's "Florida Execution of 350-Pound Inmate Turns Bloody," *Miami Herald,* July 8, 1999. What happened after Davis's execution was covered extensively by Sydney P. Freedberg in the *St. Petersburg Times:* "Bloody Execution Leads to Stay for 2nd Inmate," July 9, 1999; "Burn May Be Key in 2nd Davis Autopsy," July 15, 1999; "Davis Execution Photos Shown," July 28, 1999; "Judge Upholds Electric Chair Use," August 3, 1999; and "Again, Justices Turn Their Eyes to the Electric Chair," August 25, 1999. Also helpful was Rick Bragg, "Florida's Messy Executions Put the Electric Chair on Trial," *New York Times,* September 18, 1999, and Carl S. Kaplan, "Execution Debate Is Broadened by Photos on Web," *New York Times,* October 29, 1999.

Judge Learned Hand's comment dismissing the likelihood of a wrongful conviction appears in his opinion in the 1923 case *United States v. Garsson.*

My discussion of the emergence of DNA exonerations drew on Brandon Garrett's *Convicting the Innocent* (Harvard University Press, 2011), the Innocence Project's online summary of Kirk Bloodsworth's wrongful conviction and subsequent exoneration, and the Death Penalty Information Center's innocence database.

Brody and Hazen recounted James Leitner's remarks to them in their 1999 motion for post-conviction relief. Hazen also described the conversation in a sworn affidavit submitted two decades later, as part of Jim Dailey's later post-conviction proceedings. The affidavit notes that Hazen went to see Leitner with either Brody or the investigator Mike Cochran; Hazen now feels certain that it was Brody, which Brody confirmed to me. I contacted Cochran, who said he had not met with Leitner. I have therefore described the visit as one conducted by Brody and Hazen. Leitner, who has never publicly recanted his testimony, did not respond to my requests for comment.

CHAPTER 17: SIX BY NINE FEET

My interviews with Harry Brody, Jeff Hazen, and Mary Kay Dollar informed much of this chapter.

To describe the firings at the Capital Collateral Regional Counsel's Tampa office, I consulted Graham Brink, "New Chief Shakes Up Death Row Legal Staff," *St. Petersburg Times,* May 9, 2001, and Editorial, "Gambling with Lives on Death Row," *St. Petersburg Times,* May 14, 2001.

Bradford Thomas's remarks are drawn from "Bush's Adviser Key in Push for Quicker Death Row Appeals," *St. Petersburg Times,* January 6, 2000.

At the end of the chapter, I note that the Florida Department of Corrections used to require married women visiting male inmates to be accompanied by their husbands, and that only female blood relatives could visit alone. Although a Department of Corrections spokesperson informed me that the agency has no record of this policy, I located an archived copy of its 1998 regulations on the Wayback Machine. It states, "Married or unmarried inmates may have non-immediate family member couples on the visiting list after approval, but the member of the couple who is the opposite sex of the inmate may not visit the inmate without the spouse."

CHAPTER 18: SMALL FICTIONS

The beginning of this chapter draws on my interviews with Misty Anderson and letters that she wrote to the Texas Board of Pardons and Paroles, which she shared with me.

My description of Skalnik's life in Massachusetts comes from a detailed incident report written on May 22, 2003, by an officer with the Marlborough Police Department and court records showing the criminal charges brought against Skalnik by the Middlesex County District Attorney's Office.

The rest of the chapter is drawn from transcripts of Jim Dailey's first evidentiary hearing, which was held over five different days in circuit court in Clearwater: March 19, 2003; November 7, 2003; December 11, 2003; June 29, 2004; and November 5, 2004. It also draws on a video recording of the subsequent oral arguments that took place before the Florida Supreme Court on February 2, 2007.

I also relied on a 2019 affidavit in which David Gemmer assessed his performance before the Florida Supreme Court that day. It read in part, "My widowed mother, in her eighties at the time and infirm, was unexpectedly hospitalized the afternoon before the argument. I left the Tampa airport to attend to her as I was her sole family caregiver and healthcare surrogate and I was very concerned about her well-being. I was unable to properly prepare for the argument and got very little sleep the night before the argument as I took an early morning flight from Tampa. I was extremely fatigued. It was not my best performance."

CHAPTER 19: FAIL-SAFE

My account of Jim Dailey's interview with commissioners from the Florida Commission on Offender Review is based on a transcript of that meeting, held on September 10, 2015, at Union Correctional Institution in Raiford. Jim also shared a few additional details so I could describe the meeting more fully. My description of his behavior during his incarceration comes from his Florida Department of Corrections disciplinary records.

As for the expectation that clemency boards have for defendants to express remorse, Daniel S. Medwed explores a similar dynamic with parole boards in "The Innocent Prisoner's Dilemma: Consequences of Failing to Admit Guilt at Parole Hearings," *Iowa Law Review* 93 (2008). Medwed explores this idea further, focusing on the clemency process, in "Not Just Mercy: The Untapped Potential of Clemency to Right Wrongful Convictions," *Law Journal for Social Justice* 17 (Spring 2023).

That the clemency process is a "fail-safe," as the former U.S. Supreme Court justice William Rehnquist characterized it, comes from his majority opinion in 1993 in *Herrera v. Collins.*

CHAPTER 20: E. PAUL SMITH, ESQ.

This chapter is based on interviews with the U.S. marshal Shirley Saathoff and Lieutenant James Ferris of the Panola County Sheriff's Department in Texas, as well as their detailed reports, notes, and photographs of evidence, including Skalnik's cache of fake IDs. Particularly helpful were the audio recordings they shared with me of their interviews with several of Skalnik's victims. I also benefited from several interviews with Judy Smith, whom I've identified as his ninth wife. She believed herself to be married to Skalnik, and they lived together as husband and wife for many years, though she later learned their wedding had been a sham. Under Texas law, their union met the criteria for a common-law marriage.

That Skalnik worked as a jailhouse lawyer was confirmed by a lieutenant at the Federal Correctional Institution in Seagoville. Details of how he ran his legal operation were provided by a former cellmate who served as his typist. Skalnik's King James Bible was given to me by Donna Mackey, whose story I tell in chapter 22.

CHAPTER 21: THE CALL

Interviews with Chelsea Shirley, Laura Fernandez, Colin Kelly, and Cyd Oppenheimer formed the foundation of this chapter. I also relied on the affidavits of Juan Banda, Travis Smith, Michael Sorrentino, and James Wright, along with my conversations with Sorrentino. This chapter further draws on Jack Pearcy's 2017 affidavit, his testimony at the 2018 evidentiary hearing in Jim Dailey's case, and John Halliday's testimony at the same hearing.

My claim that Florida prisoners, on average, receive only two visits, total, from family and friends comes from Joshua Cochran et al., "Who Gets Visited in Prison? Individual- and Community-Level Disparities in Inmate Visitation Experiences," *Crime & Delinquency,* May 2017. As for the long odds against parole in Florida and for prisoners serving life sentences, I relied on Dan Sullivan, "In Tampa Hearings, the Long-Imprisoned and Their Families Chase a Slim Chance at Parole," *Tampa Bay Times,* May 10, 2019, and the Sentencing Project's 2017 report "Delaying a Second Chance: The Declining Prospects for Parole on Life Sentences." The comments of Pearcy's mother, Sally Simon, to the Florida Commission on Offender Review are drawn from Pearcy's parole records.

Fernandez provided me with a recording of the voicemail she received from the Florida governor's office on September 24, 2019.

CHAPTER 22: ELEVENTH HOUR

This chapter draws primarily on my October 2019 interview with Paul Skalnik, as well as multiple interviews with Donna Mackey, who generously shared her memories and insights.

CHAPTER 23: ZOMBIE CASE

Specific details about what Jim Dailey experienced after his death warrant was signed came from my correspondence with him, and interviews with Mary Kay Dollar and Laura Fernandez. Information on the procedures and protocols of death watch came from the Florida Department of Corrections' death-row web page and Michael Lambrix's firsthand account of death watch, particularly his five-part "Letter from Death Watch," *Death Row Journals* (blog), from December 2015 and January 2016.

The account of Marieke Laauwen learning of Jim's execution date and the correspondence that followed is drawn from interviews with her.

The discussion of the toll that death-penalty cases take on victims' families draws on my reporting on capital punishment for more than two decades, as well as the Death Penalty Project's September 2025 report, "Procedural Trauma, the Illusion of Closure, and Myth of Consensus: Understanding Victim Experiences in Capital Punishment Cases." That some death sentences may not be carried out for decades, if at all, is supported by Florida's death-row roster, which is available on the state's Department of Corrections website, and data on the Death Penalty Information Center's "Time on Death Row" web page. Florida's death-row roster shows that some prisoners who remain on death row committed their crimes as far back as the 1970s. An interview with the capital defense attorney and Yale Law School visiting lecturer Stephen Bright helped me better understand these "zombie cases."

As for the arbitrary nature of who is selected for execution in Florida, I relied on Sarah Lundy, "Only Florida's Governors Can Say How They Pick Execution Order," *Orlando Sentinel*, May 19, 2009; Melanie Kalmanson, "First DeSantis Death Warrant of 2024 Shows Randomness of Capital Punishment in Florida," *Tallahassee Democrat*, August 1, 2024; and the editorial "Troubling New Questions Cloud Death Penalty," *South Florida Sun Sentinel*, June 23, 2025. The editorial noted that "the black hole at the center of our galaxy is hardly more inscrutable than the mysterious process by which Gov. Ron DeSantis decides which condemned prisoner will be put to death next."

Governor DeSantis's comments regarding the Dailey case were reported by Dan Sullivan, "Death Row Exonerees Ask DeSantis to Halt Execution," *Tampa Bay Times,* October 23, 2019.

The passage about James Slater and what he told the Dailey defense team is based on his sworn affidavit, his subsequent testimony, and interviews with Chelsea Shirley and Colin Kelly.

CHAPTER 24: CATCH THE DEVIL

Robert Heyman's comment—"As the old saying goes, 'You've got to make a deal with a sinner to catch the devil' "—was made to the reporter Saundra Weathers of Bay News 9, and aired on January 9, 2020, in a segment titled "Future of James Dailey's Execution Hangs in the Balance."

My account of Jack Pearcy's meeting with Josh Dubin during the lawyer's visit to Sumter Correctional Institution on December 18, 2019, is based on the written statement Pearcy signed that day, which was subsequently entered into evidence, and interviews with Dubin. My account of the evidentiary hearing that followed is based on my in-person reporting in Clearwater on March 5, 2020.

For my description of Clemente Aguirre-Jarquin, I relied on my conversation with him at the hearing, the Innocence Project's web page about his case, and Dan Sullivan, "In Tampa, Man Embarks on Life After Years on Death Row," *Tampa Bay Times,* November 16, 2018.

Brittany and Kalli Boggio's comments about wanting to see the execution move forward were included in a local TV news segment, "Before His Execution, Victim's Family Will Tell James Dailey How He Ruined Their Lives," Fox 13 Tampa Bay, September 27, 2019.

Sally Simon's phone calls with Pearcy, following his meeting with Dubin, were recorded by the Florida Department of Corrections, and some were later entered into the court record. Simon disclosed at the March 2020 evidentiary hearing, in comments to the court, that she learned of her son's signed statement taking responsibility for the murder from the newspaper.

CHAPTER 25: LOCKDOWN

This chapter grew out of my firsthand reporting in the early months of the pandemic. Additional information came from my correspondence with Jim Dailey; interviews with Laura Fernandez; and the transcript of a status hearing in Jim's case that was held in Clearwater on February 20, 2020.

Regarding Robert Heyman's handwritten notes from the trial, Heyman emphasized in his comments to me that the lewd-and-lascivious charge involving Skalnik (in which he played no role) was a matter of public record.

I sent a detailed letter to the state attorney's office, including assistant state attorney Sara Macks, describing my account of the 2020 status hearing and offering an opportunity to respond. Neither Macks nor the office provided comment.

EPILOGUE

To tell the story of Jim Dailey's life after death watch, I relied on my correspondence with Jim and interviews with Mary Kay Dollar, Laura Fernandez, and Marieke Laauwen.

Insights into how the coronavirus pandemic affected Florida's prisons and death row came from sources that included Laura Cassels, "COVID-19 Death Toll Rises in Florida Prisons; Inmate Advocates Demonstrate, Families Grieve," *Florida Phoenix,* August 28, 2020; and Leonora LaPeter Anton, "Inmates Say the Coronavirus Has Hit Florida's Death Row, Tommy Zeigler," *Tampa Bay Times,* September 11, 2020.

My examination of the politics surrounding executions in Florida, both before and after President Donald Trump took office on January 20, 2025, relied on the following sources: Caden DeLisa and Brian Burgess, "On the Death Penalty, DeSantis Trails GOP Rivals, Predecessors—and Yes, Even Charlie Crist," *Capitolist,* September 1, 2022; Gray Rohrer, "Not So Deadly DeSantis—Law and Order Governor Has Signed Fewer Death Warrants Than Predecessors," *Florida Politics,* September 14, 2022; "Restoring the Death Penalty and Protecting Public Safety," White House, January 20, 2025; Editorial, "Gov. Ron DeSantis Goes on an Execution Spree," *South Florida Sun Sentinel,* June 10, 2025.

Key sources for my discussion of jailhouse witnesses included "The

Snitch System," a 2004 report by Northwestern University School of Law's Center on Wrongful Convictions; Alexandra Natapoff, *Snitching: Criminal Informants and the Erosion of American Justice* (New York University Press, 2009); Jeffrey S. Neuschatz and Jonathan M. Golding, *Jailhouse Informants: Psychological and Legal Perspectives* (New York University Press, 2023); and "Jailhouse Informants," a report by the National Registry of Exonerations, October 2, 2024.

To provide a detailed account of Florida's execution procedures, I consulted Romy Ellenbogen, "How Florida Carries Out Lethal Injections," *Tampa Bay Times*, February 23, 2023; and "Execution by Lethal Injection: Procedures," Florida Department of Corrections, 2025.

IMAGE CREDITS

10 Lisa Rogers
18 Harris County (Texas) Sheriff's Office
30 *St. Petersburg Times* via ZUMA Press
40 Karen Parker
57 Pinellas County (Florida) Sheriff's Office
70 Mary Kay Dollar
72 Mary Kay Dollar
79 Jose Font/*Tampa Bay Times* via ZUMA Press
80 *St. Petersburg Times* via ZUMA Press
95 John P. Jones/*Tampa Bay Times* via ZUMA Press
103 Pinellas County (Florida) Sheriff's Office
107 Pinellas County (Florida) Sheriff's Office
123 *Tampa Bay Times/Tampa Bay Times* via ZUMA Press
145 Marieke Laauwen
159 Misty Anderson
174 *Tampa Bay Times* via ZUMA Press
187 Mary Kay Dollar
220 Eli Durst
231 Scott Keeler/*Tampa Bay Times* via ZUMA Press
257 Lisa Rogers
266 Mary Kay Dollar

A NOTE ABOUT THE AUTHOR

PAMELA COLLOFF is a reporter at ProPublica and a staff writer at *The New York Times Magazine*. She was the recipient of a National Magazine Award for Reporting in 2020 and for Feature Writing in 2013. Her work has been anthologized in *The Best American Magazine Writing*, *The Best American Crime Reporting*, and *Next Wave: America's New Generation of Great Literary Journalists*. Colloff holds a bachelor's degree in English from Brown University. She lives in Austin, Texas, with her husband and their two children.

A NOTE ON THE TYPE

This book was set in Minion, a typeface produced by the Adobe Corporation specifically for the Macintosh personal computer and released in 1990. Designed by Robert Slimbach, Minion combines the classic characteristics of old-style faces with the full complement of weights required for modern typesetting.

Composed by North Market Street Graphics,
Lancaster, Pennsylvania

Designed by Betty Lew